Politician Civil Servant Relationship and Public Administration in India

Politician Civil Servant Relationship and Public Administration in India

Edited by

S.N. Singh
S.S. Chauhan
K.K. Srivastava

GYAN

First Published, 2017

Published by

Gyan Publishing House
5, Ansari Road
Daryaganj, New Delhi-110002
Phone: 9811692060
E-mail: books@gyanbooks.com

Printed at: G. Print Process, Delhi.

Cataloging in Publication Data—DK
Courtesy: D.K. Agencies (P) Ltd. <docinfo@dkagencies.com>

"The Changing Paradigm of Governance with Special Focus on Politician-Civil Servant Relationship" (Seminar) (2014 : Lucknow, India)
Politician civil servant relationship and public administration in India / edited by S.N. Singh, S.S. Chauhan, K.K. Srivastava.
pages cm
Seminar papers.
Includes bibliographical references.
ISBN 9788121213578

1. Public administration—India—Congresses. 2. Civil service—India—Congresses. 3. Politicians—India—Congresses. I. Singh, S. N. (Surya Narain), 1941- editor. II. Chauhan, S. S. (Writer on democracy), editor. III. Srivastava, K. K. (Teacher of Public Administration), editor. IV. Institute for Applied Research & Development (Lucknow, India), organizer. V. Indian Council of Social Science Research, sponsoring body. VI. Title.

JQ231.A17 2014 DDC 351.954 23

Contents

Preface

There are quite a few core areas in the academic discipline of public administration. The politician-civil servant relationship has been a consistent component in the academic discussion for several decades now. It has remained a core concern and continues to be so as it influences the quality of governance. There is therefore, a genuine need for a regular discussion so as to address the current problems emerging out of ongoing changes in the socio-political scenario. In view of this we made an attempt to organise a national seminar on the changing paradigm of governance with special focus on politician-civil servant relationship sometimes back. The national seminar was well attended in which academic fraternity from across the country contributed their valuable thoughts.

Since the debate about the politician-civil servant relationship has been part of the academic discussion for quite some time now, it may be pertinent to have an overview of the same in order to place the theme in a perspective. In this context it is worth recollecting the kind of political leadership as well as the civil servants during the early post-independence period. It was a period of national reconstruction in which both played their respective roles with responsibility and dignity. But gradually things started changing as the socio-political process went through several changes. A marked difference became visible in the administrative decision-making in which politician-civil servant relationship played its part as well. A political culture as well as the administrative culture developed in which earlier values were under strain. There appeared a new class political executives which preferred its own people in positions of authority. The relationship between the two, thus, experienced a new approach towards public life and governance.

The present book makes an attempt to look into various aspects of the politician-civil servant relationship penned by different scholars who have their own thoughts and opinion. It is an important area in the study of public administration and therefore, should attract the attention of the not only of the students of public administration but public policy-makers as well.

Acknowledgement

Any activity of such a dimension needs cooperation and support from individuals as well as institutions to make it successful venture. We, therefore, take this opportunity to express our grateful thanks to those whose help and support made this effort a success. Our thanks are due first of all to the Indian Council of Social Science Research, New Delhi for providing the financial support to organise the said national seminar as without this it would not have been possible to organise the seminar on that scale.

We are thankful to Pandit Ram Kishan Dwivedi, former Home Minister in the Government of Uttar Pradesh for inaugurating the national seminar. We express our gratefulness to Professor D.P. Singh, former Head of the Department of Public Administration, Lucknow University and UGC Member for gracing the occasion. We express our thanks to Professor K. Kishore, Professor Manoj Dixit, Professor N.L. Bharti, Dr Vaishali Saxena from the Department of Public Administration, Lucknow University for their continuous encouragement and cooperation not only in this particular Seminar but also in other academic activities of the Institute. We would also like to thank Professor S.K. Singh of the Department of Public Administration, Lucknow University, Professor I.D. Mishra from Gorakhpur University and Professor B.K. Tewari from Lucknow University for their active interest and interaction in the activities of the Institute for all these years. We are grateful to our contributors who have enriched the deliberations with their thoughts. We thank Dr A.K. Singh of RCUES, Lucknow for his support in our venture. We thank Sri Pramod Kumar for getting the manuscript computer typed in record time. In the end we express our thanks to the publisher for getting the book see the light of the day.

About the Contributors

1. **P.N. Gautam,** (Retired Professor, Department of Public Administration, H.P. University) Gautam Kuteer, Sanjauli, Shimla-171 006.
2. **Shiv Raj Singh,** Professor (Retd.), H.P. University, Shimla – 171 005.
3. **Ashok Ranjan Basu,** IAS (Retd.), Ph.D., D.Litt., F.I.M.A.; F.R.A.S. (London), Former Member of the Central Administrative Tribunal.
4. **S.K. Chaturvedi,** Former Head, Department of Political Science and Public Administration, C.C.S. University, Meerut.
5. **Harbans Pathak,** Formerly Professor and Head, Department of Public Administration, Punjabi University, Patiala, Director, Punjab School of Public Administration.
6. **S.K. Singh,** Former Professor of Public Administration, Lucknow University and Former Professor of Public Management, Ethiopian Civil Service University, Addis Ababa.
7. **S.N. Singh,** Emeritus Professor, Department of Public Administration, Lucknow University.
8. **U.B. Singh,** Formerly Joint Director, Regional Centre for Urban and Environmental Studies, Lucknow University, Lucknow.
9. **Abhinav Sharma,** Associate Professor, Department of Political Science, Banaras Hindu University, Varanasi.
10. **K.K. Srivastava,** Faculty Member, Department of Public Administration, University of Lucknow, Lucknow.
11. **S.S. Chauhan,** Faculty Member, Department of Public Administration, University of Lucknow, Lucknow.
12. **Nimish Gupta,** Associate Professor, Amity Business School, Lucknow.

13. **Noor Fatima Ansari,** Research Scholar, Department of Public Administration, University of Lucknow, Lucknow.
14. **Stuti Saxena,** Research Scholar, Department of Political Science, Central University of Haryana.
15. **N.L. Bharti,** Professor, Department of Public Administration, University of Lucknow, Lucknow.
16. **Ram Jeet,** Assistant Teacher, B.N.Lal Vocational Inter College, Lucknow.
17. **Kamlesh Gupta,** Former Post Doctoral, Research Associate, Allahabad University, Allahabad, U.P.
18. **Manjari Damele,** Senior Lecturer, Department of Economics, Bundelkhand Degree College, Jhansi, U.P.
19. **Reena Singh,** Research Scholar, Department of Public Administration, University of Lucknow, Lucknow.
20. **Deepti Srivastava,** SRF, Research Scholar, Department of Public Administration, University of Lucknow, Lucknow.

Introduction

There is no denying the fact that adoption of Federal Parliamentary Democracy for the politico-administrative system of India emerged as a conscious decision during the Constitution Assembly debates. Consequent upon the adoption of Constituent by the People of India, parliamentary system of governance was formalised in the country. In a democracy, power vests with the people as they enjoy the sovereign power. In a representative system, this power is exercised by the people through their elected representatives who have the mandate to govern them for a specific period. The civil service by virtue of its knowledge, experience and understanding of public affairs assist the elected representatives in formulating policies and are responsible for implementing these policies. Parliamentary democracies are usually characterised by a permanent civil service which assists the political executives.[1] A proper, rational relationship is considered a *sine qua non* for an efficient and effective governance.

Before taking up the question of relationship between the politician and civil servant it may be pertinent to note the advantages of having independent, permanent and impartial civil service. In this context we can recollect the experience of Spoils System of U.S. Civil Service which did not have these features and suffered. In India, therefore, the Constitution-makers were quite aware of the importance of the independence of the civil service system. The following could be noted as advantages of having an independent and permanent civil service.[2]

(a) The spoil system has the propensity to degenerate into a system of patronage, nepotism and corruption. Having a credible recruitment process through an impartial agency provides a defence against such abuse.

(b) Public policy today has become a complex exercise requiring in-depth knowledge and expertise in public affairs. A permanent civil service provides continuity and dumps expertise as well as institutional memory for effective policy making.

(c) A permanent and impartial civil service is more likely to assess the long-term social payoffs of any policy whereas the political executive may have a tendency to look for short-term political gain.

(d) A permanent civil service helps to ensure uniformity in public administration and also acts as a unifying force particularly in vast and culturally diverse nation.

(e) A permanent civil service like any other reputable profession is likely to evolve over time ethical basis for its functioning.

There is a general agreement amongst the intelligent circles that a healthy working relationship between minister and civil servants is essential for good governance. It is also true for the politician as a class who operate at different levels of the body politic, a similar kind of relationship would positively help the process of good governance while the principles governing the roles and responsibilities of ministers and civil servant are well defined in political theory, in the actual working of their relationship this division of responsibility becomes blurred with both sides often encroaching upon the other's sphere of responsibility. In any democracy, ministers are responsible for the people through Parliament and therefore, the civil servants have to be accountable to the minister. However, an impartial civil service is responsible not only to the government of the day but to the Constitution of the land to which they have taken an oath of loyalty. At the same time, implementing the policies of the duly elected government is a core function of civil servants. In the context of responsibility, policy formulation forms part of ministerial responsibility while its implementation is the concern of the civil servant.

Constitutional Provision in India

It may be worth noting here the provisions of the Constitution of India which provides for governance system in the country. The Indian Constitution provides for separation of power between the legislature, executive and judiciary with well defined roles and responsibilities for each one of them. Since India is a parliamentary democracy, there is an interface between the legislative and the executive at the level of the Council of Ministers, which is collectively responsible to the legislature. In terms of Articles, 53 and 54, the executive power of the Union and the States vests in the President or the Governor directly or through offices subordinate to him. Thus, officers constitute the permanent civil service and are governed by Part XIV of the Constitution. The other part of the executive is the 'political' one. The President or Governor is required to act according to the aid and advice of his/her Council of Ministers, appointed under Articles, 73 and 163 of the Constitution. The President or Governor frames rules for the conduct of business in the government. Moreover, there are also rules under which the Ministers and the civil servants have to discharge their prescribed functions and responsibilities. The minister has the mandate of the people to govern, but the Secretary has an equivalent Constitutional mandate to advice the Minister. It is important to note that his / her advice has been suitably considered, unless the Minister passes an illegal order, the Secretary is bound to implement it. This is the stated position.

The Post-Independence Scenario

There are bound to be some areas which need mention so far as the question of relationship between the Minister and the civil servant is concerned. It is alleged that in the initial years after independence, relations between Minister and Civil Servants were characterised by mutual respect and understanding of each others' respective roles, with neither encroaching upon the others' domain. It might be because of the fact that the Ministers during those days were politicians who had fought for the independence of country and were genuinely concerned about the people's cause in the areas of governance. Same could be said about the class of the civil servants who constituted the permanent civil service system. However, in subsequent years, matters started changing for the worse.

There is a marked change in the area of relationship between the Minister, in particular and the politician in general and the civil servants functioning at various levels of the government. There was a time when there was mutual respect for each other's role which was, by and large, defined through the law and also the precedence. The class of political leaders in the government otherwise in the early days of the Republic commanded respect as they were, by and large, committed to peoples' service. The civil service of those days too was by and large, honest, upright and sincere to their task. This kind of situation could not last-long and we notice a different class coming up in the political arena as well as in the civil service for whom the earlier values seem to have had little significance. The new class of politician appears to be more interested in matters personal nor public. In order to achieve their personal and partisan aspirations, they tend to manipulate the civil servant. While a good number of civil servants might not favour their political boss, at the same time there could be some who could compromise their position for such causes. Such tendencies have affected the governance and have encouraged maladministration and corruption.

There was also a tendency for some Ministers at the Union and at the State levels to focus more on routine administrative matters such as posting and transfer in preference to policy making. At the same time, some civil servants learnt the art of 'maneuvering' for favour in returns for pliability in their decision making. This fraud was further accentuated by rising materialism and acquisitiveness in society as well as decline in values across the board. As a result 'political neutrality' which was the hallmark of the civil service in the pre-independence era as well as the period right after independence, was gradually eroded. These trends lead to 'polarisation of the civil service' in India. This trend might not be in the best interest of longer societal good. For example, in Uttar Pradesh we have noted that during the last twenty years or so successive governments have consciously eroded the concept of 'neutrality' of the civil service. We are given to understand that 'X' civil servant is 'his' or 'her' man indicating the fact that they are close to Chief Minister belonging to different political parties. Often this has resulted in large scale transfers in the administration. This has generated demoralising effect on the civil service and there goes a perception in the public that transfer and posting in U.P. has developed into an 'industry'. It cannot be taken as a positive signal for governance.

It is worth recommending this observation made by Sardar Vallabhbhai Patel in the Constituent Assembly to support the continuance of pre-independence civil service structure.

> "It needs hardly to be emphasised that an efficient disciplined, and contended civil service assured of its prospects as a result of diligent and honest work, is a *sine qua non* of sound administration under democratic regimes even more than under an authoritarian rule. The service must be above party and we should ensure that political consideration, either in its recommitment or in its discipline and control, are reduced to the minimum if not eliminated altogether".

Unfortunately, this vision of civil service neutrality no longer holds good. Change in government particularly at the state level often lead to wholescale transfer of civil servants. Political neutrality is no longer the accepted norm with many civil servants getting identified, rightly or wrongly, with a particular political dispensation. There is a perception that officers have to cultivate and seek patronage from political people for obtaining suitable positions even in the Union Government. As a result, the civil service in public perception is often seen as increasingly politicised[3]. Such a perception in public affects the governing process and damage the attainment process of public good.

There is no denying that the politician civil servant relationship has undergone considerable change and that change is perceptible in public view. There is also no denying that it has encouraged inefficiency and corruption in public administration. While the situation at the Union level might not be that serious, but it does have serious connotations at the State level. Also, it might not be that serious in some states, but in some, it does have serious concerns. In view of this we feel that its high time to look into the question of politician-civil servant relationship for a better governance so that public good and public welfare can come up to the centre stage of governance.

There are several areas and issues which can be taken up in this discussion. However, we identified only the following for the participants to help their thought process. The following sub-themes were provided for the purpose.

(a) The Concept of Neutrality

(b) Advisory role of civil servants in public policy
(c) Statutory Role of Civil Servants
(d) Discharge of Delegated Function
(e) Appointment/ Recruitment to the Civil Service
(f) Transfer and Posting of civil servants

With the above sub-themes and the broader theme on "The Changing Paradigm of Governance with Special Focus on Politician-Civil Servant Relationship" a two-days National Seminar was organised by the Institute for Applied Research and Development, Lucknow on November 7-8, 2014. The Seminar was sponsored by the Indian Council of Social Science Research, New Delhi. We briefly present the proceedings of the same which is followed by articles from eminent academicians and scholars.

The Seminar was inaugurated by Pandit Ram Kishan Dwivedi former Home Minister, in the Government of Uttar Pradesh. Professor D.P. Singh, former Head of the Department of Public Administration, Lucknow University and UGC Member was the Guest of Honour in the Seminar. A large number of scholars and academicians from different parts of the country participated in the Seminar. A Souvenir was also released by the Chief Guest on this occasion which published the Abstract of the papers received alongwith Activity Photographs and a brief report about the Institute.

Proceedings of the Seminar began with the welcome address delivered by Professor S.N. Singh, Director of the Seminar and the Institute. He also gave a brief account of the activity being conducted by the Institute over the years followed by a brief comment on the theme of the Seminar. After the welcome address, Professor D.P. Singh, the Guest of Honour of the seminar, spoke about the genesis of the Department alongwith personal observations about the politician-civil servant relationship. This was followed by an introductory remarks by Professor Kumkum Kishore, Head, Department of Public Administration, Lucknow University. Professor Kishore gave a theoretical setting of governance and the importance of relationship between politician and the civil servants.

While inaugurating the Seminar Pt. Ram Kishan Dwivedi, the Chief Guest, laid stress on keeping public interest uppermost in minds of both politicians and civil servants before taking any policy or administrative decisions. He recalled the vision of our freedom fighters and national leaders, particularly, Mahatma Gandhi who was universally acknowledged as the leader of masses, Pt. Jawahar Lal Nehru, the architect of modern India, Jai Prakash Narain, the pillar of socialism in the Indian polity. The minister also recalled the basic spirit of the Constitution of India i.e. Unity, Integrity, Coexistence and Equality of Opportunity etc. and said that the entire administrative and political structure which has in the form of an organised civil services and a well structured parliamentary democracy aim at the greatest benefit of the greatest number. He, therefore, stressed that both civil servant and the politician should take every decision cautiously, in public interest and not on the basis of vested interest. He lamented the fact that today most of the decisions are taken on the basis of consideration other than public interest. The relationship between civil servants and politicians is being jeopardised. The politicians often use civil servants as a tool to manipulate decision of their liking. The Minister, however, said that many new steps have been taken which can help us in improving politician and civil servant relationship such as Lok Pal, RTI, Citizen Charter etc. The inaugural session was also addressed by Professor D.P. Singh, Former Member, University Grants Commission, New Delhi, who narrated various instances of civil service-politician confrontation and requested the participants to deliberate on the issues pertaining to their relationship. Earlier the participants at the Seminar were introduced to the subject by Dr Vaishali Saxena, Assistant Professor in the Department. At the beginning Professor K. Kishore, Head, Department of Public Administration, welcomed the Chief Guest and the Guest of Honour. She also spoke of the distinct role of civil service and the politician and said that the main role of the civil servants is a facilitator, consultant and executive of the policies of the government. She laid an added emphasis on the need of ethics in both politician and civil servants. The session ended with a formal vote of thanks proposed by the Professor S.N. Singh, Director of the Institute.

The inaugural session was followed by the first Technical Session. The session was presided over by Professor I.D. Mishra. During this session only one major paper was presented by Professor B.K. Tewari who dwelt upon different forms of government viz. the parliamentary and the presidential. He discussed the nature of the bureaucracy and the role in both the systems of government. He advocated for accountability of the civil service as is utmost missing in the contemporary scenario. He made out a case for a code of conduct by the politician to help better governance. Several interventions followed the presentation, particularly by Professor Ramesh Dixit, of Political Science Department and Professor J.M.S. Verma of Sociology Department of the University. The session ended with the remarks of the Chairperson Professor I.D. Mishra of Gorakhpur University.

The post-lunch session was the Second Technical Session of the day. This session was presided over by Professor P.N. Gautam of Himachal University, Shimla, Professor Y.S. Bhadauria acted as the Co-chairperson, whereas the Raporteur of the Session was Dr Anurag. First paper in this session was presented by Professor Harbans Pathak of Patiala University. He focused on the paradigm of governance with special mention of LPG (liberation, privatisation and globalisation). His paper emphasised on four significant factors viz. policy-making, localised trends, total accountability and the treatment of individuals. He concluded his paper with Modi Model of development which is yet to take shape. The second paper of the session was presented by Professor A.D. Mishra of Gandhian Institute, Delhi. His paper explained the context of bureaucracy in Kautilya as well as in contemporary world. He said that it was Kautilya who for the first time gave the concept of Neutrality. The concept is relevant even in today's context. He laid emphasis on ethics in governance which is lacking in the present day systems of governance. He said that three important things are necessary for changing any thing: (a) Knowledge (b) Wealth and (c) Cooperation. These factors need consideration in the present context. Another paper was presented by Mr Digvijay, S.R.F. in the Department. He discussed the concept of anonymity and neutrality in the context of politician-civil servant relationship. He further dwelt upon the question of policy-making and discussed that it should be more representative rather than restructured. He argued for a different pension scheme for the politician and the civil servants. This was followed by interventions from the participants who put their questions to the paper presenters. The session ended with the remarks and comments by the Chairperson.

The Seminar continued its third Technical session wherein Professor Harbans Pathak, presided over the session and Professor A.D. Mishra acted as the Co-chairperson of the session. Sri F.H. Siddiqui, former faculty of SIRD, Lucknow became the Rapporteur. During this session Professor P.N. Gautam of Himachal University presented his paper. He explained the concept of Bureaucracy and discussed various models of bureaucracy. He discussed that presently there is a 'Hand-in-Glove' in bureaucracy. This has affected the relationship as well as governance. Another paper was presented by Dr A.R. Basu, a former IAS of Himachal Cadre. His focus was on the question of delegated legislation. He made an attempt to establish a relationship between the parliamentary democracy and delegated legislation. He said that this is an important factor in governance. Dr M.A. Beg from Jamia, Delhi presented this thought on Modi's concept of governance in which it is advocated – "Minimum Government and Maximum Governance". He also focused on the role of public sector and the role of civil servants in achieving goals of good governance. A detailed discussion took place on the issues raised by the paper presenters. Several interventions were allowed during the session. In the end of the session the Chairperson Professor Harbans Pathak gave his presidential remarks and thanked the participants for their contribution.

This was followed by "Open House Session", in which participants were asked to put their views on the theme of the seminar. This session was chaired by Dr A.R. Basu. During the session several participants came out with their views who could not present their papers in the earlier session. It may be reported that a lively discussion took place during this session. It is encouraging that large number of young scholars presented their views.

This in brief, is the proceeding of the national seminar on the said topic conducted by the Institute.

Notes

1. Second Administrative Reforms Commission, Government of India, Tenth Report, November 2008, New Delhi, p. 272.
2. *Ibid.*
3. *Ibid.*, p. 274.

1

The Changing Paradigm of Politician-Civil Servant Relationship

— *Professor P.N. Gautam*

Present papers aims at discussing the paradigm shifts in the political-civil servant relationship right from the pre-independence days when the ICS was very much efficient, authoritarian, and full of integrity to the present turbulent times of coalition governments when most of the civil servants have become highly corrupt and inefficient and "there is hardly any room for the average officer to display any sign of independence or candour in decision-making."

Colonial Rule and First Two Decades After Independence

Colonial rulers everywhere in the world were interested only in the maintenance of law and order, collection of taxes and safeguarding and preserving their empires. So their emphasis was only on the establishment of legal and administrative structures of the governments in the slave countries. The task of building coherent political processes was not their concern. When the colonial rulers left, the newly independent countries faced imbalanced polities where the administrative systems were well developed but the political systems were not developed to play a directional role in nation-building in the nascent nations. In this context, Lucian Pye has rightly pointed out that these countries have neither effective administration nor stable polities and that public administration cannot be greatly improved without a parallel strengthening of the democratic, representative political process.[1]

In case of India, Indian Civil Service (ICS), eulogised as the "steel frame" of British Empire, selected on the basis of merit, trained in the virtues of integrity, functional efficiency, and civil service neutrality served well for protecting the British interests. Top Indian political leaders and freedom fighters like Pt. Jawaharlal Nehru and Sardar Vallabh Bhai Patel, were men of great vision and integrity. They, however, did not like the civil servants working for the British Empire. In this context it is the views of Pt. Nehru may be quoted, "The ICS were a curious set of persons. They were efficient in some ways. They organised the government, strengthened the British rule and incidentally profited greatly by it themselves. Not being appointed by, or responsible to people, the ICS paid little attention to those other departments which concerned people most. As was natural under the circumstances, they became arrogant and overbearing and contemptuous of public opinion. Narrow or limited in outlook, they began to look upon themselves as the wisest people on earth."[2]

After India got independence, the colonial administration was geared to fulfill the rising needs and expectations of the people. The same political leaders, like Nehru and Patel who earlier did not like the ICS, realising the need of "an efficient, disciplined and contended civil service" wanted that the civil service worked above party and ensured that "political considerations, either in its recruitment or in its discipline and control, are reduced to its minimum if not eliminated altogether." They wanted the higher civil servants to give their opinions frankly without any fear and also welcomed the opinions contrary to their ideas. Article 311 was introduced in the Constitution of India to protect the rights of civil servants.

The first generation politicians, who possessed high morals and dedication took care "to see that the public services adopted to the new co-existent chain of command from the political leadership at the local level up to the national level – the rhythm and balance of the two hardly disturbed." In 1953, Paul H. Appleby rated Indian administration as "among the dozen or so most advanced governments in the world." Immediately after independence, "the leadership available to the nation from such spheres as the Indian National Congress and the administration was competent, cohesive and committed to national objectives and constitutional values. Such leadership continued up to two decades or so after independence. After this, the country witnessed a gradual disappearance of 'old guards' and assumption of leadership both at the Centre and in the states by men who were much inferior in their commitment and ability."[3]

Formation of Multiparty Governments in States

The traditions of open minded discussions and cooperation between the politicians and civil servants laid down by Nehru and Patel were not followed sincerely by many of their colleagues and successors which resulted in open conflict between the ministers and their secretaries. Open rifts and quarrels between Union Finance Minister, T.T. Krishnamachari and the Principal Secretary, H.M. Patel in 1957, Gulzari Lal Nanda, the Union Home Minister and the Home Secretary, L.P. Singh in 1966, Union Railways Minister, K. Hanumanthaiya and the Chairman of the Railway Board, Bankim Chandra Ganguli in 1971, Revenue Minister of Punjab, Jiwan Singh Umranagal and the Financial Commissioner (Revenue), R.S. Talwar in 1977 and many other such examples point out the acrimonious relations between the politicians and the civil servants.

A severe blow to the cordial and harmonious relations between politicians and civil-servants was given after the late 1960s when a period of political turbulence started. One-party dominance was weakened with the splits in Congress Party in 1969 and 1978. Many states had non-Congress governments composed of multi-parties called Sarv-Vidhayal Dals (S.V.D.) in 1967. Referring to Uttar Pradesh, S.K. Singh has pointed out that "in 1967 the first challenge to hitherto single party Congress government in the state was posed and a S.V.D. government was formed under the leadership of Chaudhary Charan Singh. This marked the beginning of an era of defections and instability."[4] Haryana, perhaps was the most notorious of all the states with the emergence of the phenomenon of "Aya Rams and Gaya Rams", an usually quoted phrase for the turn-coats who would quickly change their party affiliation for the lure of money or ministerial positions. To further quote Singh, "During 1967-76 U.P. had six different Chief Ministers with four spells of President Rule. From 1977 to 2002 state witnessed sixteen changes in government with varying duration of President Rule in between. 1967 became the watershed at the national and state level as the era of instability appeared on the political scene which is troubling even today's government and administration. As a consequence, political and social fragmentation multiplied, caste and communal factors became dominant resulting in the services getting heavy dose of influence. Officers of the services started to be identified as loyal to different political parties in power and consequently were rewarded or punished accordingly. With the passage of time they began to be identified with political leaders, castes, classes and group interests. The greatest casualty in the process was integrity, independence, objectivity, fairness, impartiality and of course anonymity which constituted hitherto the great strength of the services. A kind of spoils system emerged which is destructive of essential qualities of sound administration, viz., continuity, credibility, fearlessness and impartiality."[5] The above situation prevailed more or less in all the states of the country.

Nineteen Months of Emergency

Internal emergency declared by Mrs Indira Gandhi on the night of 26th June, 1975 did a great damage to the cordial relations between the politicians and the civil servants. Arbitrariness let loose by the politicians, not fearing even God, made the civil servants humble and meek. They developed a fear psychosis which led to the degeneration of their courage, integrity, discipline, devotion to duty, and all such virtues. Mrs Indira Gandhi gave a call for a "committed bureaucracy" and during emergency the politicisation of bureaucracy became even more intense. The civil servants had to be committed to the ruling party's ideology, policies and programmes. Men like Jagjivan Ram, Mohan Kumaramanglam too held such views. In the words of K. Subrahmanyam, "Mrs Indira Gandhi destroyed the concept of an independent and apolitical civil service...career advancements were made in favour of civil servants committed to the authoritarian rule of the leader. Those who asserted their independence or remained apolitical were quietly sidelined and the opportunists in the civil services started making tacit alliances with politicians."[6] A very senior retired IAS officer, M.N. Buch has also observed, "Mrs Gandhi was shrewd enough...to realise its (Civil Service) potential as an instrument to convert the Indian state into her private fiefdom."[7]

The 'Yes Minister' syndrome was fully evident everywhere during the period of the Emergency. Ruthless juggernaut of political machinery of the time cowed down all the voices of dissent in the society and the civil servants willy-nilly danced to the tune of the politicians. Inquiry Commission appointed by Government of India under the chairmanship of Justice Shaw to probe into the excesses done during the Emergency, in its report submitted in two volumes in 1978 has clearly shown that in case after case, the civil servants who were merely asked to bend the rules chose to crawl to ingratiate themselves with their bosses.

After Emergency to the Beginning of Era of Liberalisation

When the Janata Party succeeded the Congress Party in 1977, it also went the Congress way. The arrest and suspension of senior officers like Secretary to Petroleum Ministry, B.B. Vohra and Secretary of Communications S.S. Aggarwal, on the formation of Janata Government after the end of Emergency, further had a great demoralising effect on the civil servants. Change of governments, thereafter, made the civil servants timid and dancing to the tune of the politicians to save their careers. Many of the civil servants found the situation as an opportunity to have pliable posts and enjoy pelf, power and position. So they went out of the way to please the politicians. Marina Pinto has discussed this phenomenon of hobnobbing between the politicians and the civil servants in the following words: "When Mrs Gandhi returned to power in 1980, she brought back her old faithful followers. The unmistakable message was that to survive one can never be defiant...During the time of Rajiv Gandhi, the time-tested approach of loyalty to the political boss was upheld. Not only were favourites rewarded even if undeserving and those critical or neutral side-tracked, the near total negation of the doctrine of civil service neutrality was seen in the coterie that surrounded Rajiv Gandhi and which played a key role in the governance of the nation."[8]

Phenomena of criminalisation of politics and politicisation of criminals emerged and prospered during this time. Politicians made good use of the criminals for catching votes- booth capturing, bribing the voters, intimidating by not allowing the opponents to vote, violence during the elections, etc. were the known methods of the criminals. After the elections were over, these criminals protected by the politicians made it difficult for law enforcing agencies to control them. After some time the criminals finding politics a profitable business themselves joined political parties and fought elections and won, many of the won even when they were in jails, of course, with the help of their powerful gangsters. License-permit raj facilitated the hands-in-glove relation of the politicians and civil-servants for the benefit of both. Transfers and postings of the officials became a big industry and a tool in the hands of the politicians to use the civil servants. The situation became worse in the states of U.P. and Bihar where there were frequent transfers to post the pliable officers to various important posts. Various mafias working under the protection and connivance of powerful politicians made the situation more unbearable.

From the Era of Liberalisation to the Present Times

Economic reforms were introduced in the Indian economy due to the conditions imposed by World Bank and IMF. Politico-administrative scenario of criminalisation of politics, politicisation of criminals and transfer industry continued as usual. However, the license-permit raj had to be dismantled again because of the compulsions forced by the loaning authorities. As for the relationship between the politicians and civil servants during this period, there are two broad opinions. Firstly, with the starting of economic reforms financial lay out of the governments increased manifold, so lure of money led to increased corruption which further led to strained relation between politicians and civil servants. License-permit raj was dismantled to end the corruption. But this did not happen. With liberalisation the revenues of the government increased and the corruption also increased perhaps in the similar proportion. We come across multi-thousand crores of scams. 2G scam, Adarsh Colony scam, Commonwealth Games scam, Coal-allocation scam are some of the recent scams which may be called as the tips of the icebergs. Private-Public Partnership (PPP) model which was adopted following the economic reforms further increased the level of corruption. Transparency International India in its reports have exposed the unholy alliance between the civil servants and corporate houses leading to enormous corruption. One of the reports related to the 2G scam which resulted due to the connivance between the ex-Communication Minister A. Raja and the corporate houses.

Other opinion about the relationship between the politicians and civil servants and increasing corruption during this period is that it is because of greater awakening in public life, Right to Information Act (RTI) and media exposures that we come across the cases of strained relationship between them and increased level of corruption. Rising level of inflation and decreasing value of the rupee may also be another cause of the seeming high level of corruption. Some persons are also of the opinion that RTI and decreasing the discretion with the civil servants have lowered the level of corruption as well as saved them from a lot of political pressure. Whichever of the above two opinions may be correct or may be both are correct, we clearly observe that the politico-administrative phenomenon is going worse day by day.

A former Director of Central Bureau of Investigation lamenting on the present deplorable position has remarked that "There is hardly any room today for the average officer to display any sign of independence or candour in decision making." Memoirs of former Secretary of Union Ministry of Coal, P.C. Parekh, Crusader or Conspirator, has clearly pointed out that the relationship between civil servants and political executive has deteriorated from pre-Independence days to now.

Some examples of deteriorating relationship between the politicians and civil servants, one blaming the other, arrogating powers which do not belong to them, helping each other for their own benefit with no worry for the people whom they are supposed to serve, may be quoted here. Tensions in minister-civil servant relationship have resulted in political leaders adopting extreme positions with regard to the bureaucracy. While one Central Minister is reported to have informed the bureaucrats in his Ministry, that "(civil) servants should not speak till the master permits...(you) are not to apply your mind, you are just to do what you are told"...another Minister stated in an interview that bureaucrats are "like servants" who should not be allowed to act on their own.[9] A senior bureaucrat resigned while alleging that the entire politico-administrative system vitiated by the "greedy and power-hungry politicians and corrupt and self-seeking civil servants".[10] In another case, a senior IAS officer of Maharashtra threatened to resign and wrote to the Chief Secretary, "My spirit is not in tune with the working environment. After deep introspect, I find myself in a situation in which I am unable to adjust myself properly."[11] Director of LBSAA, Mussoorie has very candidly said, "Unfortunately many...officers are accepting the diminishing role of themselves by becoming agents of exploitation in a state structure which is callous to the needs of the poor. In the process, they would become totally indistinguishable from other rent-seeking parasites – politicians, inspectors...they are taking too much from the system and contributing too little."[12] Julio Riberio has nicely described the relationship between the corrupt politicians and corrupt officials: "Corrupt politicians are understandably very comfortable in association or axis with corrupt officials, since both sides stand to prosper with such an arrangement...When honest officials find their blatantly corrupt colleagues move up the promotion ladder, they are bound to be influenced. If they are themselves weak or fence-sitters, they would join the bourgeoning ranks of the dishonest."[13] This unholy alliance between corrupt politicians and corrupt officials has been blatantly remarked by T. N. Seshan by saying that the civil servants are like "polished call girls who continuously prostitute their position."[14]

Peters's Models of Politicians and Civil Servants Relationship

After the brief history of the relationship between the politicians and civil servants, let us discuss the five models of their relationship as pointed out by Gye Peters. In the first model the clear separation between politicians and administration exists, in which the civil servants are ready to unquestionably follow the orders of the political appointees. This mode of interaction aligns clearly to the Weberian formal-legal model and the traditional Wilsonian approach to public administration whereby 'the field of administration is a field of business. It is removed from the hurry and strife of politics'. In this model, politicians make policies and civil servants implement them. Peters notes that while this model is advocated by many contemporary political executives it also serves a useful fiction, allowing civil servants a great deal of functional responsibility while retaining political responsibility in the hands of the elected politicians.

The second model ("village life") assumes that civil servants and politicians are both part of unified state elite and they should not be in conflict over power within the government structure itself. Senior civil servants and political executives are conceptualised as having relatively similar values and goals that contributes to the maintenance and functioning of government. In this instance this horizontally connected elite coalesce against external interference in their affairs and common interest in the management of the state.

The third model ("functional village life") assumes a degree of some integration of civil service and political careers. Peters refers to model three as a subset of the 'village life' model with the difference that while 'village life' assumes an integration of political and administrative elites in the higher echelons of government, the 'functional' model places this integration along functional lines. To illustrate, a politician and civil servant from one government department have more in common than a minister with his political cabinet colleagues heading different governmental portfolios. This model is oriented toward vertical integration and more extensive contacts with society whereby political and administrative elites within a specific policy sector will be allied against political and bureaucratic elites from other policy sectors. The village life and functional models need not be mutually exclusive and in reality are closely intertwined.

The fourth model ("adverse model") assumes a significant separation between the two groups (politicians and bureaucrats) who are assumed to be competitors for power and control over policy. Such conflicts may arise in several ways – via the challenge of the bureaucracy to an incoming political executive, conflicts over the shape and content of policy, resources and the impact of politicisation.

The fifth model ("administrative state model") of the interactions between politicians and civil servants indicates the clear separation between policy-makers and administration, but in which civil servants are the dominant force. This model conceives that the dominant role of the bureaucracy in decision-making has been exacerbated by the growth and complexity of government and the decline of the legislature in contemporary times. This model differentiates from the 'adverse model' in that the latter assumes that the political executive is the principal motivator in the decision-making process (as imputed in their role).

After discussing the five models pointed out by Peters, let me discuss another model relationship between the politicians and civil servants which I find relevant to present day situation in India. Sixth model, I would call it, Hand-in-Glove Model. Herein, both the politicians and civil servants conspire and collaborate for their respective benefits looting the public wealth to the callous and criminal disregard for their duties towards the voiceless suffering millions following the transactional analysis ideal of "I am O.K. You are O.K."

Jayanta Kumar Ray in his Administrators in a Mixed Polity has dealt with about 160 cases on interaction between politics and administration. On the basis of these cases, he has divided the administrators into four categories- promoters, resistors, accommodators and detractors.[15] P.R. Dubhashi has briefly described these four categories as follows: "The civil servants of the first category are loyal to the public purpose and seek to promote public good in the best possible manner. The resistors even go one step further in the pursuit of the public purpose even at the cost of their own career, by putting stiff resistance to undue pressures. The accommodators buckle down under pressures while the detractors go out of way to curry favour of the politicians in power by all kinds of wrong advice and misdeeds in order to butter their own bread."[16]

Different Categories of Present Civil Servants

On the basis of observation, the present civil servants may be divided into following categories:

1. Honest, Sincere and Non-Attached.
2. Honest, Sincere and Attached.
3. Dishonest and Attached.
4. Dishonest and Non-Attached- Self-Seekers.
5. Listless-Ineffective.
6. Whistleblowers.
7. Enterprising/Innovative- Effective.
8. Politicking

Conclusion

Present scenario of the relationship between the politicians and the civil servants is quite dismal. Indian Civil Service (ICS) and later Indian Administrative Service (IAS) was retained in the free India with the hope that the "steel frame" which maintained the British Empire was essential for the socio-economic development of the country and the idealists like Pt. Jawaharlal Nehru and Sardar Vallabh Bhai Patel wanted the civil servants to express their frank and honest opinion. C.D. Deshmukh who strongly defended the retention of All India Services in 1951 lamented in 1974 that, "No civil servant is any longer appreciated for speaking or writing without fear or favour."[17]

Tradition of mutual respect diminished with the old guard going away from the scene. Formation of multi-party governments in the states led to the deterioration of cordial relationship between the civil servants and politicians. Declaration of internal emergency in 1975 gave a serious blow and opened the floodgates of mutual distrust and acrimony. Formation of coalition governments at the Centre led to further tensions between their relationship. Our former Prime Minister Dr Manmohan Singh asked the senior officers to be honest and fearless in advising political leadership. So did the present Prime Minister, Sh. Narendra Modi, in his first meeting with the Secretaries of all the Ministries of Government asked them to be fearless and come out openly with their innovative ideas to him for making administration effective and poor centric. Whatever the top political personnel may say, it is a well known fact that the honest officials concerned with the maintenance of law and order, protection of mines, minerals, forest and environment, find it very difficult to do their duties according to the rules and regulations. We have to agree with what a former Director of Central Bureau of Investigation lamenting on the present deplorable position has remarked that "There is hardly any room today for the average officer to display any sign of independence or candour in decision making." We have also to agree with what Stella Manzie has said about UK, the same situation prevails in India too where she has likened the partnership between a politician and a senior public servant to an ice-skating duo. The metaphor evokes the delicate, symbiotic, sometimes precarious, relationship that politicians and public servants must have if they wish to be successful.[18]

References and Notes

1. Lucian Pye, "The Political Context of National Development in Irwing Swerdlow" (ed.) *Development Administration: Concepts and Problems,* Syracuse University Press, 1963.
2. S.K. Singh, The Civil Service in U.P. : Perspective and Challenges, in P.S. Bhatnagar (Ed.), Indian Administration: Issues and Opinions, Jaipur, Mangal Deep Publications, 2003, pp. 127-28.
3. C.N. Bhalerao, Some Political and Administrative Issues in India's Governance, in Ramesh K. Arora and Meena Sogani (Eds.) *Governance in India: Paradigms and Practices*, Akhilesh Publishers, Jaipur, 2011, p. 57.
4. *Op.cit*, p. 133.
5. *Ibid*, pp. 133-34.

6. K. Subrahmanyam, "Servile Stagnancy", *Economic Times*, Banglore, 15 November, 1992.
7. *Indian Express*, 1 October,1990.
8. Marina R Pinto, Civil Servants in India- Anonymous Ciphers or Questioning Neutrals?, in Ramesh K. Arora and Meena Sugani (Eds), *Governance in India: Paradigms and Practices*, Jaipur, Aalekh Publishers, 2011, p. 91.
9. Sandeep Shastri, Political Control of Bureaucracy in India: Emerging Trends, in Ramesh K. Arora, *Public Administration: Fresh Perspectives*, Jaipur, Aalekh Publishers, 2004, pp. 133-34.
10. S.R. Maheshwari, "Bureaucracy under Pressure" *Indian Express,* March 17, 1992.
11. *Times of India,* February 29, 2004.
12. Anil Agarwal, "IAS is Indifferent to the Needs of the Poor People", *Hindustan Times*, April 29, 1996.
13. Julio Riberio, "Circumventing the Axis", *Telegraph,* New Delhi, May 12, 1995.
14. T.N. Seshan, *The Times of India*, January 23, 1994.
15. Jayant Kumar Ray, *Administrators in a Mixed Polity*, Delhi, Macmillan, 1981.
16. P.R. Dubhashi, *Essays in Public Administration*, New Delhi, N.B.O. Publisher's Distributors, 1985, p. 309.
17. S.K. Singh, *op. cit*, p. 129.
18. Stella Manzie, *The Guardian*, September,18, 2013.

2

Role of Bureaucracy in Public Policy Making in India

— ***Shiv Raj Singh***

Bureaucracy as an archetype of rationality is a prerequisite of modernisation of every society. It has always been a dominant force in all the systems of government and has emerged as a powerful institution in the contemporary world. Bureaucracy in India at the time when India became free was groomed for a "law and order state" or a "police state" or "a night-watchman state" rather than a welfare state or development state. The priorities underwent a total change after the end of colonialism and emergence of freedom. Mass primary education, a network of health facilities, rural employment and development programmes, cooperative development programmes, rural local government known as Panchayati Raj, agriculture modernisation, land reforms, industrial diversification, development of economic infrastructure like electrification, irrigation, transport and communication, all these and many more become the responsibilities of public administration. Bureaucracy was expected to be governed and oriented to the new function of development.[1]

On many functions of governance of any country, that of policy making is certainly the most important. Policy is very essential in administration for it gives a concrete shape to the political and social objectives which the government lays down in the form of laws, rules, regulations etc. Being a federal polity policy-making activity is assumed at the central, state and local government levels. The success of any government depends upon the well thought, clear and sound policies.

By public policy is meant a government policy. Public policies have been defined as guidelines for public action, prescribing in general term the means for moving toward a desired course of events or outcome.[2] Policies are not just wishes or declarations of objectives. They have to be implementable and should indicate the availability of resources, organisation and personnel, allocation of responsibility and time-limit for implementation.

In any organisation, the task of policy formulation has necessarily to be fairly widespread and complex in nature the ultimate responsibility for policy formulation, is with the parliament in the centre and in the states with the state legislatures, but in the discharge of this responsibility, it is aided and advised by a number of agencies and individuals. Bureaucracy is one such agency which plays a vital role in policymaking both in developing and developed countries. The Fulton Committee in U.K. feels that the permanent secretaries of the departments and their deputies and assistants were so much preoccupied with day-to-day administration that they had hardly the time or the inclination to address the policy matters. The position in India is no different. The Fulton committee recommended that every department should have a technocrat secretary (apart from the administrative secretary) who should be solely concerned with long-term policy aspects. This particular recommendation was never implemented because of the opposition registered by the bureaucracy but also because it is, in the very nature of policy formulation that it can never be divorced from the day-to-day issues. A better alternative would be the constitution of a small policy group in every department comprising top administrators who could keep a close on the emerging policy issues, the ongoing impact of existing policies and the formulation of new policies.[3]

A series of new policies were framed in past independence India such as Industrial Development and Regulation Policies, policies for agricultural modernisation, cooperative development and promotion of Panchayati Raj, educational policies at all levels (primary, secondary and higher) manpower development, policies to provide health for all, policies for a amelioration of poverty etc. Since the policies had a great deal of technical content, the government did find it necessary to call in the services of experts like economists and scientists in different fields as advisors, what was the relative role of generalist secretaries of departments and the new technical advisors in the field of policy making? The answer cannot be given categorically as very little empirical work in the field is available. Research studies in different fields of activity are needed to bring out the relative roles of politician, the general administrator and the advisor in policy making.

In order to sharpen the skills of bureaucracy, at the initiative of late Rajiv Gandhi a comprehensive programmes of training was advised for IAS officers-training in programmes implementation for junior officers, in programme management for middle level officers and in policy-making for senior officers of the level of Joint Secretary and above.

The programmes continue even today in intuitions like the Lal Bahadur Shastri Academy of Public Administration at Mussorie, The[4] Indian Institute of Public Administration at New Delhi, the Administrative Staff College at Hyderabad and the Institute of Management. How far have these programmes improved the quality of policy-making in India should be a matter of systematic research.

A recent phenomenon especially in the USA is the emergence of "think-tanks" in various areas of administration which can offer expert policy analysis and suggest ideas for fresh policies. Apart from the fact that in India, such 'think-tanks' are available only to a limited extent, a major handicap is that we have not yet established a tradition of government agencies drawing on the analysis and recommendation of the "think-tanks" since the former tend to think policy-making as their exclusive preserve in which outsiders cannot be allowed to intrude and more so because most of these matters are labeled as "confidential and top secret. For a think tank or for that matter for even a governmental agency to make any contribution to policy-making it should have an access to what Yezkel Dror has called the CMG-Central Mind of Government. In very governmental set-up the CMG has to be identified. In our set-up, it is easily identified with Prime Minister himself and those to whom "policy window" is open, for the exercise of their "policy entrepreneurship".[5]

So we have to agree that the role of bureaucracy had been crucial both in the initiating and shaping policy too, not to speak of affecting the state of policy effectiveness at implementation stages. Bureaucracy plays a major role in shaping policy outcomes by influencing the definition of decisional problems as well as organisation of issues. In the process it manages to accommodate certain interests to the exclusion of certain others, thereby providing or denying them the opportunity to benefit from policy. Except when certain issues become politically visible and quite activated in public domain, the capacity of bureaucrats to determine their substance is quite significant. Their role has been particularly relevant in respect of regulatory policy. It is for this reason that powerful business lobbies rely on bureaucratic support for more than politicisation of issues.[6]

This is more true for developing country like India which has engaged itself in development administration, with the result that the government function have increased manifold and the parliament with limited time at its disposal makes the legislation of very general kind; in order that it may be effectively implemented bureaucracy must work out regulation or regulatory codes elaborating its policy which has been adopted by the political branches of the government. This, much of substance of policy is a matter of decision by bureaucrats and the effectiveness of policy is the consequences of the spirit and the will of bureaucrats. Apart from its primary function of policy implementation and policy-making the bureaucracy may perform important functions as articulators and aggregators of interests. In parliamentary democracy the top bureaucracy must advice the ministers. The secretariat is the key organisation in the governmental hierarchy, engaged in assisting the ministers in formulation of policies. In addition, it translates those policies in issues or programmes and ensures their efficient execution.[7]

Conclusion

From the above discussion with regard to policy-making analysis, it can safely be said that no political system can function or survive without well organised, efficient and impartial bureaucracy which not only implement the policies but also plays very important role in policy-making which is the primary function of legislature or political executive. In the absence of an elaborate machinery at the disposal of legislature which would be able to investigate collect and analyse information independently, the legislature is compelled to accept the authority of bureaucracy for making certain policies which are based on information collected, marshaled and supplied by the bureaucracy itself, whatever its nature. Moreover the term of elected representatives is comparatively very short and affords little opportunity to them to specialise in any matter of such an extent as to actively compete with the bureaucracy. Dyal and Mathur and others have suggested that the political system contributes towards the articulation in of goals and has limited the contribution in formulating the content of policy. The administrators and specialist inputs are greater in recommending the content of policy.

Notes

1. P.R. Dubhashi, Bureaucracy and Policy making in India in edited book of Hoshiar Singh, Higher Civil Services in India, Nirmal Book Agency, Kurukshetra, 1995, pp. 13-14.
2. R.B. Jain, "Parliament and policy in India (Accountability Syndrome, The Indian Journal of Policy Administration, Vol. XXIV, No. 3, July-September 1983, p. 559.
3. Romesh K. Arora (ed), Indian Administration Perceptions and perspectives, Aalekh Publishers, Jaipur, 1999, pp. 59-60.
4. P.R. Dubhashi, op.cit., pp. 14-15.
5. Romesh K Arora (ed) op.cit. p. 61.
6. Noorjahan Bava (ed.), Development policies and Administration in India, Article by Dolly Arora, Policy process in India: Patterns and problems, Uppal Publishing House, New Delhi, 2000, pp. 95-96.
7. G.A. Almond and G.B. Powell, Comparative Policies; A development Approach, A Merind Publishing Co., New Delhi, 1975, p. 154.

3

Discharge of Delegated Functions

—Ashok Ranjan Basu

In the eighteenth century the study of governmental functions led to the famous theory of separation of powers, ascribed to Baron de Montesquie[1]. According to Montesquieu's theory, powers of the government are of three kinds: legislative, executive and judicial and each of these powers should be vested in separate and distinct organ. According to the traditional theory, the function of the executive is to administer the law enacted by the legislature, and in the ideal state, the legislative power must be exercised exclusively by the legislators who are directly responsible to the electorate. As per Halsbury's Laws of England[2], when an instrument of a legislative nature is made by an authority in exercise of power delegated or conferred by the Legislature, it is called subordinate or delegated legislation. According to the Committee on Minister's Power[3], the expression delegated legislation is used in two senses. In one sense the delegated legislation means the exercise of power of rule making delegated to the Executive by the Legislature. In the other sense, it means the output of the exercise of that power.

In the first sense, it means that the authority, making the legislation is subordinate to the Legislature. Thus, the legislative power exercised by an another authority, in the exercise of the powers delegated on them by the legislature itself, is also known as subordinate legislation, because the powers of the authority which makes it are limited by the statute which conferred the power and consequently it is valid in so far as it kept within those limits[4]. In the second sense, delegated legislation refers to all law-making which is generally expressed as rules, regulations, bye-laws, orders, schemes, directions, circulars, or notifications etc. Thus, when the function of legislation is entrusted to organs other than the legislature itself, the legislations made by such organs is called the delegated legislation.

According to Salmond[5], legislation is either supreme or subordinate. Whereas the former proceeds from the sovereign or superior power, the latter flows from any authority other than the sovereign power, and are therefore dependent for its existence and continuation on superior or supreme authority. Whereas an Act, enactment or statute is made by a legislature, subordinate or delegated legislation is created by an executive or administrative authority. Both, in wider sense, are products of 'legislative function' of the State having the "force of law" in their application to subjects. However, an Act of Legislature proceeds from the supreme power of the State and has no rival, in the field and also does not derives its authority from any other organ of the State, whereas delegated or subordinate legislation, on the other hand, is framed by the executive and owes its existence, continuance and validity on superior or supreme.

Calcutta Bench and Vice President, RC 48 on Administrative Culture, International Political Science Association, Montreal, Canada authority i.e. legislature. An executive can make a subordinate legislation only if such power is conferred on it by the competent legislature and not otherwise. Moreover, the subordinate law-making body is bound by the terms of its delegated or derivative authority.[6]

Delegated Legislation as Distinguished from Administrative Power

The delegated legislation can be distinguished from administrative functions. An administrative order refers to a particular individual and in this respect it is required to be served only on the individual concerned. In the case of adjudication, the administration is required to follow the principles of natural justice, while in case of legislation no such requirement is necessary. An administrative action may be challenged on the ground of malafides but it is unlikely for such a challenge to prevail in case of delegated legislation. The requirement of duty to give reasons, applies to administrative orders but not to legislative orders. If an order is legislative in character, it has to be published in a certain manner which is not necessary if it is administrative in nature. Differences between legislative and administrative actions also may become significant when questions of sub-delegation of powers arise. Only in most exceptional circumstances can legislative powers be sub-delegated but administrative powers can be sub-delegated. Thus, it can be inferred that a power to make rules of general "applicability" is legislative, while the power to make orders in specific cases is "administrative."[7] Thus, the distinction is often made between legislative and administrative acts as those between general and particular.[8] Thus, with the help of these tests it is possible to distinguish between legislative function and administrative action, though there are cases where the test may break down for it is not always easy to distinguish "general" from "particular"[9], as the difference is only a matter of degree.

Administrative Action

The nature of administrative action has been defined by Supreme Court in Ram Jawaya v State of Punjab[10]. Ordinarily executive power connotes the residue of governmental functions that remains after legislative and judicial functions are taken away. Thus:

(i) Administrative action is generally based on governmental policy or expediency;

(ii) Administrative action is subjective rather than objective. The ground on which the action is taken and the procedure for taking the action are a matter of discretion of the authority which is taking action;

(iii) While taking action, an administrative authority may not only consider the evidence adduced by the parties to the controversy but may also use its discretion;

(iv) Administrative action is not required to follow the elaborate procedure of collecting evidence and weighing arguments;

(v) An administrative decision may be held to be invalid on the ground of unreasonableness;

(vi) Administrative action may be delegated and sub-delegated;

(vii) Administrative action will not become a quasi judicial action, even if it has to be performed after forming an opinion as to the existence of any objective fact;

(viii) Administrative action is concerned with the treatment of a particular situation and is devoid of generality;

(ix) Administrative action does not decide a right though it may affect a right.

The distinction between the administrative power and quasi judicial power is quite thin and is being gradually obliterated. However, in A.K. Karaipak v Union of India[11], it was held that "For determining whether a power is an administrative power or a quasi judicial power, one has to look to the nature of power conferred, the person or persons on whom it is conferred, the framework of the law conferring that power, the consequences ensuing from the exercise of that power and the manner in which that power is expected to be exercised. In Province of Bombay v Khusaldas Advani[12], Das J, observed that "If a statute empowers an authority —— to decide disputes arising out of a claim by one party under a statute which claim is opposed by another party and to determine the respective rights of contesting parties, who are opposed to each other, there is a lis ——"

Administrative authority has not in all cases to decide "lis inter partes". Sometimes, the Administrative authority decides a lis between itself and another party which is called a quasi lis. A general test adopted for distinguishing 'quasi judicial' from 'administrative' is the duty to act judicially. In D.K. Yadava v J.M.A. Industries Ltd.[13] It has been held that the rules of natural justice are applicable to a quasi judicial as well as administrative action.

Ministerial Action

A power with the administration, the exercise of which involves no element of discretion is characterised as ministerial. In this sense, ministerial action is that action of the administrative authority which is performed as a matter of duty imposed upon it by the law leaving nothing to the judgement of the authority. In Kavita v State of Maharashtra[14] the Supreme Court held that the task of referring the question of detention to an advisory board under COFEPOSA was a ministerial act which involved no exercise of discretion.

Administrative Instructions

Administrative operation of government proceeds on the assumption that the superior administrative authorities issue administrative instructions to their subordinates. The executive functions comprise both the determination of policy as well as carrying it into execution. The executive power of the Union extends to all the matters in respect of which Parliament has power to make laws (Article 73 of the Constitution of India) and similarly the executive power of the State extends to all the matters in respect of which the state legislature has power to make laws (Article 162 of the Constitution of India). Generally speaking, administrative rules, regulations or instructions which have no statutory force do not create any legal right in favour of aggrieved party and cannot be enforced through court of law against the administration. The violation of such instructions cannot be enforced in a court of law, yet on account of violation thereof, disciplinary action can be taken against the concerned.[15]

Growth of Delegated Legislation

Initially there had been a lot of criticism on the growth of delegated legislation being termed as undemocratic[16], but with the change of time and with the involvement of the government in various welfare activities, much of antipathy has died down. There are various factors which have led to the growth of delegated legislation. With the phenomenal increase in State functions there has been a tremendous increase in legislation as a result of which, it has become difficult for the legislature to devote sufficient time to discuss all the matters minutely and therefore, the legislature passes the legislation in skeleton form containing general policy and empowers the executive to fill in the details. Many a times, the subject matter of legislation is highly technical in nature and it becomes difficult for the legislators to deal with such matters. In such cases the legislative power are delegated to experts to deal with such problems.

The Parliament does not function on a continuous basis, and at the time of passing of any enactment, it is not always possible to foresee all the contingencies that may arise. Therefore, it becomes imperative to give the powers to the Executive to meet the unforeseen contingencies and to adjust to new circumstances. Moreover while the parliamentary process involves delays, the delegated legislation offers rapid machinery for amendment. Whereas the legislative process suffers from the limitation of lack of viability and experimentation, the delegated legislation enables the executive to experiment. This permits rapid utilisation of experience and implementation of necessary changes in the application of the provisions in the light of such experience. During emergency quick action is required to be taken. Legislative process is not equipped to provide for urgent solution to meet the situation. In some situations, public interest demands that the law must not be known till it comes into operation. Due to these reasons delegation of power to the executive becomes necessary. Finally, the complexity of modern day administration has led to the growth of delegated legislation.

Classification of Delegated Legislation

There are various ways by which delegated delegation can be classified, e.g. (i) Title based classification; (ii) Nature based classification; (iii) Discretion based classification; (iv) Purposed base classification; (v) Authority based classification, etc.

(i) Title based classification

Parliament does not follow any particular policy in choosing the forms of delegated legislation. Therefore, the delegated legislation appears in several forms viz. rules, regulations, orders, notification, bye law, scheme and direction. The Committee on Minister's Powers (Donoughmore Committee)[17], recommended for simplification of nomenclature. It suggested for confining the term "rule" to statutory instrument regulating procedure, the term "regulation" to substantive administrative rule making and the term "order" to be confined to instruments exercising executive and quasi judicial decisions.

(ii) Nature based classification

According to the Committee on Minister's Powers, there are two types of parliamentary delegation: (A) Normal delegation and (B) Exceptional delegation. Again Normal delegations are of two types i.e. (a) Positive delegation: where the limits are clearly defined in the Parent Act; and (b) Negative delegation: where the delegated power does not include power to do certain things e.g. power to legislate on matters of policy or power to impose tax.

Exceptional delegation is also known as Henry VIII clause. Instances of exceptional delegation may be as follows: (i) power to legislate on matters of principle; (ii) power to amend Acts of Parliament; (iii) power giving such a wide discretion that it is almost impossible to know the limits; (iv) power to make rules which cannot be challenged in a court of law etc.

The classification may be based on the nature and extent of power conferred and the purposes for which such power can be exercised. The executive, thus can be empowered to fix an appointed day for the Act to come into force, to supply details, to extend the provisions of the Act to other areas, to include or to exclude operation of the Act to certain territories, persons, industries, commodities, to suspend or to modify the provisions of the Act, etc. A statute may also empower the executive to delegate further powers conferred on it to its subordinate authority. This authority based classification is known as "sub-delegation".

(iii) Permissible and Impermissible Delegation

There are two modes of permissible delegation viz. conditional and subordinate. In America, they are known as contingent and subordinate, whereas in India they are known as conditional and subordinate. In India, conditional legislation represents nearly the same idea as contingent legislation in America. Contingent legislation is defined as a statute that provides control but specifies that they are to come into effect only when a given administrative authority finds the existence of conditions defined in the statute.[18] In subordinate legislation on the other hand, the process consists of a discretionary elaboration of rules and regulations. The distinction between the two types of permissible is said to be based on the point of discretion. In contingent or conditional legislation, delegation is of fact finding. In subordinate legislation the delegation is of discretion. This implies that by delegated or subordinate legislation the delegate completes the legislation by supplying details within the limits prescribed by the statute and in case of conditional legislation, the power of legislation is exercised by the Legislature conditionally leaving to the discretion of an external authority the time and manner of carrying its legislation into effect as also the determination of the area to which it is to extend.[19] The need for safeguard against the abuse of delegated legislation in conditional legislation is as great as in the case of subordinate legislation.

Delegated Legislation in Britain

In Britain, on account of the principle of the sovereignty of Parliament, the courts cannot question parliamentary law in any ground. In R. V. Halliday[20], it has been observed that "The British constitution has entrusted to the Two Houses of Parliament, subject to the assent of the King, an absolute power untrammelled by any instrument obedience to which may be compelled by some judicial body". The remedy, however, lies in the hands of the parliament itself. Parliament can control the delegation of power by it, if it so pleases. The sovereignty of Parliament, however, does not mean that there are no principles to which the practice of law making power must conform. It has been suggested by the Committee on Ministers' Power that "the precise limits of law making power which Parliament intends to confer on a Minister should always be expressly defined in clear language by the statute which confers it: When discretion is conferred its limits should be defined with equal clearness."[21]

Delegated Legislation in United States of America

In USA, the delegated legislation is not recognised because of two doctrines i.e. (a) The doctrine of the "Separation of Powers"; and (b) "Delegatus non-potest delegare". Though in theory, it was not possible for the Congress to delegate the legislative power to the executive, but due to increase in governmental functions, it was impossible for the Congress to enact the statutes with all particular details. The U.S. Supreme Court, tried to create a balance between the two conflicting forces: doctrine of separation of power barring delegation and the inevitability of delegation due to the exigencies of the modern government.[22] The most that can be asked under the separation of powers doctrine, is that the Congress lay down the general policy and standards that animate the law, leaving the agency to refine those standards, fill in the blanks, or apply the standards to particular cases.[23] The test in the words of Justice Cardozo is "to uphold the delegation there is need to discover in terms of the Act a standard reasonably clear whereby the discretion must be governed."[24] If the statute contains no standards to limit delegation of power, it amounts to giving blank cheque to make law in the delegated area of authority and thus the agency becomes primary legislator.

Delegated Legislation in India

In India, during the pre-constitution period, Queen v. Burah[25], is the leading authority on the subject. By Act XXII of 1869, the area of Garo Hills was removed from the jurisdiction of civil and criminal courts and the law applied therein, and by Section 9, the Lieutenant Governor of Bengal, was empowered to extend mutatis mutandis all or any of the provisions of the Act applicable to Khasi, Jayantia and Naga Hills in the Garo Hills and to fix the date of such applications. By a notification dated 14th October 1871, the Lieutenant Governor extended all the provisions of the Act to the District of Khasi and Jayantia Hills. The appellants, who were convicted of murder and sentenced to death, challenged the notification. The Calcutta High Court, by a majority, upheld the contention of the appellants and held that Section 9 of the Act was ultra vires the powers of the Indian legislature as the Indian Legislature was a delegate of the Imperial Parliament and therefore further delegation was not permissible.

On appeal, the Privy Council reversed the decision of the Calcutta High Court and held that the Indian Legislature was not a delegate of the Imperial Parliament and it had plenary powers of legislation as those of the Imperial Parliament itself. It agreed that the Governor General-in-Council could not, by legislation, create a new legislative power in India not created or authorised by the Council's Act. But in fact it was not done. It was only a case of 'conditional legislation', as the Governor was not authorised to pass new laws, but merely to extend the provisions of the Act already passed by the competent legislature upon fulfilment of certain conditions. In this case, the decision of the Privy Council is open to two different interpretations. One interpretation is that since the Indian legislature is not a delegate of British Parliament, there is no limit on the delegation of the legislative power. But the other interpretation is that since the Privy Council has validated only conditional legislation, therefore the delegation of legislative power is not permissible.

However, the question of constitutional validity of delegation of powers came for consideration before the Federal Court and in Jatindra Nath Gupta v Province of Bihar; Federal Court ruled that legislative powers cannot be delegated.[26] As this decision created confusion, the question of permissible limits of delegation of legislative powers became important. The Supreme Court was called upon to determine the constitutional validity of the provisions of three Acts, i.e. (i) Section 7 of the Delhi Laws Act,1912; (ii) Section 2 of the Ajmer – Mewar (Extension of Laws) Act,1947 and (iii) Section 2 of the Part C States (Laws) Act were in issue in Delhi Laws Act Case, Re[27]. It was propounded that:

(i) Parliament cannot abdicate or efface itself by creating a parallel law body;

(ii) Power of delegation is ancillary to the power of legislation;

(iii) The limitation upon delegation of legislative power is that the legislature cannot part with its essential legislative power that has been expressly vested in it by the Constitution. Essential legislative power means laying down policy of law and enacting that policy into a binding rule of conduct.

(iv) Power to repeal is legislative and it cannot be delegated.

Forms of Delegation

Thus, the theme of the Re Delhi Laws Act case is that essential legislative function cannot be delegated, whereas non-essential functions can be delegated. Moreover, the legislature should not delegate its essential legislative function which means laying of policy and enacting it into a binding rule of conduct. The executive cannot be authorised to repeal a law in force and by exercising the power of modification, the legislative policy should not be changed. Thus, in the Re Delhi Laws Act case the doctrine of excessive delegation was propounded. The various forms of delegation are:

(a) **Amplification of policy:** Delegated legislation, to some extent involves abandonment of the function by the legislature and enhancement of the power of administration. Many a time the legislature passes an Act in 'skeleton form' containing only the barest of general policies and leaves to the executive the task of not only filling in 'details' but even that of amplifying the policies. The vires-the limits-of the authority delegated have become so broad as to cover almost all administrative rules making within the particular area of legislation.

(b) **Modification:** Sometimes, a provision is made in the statute conferring power on the executive to modify the existing statute itself. This sometimes amendment of the Legislative Act. But sometimes such power is necessary for flexibility of approach to meet the changing circumstances. In Indian legislative practice the power to modify the statute has mostly been delegated as sequel to the power of extension and application of laws.

(c) **Removal of difficulties (Henry VIII Clause):** Power, sometimes, is conferred on the government to modify the existing statute for the purpose of removing difficulties so that it may be brought into full operation as the legislature while passing the act can not foresee all the difficulties which may arise during the implementation process. Legislature, therefore, introduces in the statute a 'removal of difficulties' clause envisaging that government may remove any difficulty that may arise in putting the law into operation. There are two types of 'removal of difficulties' clauses. The first one, which is quite narrow, empowers the executive to exercise the power to remove difficulties consistent with the provisions of the enabling Act and in such case; the government cannot change the provisions of the statute. The second one which is quite broad empowers the executive in the guise of 'removal of difficulties' to modify even the Parent Act or any other Act. This is nicknamed as 'Henry VIII clause' as personifying "executive autocracy".

(d) **Inclusion or exclusion:** As a matter of common practice, legislature passes a law to confer the power on the government to bring individuals, bodies or commodities within or to exempt them from the purview of a statute. In this way the range of a statute can be enlarged or reduced through the operation of delegated legislation.

(e) **Taxation:** In a democratic system of government, taxation is the exclusive function of the legislature. When the legislature passes a statute to levy tax, it leaves some elements of taxing power to the executive. The doctrine of excessive delegation is applied by the Court to determine the validity of the delegation of the taxing power.

Procedure for Making of Subordinate/Delegated Legislation

Originally the only provision regulating the methods by which a law making power could be exercised by the Minister or other body to whom the power has been entrusted by Parliament were those, if any, contained in the enabling statute itself. In England, the 1946 Act contemplated that any exercise of subordinate legislative power must be by way of document duly signed by the Minister or by some person in his department who has been duly authorised to sign the document on behalf of the minister. The 1946 Act makes specific provision for publication. In some cases the enabling Act may require the instrument to be laid before the Parliament. Bye laws are special form of delegated legislation which has several peculiar features which do not apply to other forms of delegated legislation.

Control of Delegated Legislation

Due to the complexities and exigencies of intensive form of government, the institution of delegated legislation has come to stay. Delegation of legislative powers to the executive, however, has to be conceded within the permissible limits. The Committee of Ministers' Powers has rightly observed that though the practice of delegated legislation is not bad, "risks of abuse and incidental to it" are there and therefore safeguards are necessary "if the country is to continue the advantages of the practice without suffering from its inherent dangers."[28] Therefore, today the question is not whether delegated legislation is desirable or not, but it is what controls and safeguards can be introduced so that the power conferred is not misused or misapplied.[29]

The control mechanism of delegated legislation is exercised at two stages: (a) at the stage of delegation of legislative power by the legislature to the executive and (b) at the stage of exercise of the delegated power by the executive. The first aspect has been described earlier. Now some of the controls and safeguards against the possible abuse of delegated legislation by the executive authorities will be considered.

The controls which are exercised over delegated legislation may be divided into three categories; (i) Judicial Control; (ii) Legislative Control; and (iii) Procedural Control.

Judicial Control

The judicial control over delegated legislation is exercised by applying two tests: Substantive ultra vires and (ii) Procedural ultra vires. It is a fundamental principle of law that a public authority cannot act outside the powers and if the authority acts, such an act becomes ultra vires and hence void. Judicial control over delegated legislation is exercised by applying the doctrine of ultra vires in number of circumstances[30] as discussed below.

1. Where the Parent Act is ultra vires the Constitution

Express Constitutional limits: The Constitution prescribes the boundaries within which the legislature can act. Invalidity of the rules and regulations arises if the Parent Act is violative of express limits prescribed by the Constitution, e.g. the legislative powers of the Union and the States are distributed in Art. 246. If either legislature encroaches upon the exclusive sphere of others as demarcated in the three lists, the legislation will be ultra vires.

Implied Constitutional limits: Implied Constitutional limits are those which were enunciated in Delhi Laws Act case, viz., laying down of policy and enacting the policy into a binding rule of conduct. Legislature cannot delegate essential legislative function to any other agency and if it so delegates, the Parent Act will be ultra vires of the Constitution. As such, in Delhi Laws Case the Supreme Court declared the later part of clause 2 bad because it conferred the power on the administrative agency to repeal a law, which is an essential legislative power.

Constitutional Rights: Any law that violates the provisions of rights conferred under the Constitution are ultra vires.

2. Where the delegated legislation is ultra vires the Constitution

(i) It may so happen that the Parent Act may not be ultra vires of the Constitution and the delegated legislation may be consistent with the Parent Act, yet the delegated legislation may be held invalid on the ground of that it is ultra vires of the Constitution[31];

(ii) Arbitrary Powers is ultra vires of the Constitution. In K. Panduranga v State of A.P.[32], it was held that compelling a person to carry on business against his will is violative of Art 19(1) (b) of the Constitution.

(iii) Theory of Derivative Immunity: In cases where Parent Act cannot be challenged before the Court because of protection of Art. 31-B of the Constitution on account of its placement in the Ninth Schedule, the delegated legislation promulgated there under can still be challenged if it violates any of the provision of the Constitution.

3. Where the delegated legislation is ultra vires the Parent Act

The general accepted principle is that the authority of delegated legislation must be exercised within the authority. In cases where (i) Delegated legislation in excess of the power conferred by the Parent Act; or (ii) Delegated legislation in conflict with the Parent Act; or (iii) Delegated legislation in conflict with the procedure prescribed in the Parent.

Act then the Delegated legislation can be challenged on the ground that it is ultra vires the Parent Act or the enabling statute or any general law.[33]

4. Malafide/Bad faith

Delegated legislation may be challenged on the ground of mala-fides or improper motives of the rule making authority.[34]

5. Unreasonableness

This rule is based on the presumption that the legislature never intended to give power to make unreasonable rules and therefore they are ultra vires. As de Smith[35] observes "there is no reason or principle why a manifestly statutory instrument should not be held to be ultra vires on that ground alone...." The elements of unreasonableness are: (a) partial or unequal operation between different classes, (b) manifestly unjust, (c) bad faith, and (d) oppressive interference with the rights of the people that no justification can be found in the minds of reasonable men. In India, Art. 14 of the Constitution guarantees equality before law and invalidates any law and action which is arbitrary and unreasonable.

Legislative Control

A three prong control is exercised by the legislature over the delegated legislation as follows: (a) Proceedings in Parliament; (b) Laying on the Table; (c) Scrutiny Committees. The underlying object of legislative control is to keep watch over the rule-making authorities so that there is no abuse of power on their part.

(a) Proceedings in Parliament

A rule of each House requires that a bill involving proposal for delegation of legislative powers shall be accompanied by a memorandum explaining such proposals and drawing attention to their scope, and stating also whether they are of exceptional or normal character. A number of proceedings are involved in exercise of control over delegation of legislative powers by the legislature, e.g.:

(i) *Debate on delegating bill:* Through debate on the Act which contains delegation. Members may discuss anything about delegation including necessity, extent, type of delegation and the authority to whom the power is delegated; (ii) *Through questions and notices:* Any Member can ask questions on any aspect of delegation of legislative power and if dissatisfied can give notice for discussion under Rule 59 of the Procedure and Conduct of Business in Lok Sabha; (iii) *Through moving resolution and notices in the House:* Any Member may move a resolution on motion, if the matter regarding delegation of power is urgent and immediate and the reply of the government is unsatisfactory; (iv) *Through vote on grant:* Whenever the budget demand of a Ministry are presented any Member may propose a cut and thereby bring the exercise of rule-making power of the Ministry under discussion; (v) *Direction by Speaker:* The Speaker may refer bills containing provisions for delegation of legislative powers to the Committee to examine the extent to which such powers sought to be delegated.

(b) Laying on the Table

One of the devices of control over the exercise of power of delegated legislation is legislative overseeing of delegated legislation.

A device to invoke the legislative supervision is a provision in the delegating statute requiring 'Laying' of the rules before the concerned legislature. Laying serves two purposes, firstly, it informs the legislature as to what rules have been framed by the administrative authorities in exercise of the law-making power, and it provides an opportunity to the legislature to question or challenge the rules already made or proposed to be made. There are seven type of laying: (i) Laying without further provision of control; (ii) Laying with deferred operation; (iii) Laying with immediate effect but subject to annulment; (iv) Laying in draft but subject to resolution that no further proceedings be taken; (v) Laying in draft and requiring affirmative resolution; (vi) Laying with operation deferred until approval given by affirmative resolution and (vii) Laying with immediate effect but requiring affirmative resolution as condition for continuance.

In India, there is no statutory provision requiring laying of all delegated legislations. There is no obligation on administration to lay the rules before Parliament. Whether the rules made under the statute are to be laid before the Houses of Parliament depends on the term of each enabling statute.

According to the Committee on Delegated Legislation, the statutes contain four manners of such provisions: (i) Requirement of mere publication of rules in the official gazette; (ii) Requirement of such publication and Laying on the Table; (iii) Over and above the aforesaid two conditions, some statutes allowed modification by Parliament; and (iv) Requirement of laying of rules for a specified period before they are published in the official gazette.[36]

As there is no uniform practice in the laying procedure, the Scrutiny Committee made the following suggestions:-[37]

(a) All acts of Parliament should uniformly require that the rules shall be laid on the Table of the House as soon as possible;

(b) This period should be uniform and should be a total period of thirty days from the date of their final publication; and

(c) The rules shall be subject to such modification as the Houses may like to make.

The legislature also exercises control over the delegated legislation through the Scrutiny Committees. Under the Constitution of India, there are two such Committees i.e. (i) The Lok Sabha Committee on Subordinate Legislation and (ii) The Rajya Sabha Committee on Subordinate Legislation. The main functions of these Committees are to examine and ensure: (a) whether the order is in accord with the general object of the Constitution or the Act pursuant to which it is made; (b) whether it contains matter which in the opinion of the Committee should more properly be dealt with in an Act of Parliament; (c) whether it directly or indirectly bars the jurisdiction of the Courts; (d) whether it contains imposition of tax; (e) Whether it gives retrospective effect to any of the provisions in respect of which the Constitution or the Act does not expressly give any such power; (f) whether it involves expenditure from the Consolidated fund of India; (g) Whether it appears to make some unusual or unexpected use of powers conferred by the Constitution or the Act pursuant to which it is made; (h) whether there appears to have some unjustifiable delay in the publication or the laying of it before Parliament; and (i) whether for any reasons its form or purport calls for any elucidation.

As Parliamentary control over delegated legislation is not very effective, Procedural control mechanism attempts to exercise more effective control by providing effective vigil over delegated legislation, by ensuring effective people participation for better social communication, acceptance and effectiveness of the rules. Procedural control mechanism has three components i.e.

1. *Antecedent Publicity:* The primary safeguard to ensure the proper exercise of power of delegated legislation lies in the development of adequate procedures to be followed by the administrative process in the formulation of rules and regulations. A means of obtaining participation in the rule making process by unorganised interests is through the device of antecedent publicity. In India, though, there is no separate law relating to the system of antecedent policy, in certain cases the enabling statutes have provided for antecedent policy. Antecedent publicity required by parent Act attracts the application of Section 23 of the General Clauses Act, 1897 which provides that (a) the authority shall publish a draft of the proposed rules in the Gazette; (b) the authority shall invite objections and suggestions by a specific date; and

(c) the authority shall take into consideration any objections or suggestions which may be received by it while finalising the rules.

2. *Publication:* Unlike, the laws passed by the legislature, the delegated legislation do not receive sufficient publicity. The affected persons come know of the rule after it has come into effect. Therefore, it is necessary that rules so framed are adequately publicised so that people are not caught unaware. The general mode of publication of delegated legislation are: (i) where there is a statutory requirement as to the mode or form of publication and they are such that in the circumstances, the Court holds to be mandatory, a failure to comply with those requirements might result in their being no effective order the contravention of which could be subject of prosecution; (ii) where there is no statutory requirement, it is necessary that it should be published in the usual form i.e. by publication within the country as generally adopted to notify all the persons of the making of the rules; (iii) in India, the publication in the official Gazette, viz. Gazette of India is the ordinary method of bringing a rule or subordinate legislation to the notice of the persons concerned. However, where the Parent Act prescribes a mode of publication, that mode must be followed. Publication of delegated legislation has been taken by the Courts as a corollary of natural justice. Unless the rule-making authority specifies otherwise, the rules generally takes effect on the date of its publication.

3. *Consultation of interests:* In order to check and control the exercise of the power of delegated legislation is the technique of consultation by which affected persons may participate in the rule making process. This makes the rule-making process more democratic and thus increases its effectiveness as well as its acceptability. The technique of consultation is thus amounts to democratisation of rule making process to some extent. Thus, the objection of bureaucratic legislation can be minimised. The consultations can be of two types i.e. Ordinary types of consultation or Extraordinary types of consultation. The ordinary types of consultation may be further subdivided into (i) individual objections and (ii) consultation with

specified interests. Similarly, extraordinary consultations can also be further divided into (a) preparation by affected interests and (b) approval by statutory body.

In India, though there is no general statutory provision requiring consultation with the affected interests before making the delegated legislation, some statutes, however, specifically provides for consultation. Consultation as required under the Indian statutes fall under the following categories: (i) official consultation, (ii) consultation with statutory boards, (iii) consultation with advisory bodies and (iv) making of draft rules by affected interest.

The general principle is that delegated legislation cannot have any retrospective effect unless such a power is conferred on the rule making authority under the Parent Act. In B.S. Yadava v State of Haryana[38], it was held that, it is not enough that the statute should authorise retrospective operation of delegated legislation, there must also exist rational and reasonable nexus between the concerned rule and its retrospectivity.

(c) *Scrutiny Committees:* The Committee on subordinate legislation of Lok Sabha and Rajya Sabha examines the delegated legislation and brings to the notice of the House whether the administrative rule-making has exceeded the intention of the Parliament or has departed from it or has affected any fundamental norm or principle. According to Rule 223, the main function of the committee is to examine: (a) whether the rules are in accordance with the general object of the Act; (b) whether the rules contain any matter which could be more properly be dealt with in the Act; (c) whether it contains imposition of tax; (d) whether it directly or indirectly bars the jurisdiction of the courts; (e) whether it is retrospective; (f) whether it involves expenditure from the Consolidated Fund; (g) whether there has been unjustified delay in its publication or in laying; (h) whether for any reason it requires further elucidation

Sub-delegation

When a statute confers legislative powers on an administrative authority and that authority further delegates those powers to another subordinate authority or agency, it is called sub-delegation. The need of sub-delegation is supported on following consideration:

Power of delegation necessarily carries with it the power of further delegation, hence; the delegate has the power to further delegate; Sub-delegation is ancillary to delegated legislation and objection to such process is likely to subvert the authority which the legislature delegates to the executive. The maxim "delegatus non potest delegare' merely states a rule of a construction of a statute and does not lay down a rule of law. The sub-delegation is subject to those controls which are exercised over the delegated legislation. The doctrine of substantive ultra vires applies to sub-delegation as well. Similarly, the publication of sub-delegation is also necessary.[39]

Exclusion of Judicial Review

Sometimes attempts are made by the legislature to limit or exclude judicial review of delegated legislation. Thus, in an Act, a provision may be made that rules regulations, bye laws etc. made under it "shall have effect if enacted in the Act" "shall not be questioned in any court". In Institute of Patent v. Lockood[40], Lord Herschell said that the jurisdiction of Courts to question the validity of the delegated legislation could be taken away. The Herschell doctrine, however, was overruled by Lord Dunedin, in Minister of Health v. R., Ex-parte Yaffe[41]. Allen is of the view that the words "as if enacted in the Act" do not preclude judicial consideration of vires[42]. In India, in some cases the Supreme Court has adopted the Herschell doctrine while in some cases Yaffe has been followed. However, it has now been held that, an Act providing that rule made there under, on publication in the official Gazette would be "as if enacted" in the Act cannot take away judicial review[43].

A number of general principles which emerge from the various judgments relating to delegation of legislative powers are summarised as follows:

1. The Constitution confers law making power to the Legislature and as such the said function cannot be delegated by the legislature to the Executive. The legislature can neither create a parallel legislature nor destroy its legislative power.
2. Delegation of legislative power is permissible provided this does not amount to abdication of legislative function and policy as laid down by the legislature.

3. The legislature cannot delegate the essential legislative function. The essential legislative function consists in the determination of legislative policy and making it a binding rule of conduct.
4. If the legislature has performed its essential legislative function of laying down the policy of law, there is no constitutional bar against the delegation of subsidiary or ancillary powers in that behalf to the executive for making the legislation effective, useful and complete.
5. A statute delegating law-making powers to the executive shall be invalid if it lays down no principles and provides no standards for guidance to the rule-making body.
6. The legislative policy can be formulated as broadly and with as little or much detail as the Legislature thinks fit. It is not necessary that the policy must be express; it may be implied as well. It may be gathered from history, preamble, title, scheme, statement of objects and reasons. Guidance may be found anywhere in the statute.
7. Power to repeal does not make the delegation valid, if otherwise it is excessive, Impermissible or unwarranted.
8. When a statute is challenged on the ground of excessive delegation, it must satisfy two tests: (i) whether it delegates essential legislative function or power, and (ii) whether the legislature has enunciated its policy and principle for the guidance of the delegate.
9. Whether the legislature has performed the essential legislative function and laid down the policy and the delegation is permissible or not depends upon the circumstances of the statute under consideration.
10. Delegated legislature may take different forms. However, these principles apply to all forms of delegation viz. conditional legislation, subordinate legislation, supplementary legislation, sub-delegation etc.

Administration has to discharge multifarious functions. Administrative legislation is one of such functions. There is no more characteristic administrative activity than legislation. However, while discharging the delegated functions, the administration has to perform the delegated functions with certain restrictions as discussed above. The delegated legislation in the changed socio-economic complexion has become a constituent element of the legislative power as a whole.

Notes

1. Montesquieu, Baron de Montesquieu; Esprit Des Lois (1748), Ch.12. (Translated by Thomas Nugent).
2. Halsbury's; Laws of England, 4th ed. Vol. 44, pp. 981-984.
3. Report of the Committee on Ministers' Power (Donoughmore Committee) Cmd.4060 1932, p. 36.
4. Basu, D.D.; Administrative Law, 1986, p. 64.
5. Salmond on Jurisprudence, 12th. Edn. 116.
6. *Ibid.*
7. Schwartz, American Administrative Law, 108, 1962.
8. de Smith, Judicial Review of Administrative Action, 17(1980).
9. Griffith and Street, Principles of Administrative Law, 696(1977).
10. Ram Jawaya v State of Punjab, A.I.R. 1955, S.C.549.
11. A.K. Karaipak V. Union of India, A.I.R.1970, S.C.150.
12. Province of Bombay v Khusaldas Advani, A.I.R. 1950, S.C. 222.
13. D.K.Yadava v J.M.A. Industries Ltd.,(1993)3SCC 259.
14. Kavita v State of Maharashtra, A.I.R. 1981, S.C. 1641.
15. A.I.R. 1971 S.C.1.920.
16. Lord Hewart; The New Despotism, 1929.
17. Report of the Committee on Ministers Power (Donoughmore Committee), supra.
18. Hart; An Introduction to administrative Law with selected cases, p. 310.
19. Hamdard Dawakhana v. Union of India, AIR 1960 SC 554.
20. R. V. Halliday; 1917, AC 260.
21. Report of the Committee on Ministers Power (Donoughmore Committee, supra.
22. Indian Law Institute: Cases and Materials on Administrative Law in India, 1966, Vol.1, pp. 188-89.
23. Rehnquist, J in Industrial Deptt. v American Petroleum Institute (1980)448 U.S.607 (675).
24. Panama Refining Company v. Ryan, 293, US 338,434(1935).
25. Queen v Burah, (1878) 3 AC 889.
26. Jatindra Nath Gupta v Province of Bihar, AIR 1949, FC 175.

27. Delhi Laws Act, 1912; AIR 1951, SC, 332.
28. Report of the Committee on Ministers Power (Donoughmore Committee), supra.
29. Committee on Subordinate Legislation (First Lok Sabha), 1954(3rd Report) p. 16.
30. Indian Express Newspapers v Union of India, AIR 1985 SC 515.
31. Narendra Kumar v Union of India, A.I.R. 1960 S.C. 430.
32. K. Panduranga v State of A.P. A.I.R. 1985, A.P. 208.
33. Wade, Administrative Law, 1988, p. 863.
34. Mc Eldowney v. Forde, 1969, 1 All. E.R. 1039.
35. de Smith, Judicial Review of Administrative Action, (1984) pp. 354-55.
36. Upadhayaya, J.J.R., Administrative Law, Central Law Agency, Allahabad, 1999, p. 89.
37. *Ibid.*
38. B.S. Yadava v State of Haryana, AIR 1981 SC 561.
39. Narendra Kumar v. Union of India, AIR 1960SC 430.
40. Institute of Patent v. Lockood, (1894) AC 347.
41. Minister of Health v. R., Ex-parte Yaffe, (1931) AC 494.
42. Allen, Law and Orders, 1965, p. 258.
43. Assistant Collector of Central Excise v Ram Krishnan, AIR 1989 SC 1829.

4

Changing Paradigm of Governance With Reference to Politician Civil Servant Relationship: An Overview

— *S.K. Chaturvedi*

Etymologically the meaning of terms 'paradigm' and 'governance' connotes a mixture of philosophical assumptions and criterion of 'valid knowledge' and 'rule with authority and conduct of policy affairs' that is to say paradigm of governance denotes a framework of ideas that establish general context of analysis of conduct of policies or affairs. In the context of a parliamentary democratic system, politicians and civil servants work in tandem to bring desired socio-economic and political changes in consonance with the values enshrined in the Constitution. A bureaucrat is answerable to popular, representative government in power while remaining politically neutral. He is supposed to carry out the approved policies and programmes of the government in power with sincerity and competence. While politicians in power are free to lay down policies according to their political commitments and manifestoes, the administrators implement these policies as also advice the politicians about the effect of such policies on the society at large. Thus, in democracy the officials play a major role not only in the execution of the policy but also in the overall management of the administrative machinery. In other words, bureaucracy dominates the output end of the political conversion processes. It is indispensable in the rule-making and adjudication processes as well as influential in the political processes of interest articulation, aggregation and communication. Other governmental structures such as political executive, legislature and courts must be viewed in relation to the functioning of bureaucracy.[1] They, without subscribing to any political ideology or programme, help political elements in the achievement of their ideals and goals on the basis of their professional competence. In brief, the two have a well knit intimate relationship.

The conventional concept of relationship between the two is based on the real division of labour. One enacts the policy and other implements it. In the process of decision-making and implementation, collection of facts, formulation of policy alternatives, discharge of responsibilities, the civil servant is supposed to be impartial and neutral whereas, politicians must have a concern to the problems being faced by the people and should be ready to take necessary and required ideological policy steps to resolve them. In post-independence period, the relationship between politicians and civil servants was rightly described by Sardar Ballab Bhai Patel '*you will not have a united India if you do not have a good All India Service which has the independence to speak out its mind, which has a sense of security that you will stand by your word and after all, there is a Parliament of which we can be proud where their rights and privileges are secure.*[2]

Prudence, practicability, moderation and avoidance of risk comprise the preferred work culture of civil servants.[3] After attainment of independence the nation changed to a mixed polity in which political administrative elements worked together. In the system of mixed polity, a civil servant is answerable to representative government in power and not to any particular person but to the system without fear or favour, thus, keeping them politically neutral. He should not tailor his views to suit the convenience of a particular political outfit and at the same time remain responsive to the masses. Briefly the relationship between Civil Servant and politician has a behavioural dimension of neutrality and objectivity. After the country became free, the civil servants opened their mind freely and fearlessly in front of political leadership before any public policy was visualised. Accordingly, the policies were drafted or amended as mutually agreed by the two. Fortunately, at that time, we had politicians who not only had a magnificent vision for the future but also had good sense of running the administration. Civil servants responded in a positive and creative way. It is due to this relationship that the most challenging incident of partition of the country could be managed successfully and millions of the people could be resettled, the shattered economy of Punjab could be rebuilt. Until 1960s, the politician and civil servant relationship moved with mutual trust. If the politicians became a willing partner with the bureaucracy, bureaucracy was omniscient as a result of which, civil servants acted with a free will within the legal and constitutional framework. However, by 1960s, the political leadership's nature changed. In place of one dominant party system, collision governments appeared on national and state scene resulting in emergence of committed bureaucracy to great extent. The civil servants became pliable tool in the hands of an unscrupulous political set up as a result of which politicisation of civil servants ensued. They took side of one or other political outfit on the basis of caste, region and even religion and whenever, their favoured political party came to power they served their own interests. Corruption of various types was compromised for serving interests of the interested quarters.

In late 1990s when the process of liberalisation started, a number of measures in the direction of social welfare were taken, however, civil servants showed a lack luster attitude giving an opportunity to the political leadership to grind its own axe in the changed situation. Consequently, the very concept of neutrality and objectivity of the civil servants became a casualty. The defection, disintegration and fragmentation amongst political parties brought uncertainty in the governance as a result of which, the civil servants failed in maintaining objectivity and neutrality in the governance. Needless to mention that politicians became more aggressive and less objective and more prone to brow beat or over do the administrator to achieve the ends. They could not be disciplined by the party set up for obvious reasons.

In coalition governments, ministers are generally busy in the power game and maneuvering for their survival. Neither they have time nor the inclination to guide, direct and control the department and ministry. But owing to the administrative structure they head the bureaucracy, in general, as a result of which they have no alternative except to accept the policy advice rendered by the civil servants and if the civil servant is pliable then use them for fulfilling their interests. Obviously, in absence of effective checks, the power of bureaucracy is bound to increase or the politician becomes a dictator. Number of cases, predominantly the Mandal Commission Report which changed socio-political structure of the political community and administration, may be cited in this respect where, the civil servants took years in coming to policy-decisions however, the politicians took hours in giving it a green signal as it served their political ends. Ministers and legislators often use civil servants to influence the recruitment, transfer and regulatory policies and in turn, bureaucracy takes advantage of the politicians for lucrative transfer and postings. This directly or indirectly influences the very concept of bureaucratic neutrality as a result of which an ulterior nexus between the bureaucracy, politicians and corporate people comes into existence where, civil servants work on oral orders and keep the politicians in good humour and toe their line.[4]

Summarily, in post-1967 period, the politician civil servant relationship which should have been known for neutrality, integrity, accountability, people's welfare and mutual respect and understanding, started to witness tensions as a result of which free and frank advice and meaningful exchange of views between the politicians and civil servants became an immediate casualty. Factionalism, group rivalry and casteism among senior politicians and bureaucrats became an important factor in public policy formulation and decision making process. Obviously, to some extent this has given rise to politicisation of bureaucracy and criminalisation of politics. Of late, due to all this the role of Constitutional institutions has also come under question mark. In this backdrop, the very query that the existing paradigm of governance particularly in the context of civil servants and politicians requires a re-consideration becomes relevant. Before pondering over the issue it may be noted that common men perceives civil servant as a person who provides a free and ready access to the aggrieved persons and exercises his authority, influence and position to remedy the situation, redress grievance and to rectify mistakes committed during the process of administration. However, with politician bureaucrat nexus grinding their own axe, over the years, people's faith in them has diminished and people have shifted to those petty politicians, who are more or less power brokers, for resolution of their problems. Obviously, the civil servant politician relationship has undergone a shift from what was envisaged when it was created.[5] If the political system, as it has now emerged, is unable to change it then there is dire need of reviewing administrative structure in general and role, function and behaviour of civil servants in particular. American pattern of bureaucratic structure could be one prospective answer to this. However, this may prove an anti-thesis to the parliamentary system of ours. Therefore, some necessary steps need to be taken immediately to mend the fences. To begin with, stress should be given on encouraging free, frank and meaningful exchange of views between the civil servant and politicians so as to arrive at constructive conclusions. Factionalism, group rivalry and casteism etc. should not be allowed to dictate the mutual relationship and public policy formulation. Politicians should desist from politicising bureaucracy and allow it to remain neutral in larger interest of the polity. The transfer, promotion, suspension and compulsory retirement of the civil servants must be transparent and may not be governed by the whims and interests of the politicians. This is possible if the politicians desist from influencing the role and functions of constitutional institutions both at state and central level.

The Apex Court of the country has time and again stressed on taking up electoral reforms immediately so as to neutralize the role of money and muscle power in the elections which may act as catalyst in breeding honest and committed politicians, who may prove to be instrumental in keeping the neutrality of civil servants alive and at the same time protect and encourage honest functionaries both in civil and political set up. Further, steps need to be taken to diffuse the process of politicisation of the civil servants and in this context political parties, particularly party in power, should take initiative by stressing on adherence of duties by all civil servants in letter and spirit. Rules in respect of posting, transfer, promotion, should be strictly followed by the political party in power so that neutrality of bureaucracy may be upheld. Recently court of law has emphasised that time period of working at the particular place be underlined and honoured. No posting be made as a consequence of punishment. In keeping the civil servant and politician's relationship in an ideal mode, it is required that sense of insecurity in facing the future should not always harm the minds of civil servants. Political leadership need to help civil servants so that they may keep public interest above all interests and serve the masses to the best of their capabilities. On the other hand, political parties need to take steps to strengthen inner party democracy and grievance redress mechanism. These are some of the emergent steps required to be taken to streamline politician civil servant relationship as envisaged by the political leadership on the floor of Constituent Assembly.

At the very outset, we began with an assumption that there is an emergent need of advocating a shift in philosophical assumptions in the conduct of policy affairs in the context of politicians and civil servant relationship in Parliamentary democratic set up. Perhaps, the answer negates assumption as in a Parliamentary democracy it is the Parliament that serves as an effective check on all powerful cabinet and bureaucracy. Parliament alone should develop and create strong traditions where politicians, i.e. ministers, and officials both could be able to serve the masses under democratically elected and constituted parliament and where, honesty, integrity, uprightness of the civil servants guarantee good and efficient administration even though they always operate from behind the curtain.[6]

One may only hope that there are politicians of higher stature and standing who will mould, influence and properly operate bureaucracy as also there are enough persons in bureaucracy who would rise to the occasion and maintain neutrality and objectivity in the services.[7]

Notes

1. Gabriel Almond and Powell, Comparative Politics, New Delhi, Amerind Publishing Company, 1972, p. 158.
2. Sardar Patel: Constituent Assembly Debates, October 10, 1949.
3. Joel D. Aberbach, Bureaucrats and Politicians in western democracies, Cambridge, Howard University Press, 1981, p. 9.
4. Report of Commission of inquiry against K.B. Sahayan, C.M. of Bihar, 1970, pp. 1200-1206.
5. S.C. Bajpayee, P.K. Kaul; Politician Civil servant relationship, IJPA, January – March 1993, p. 41.
6. Harbhajan Singh Deol, Administrators and Politicians: A critique of their roles, IJPA, New Delhi, April – June, 1984, pp. 318-19.
7. B.G. Deshmukh, Indian Bureaucracy: Facing the Future, IJPA, January – March, 1998, p. 17.

5

Changing Paradigm of Governance with a Special Focus on Politician Civil Servant Relationship

— *Harbans Pathak*

Governance

It is a fact of history that Governance always remained a constant threat, since then very inception. Autocratic rulers, authoritarian personalities, bureaucratic social formations, materially rich, ecclesiastical orthodoxy, half baked ultra radicals, police and military vested interests posed a direct threat to the doctrine of governance, both in theory as well as in actual practice.

Good Governance

Therefore, search for Good Governance has always been a concern of political thinkers, leaders, scholars and administrators throughout the world. History testifies that administration all over the World and in third World particularly, was concerned in carrying out the process of development which was basically a state led activity. This was meant conscious reduction in the rule of market and steady enlargement of the size and role of civil service. The current trend towards globalisation has led in a re-thinking about this role of the State vis-à-vis the market. The forces of Liberalisation, Privatisation and Globalisation (LPG) and the revolution in Information Technology has shattered many a myth about governance. The governments can no longer afford to support rigid bureaucratic, reactive, rules driven administrator organisations. Rather today administrative system ought to be flexible, consultative, result oriented and proactive. Hence Good Governance means competent management of a country resources and affairs in a manner that is open, transparent, accountable, equitable and responsive to people's needs.

Minister-Secretary Relationship

The relationship between the two is based on mutual trust and confidence. The administrator has to develop an approach that however close and intimate he may be with politician, he must always bear in mind that he is only his advisor, the ultimate authority to take decisions on policies must necessarily be the ministers.

Some Cases of Conflict

The genesis of politician-administrator relationship can be traced back to the year 1921, when the Montague-Chelmsford Reforms of 1919 were implemented and the relationship became more obvious after the promulgation of the Government of India Act, 1935. The experiment in Minister-Secretary Relationship did not go off entirely without friction and conflict. Many of the Ministers later complained before the Reforms Enquiry Committee (1924) about lack of cooperation on the part of the Secretary.

After independence the strained relations between Minister-Secretary first came into light in 1957, when a conflict arose between T.T. Krishnamachari and his Principal Finance Secretary H.M. Patel about the purchase of some shares of some private companies by the Life Insurance Corporation.

The discord of Minister-Secretary Relationship was witnessed once again in 1966 when the then Union Home Minister Gulzari Lal Nanda has shown discontentment over his Home Secretary L.P. Singh.

When Mrs Indira Gandhi came into power in 1980, she used Civil Service to sub-serve her political objectives. He transferred those Civil Servants who were undependable and loyal to the Janta Government to unimportant positions. She advocated the model of Committed Civil Service, when Rajiv Gandhi came to power. He said our Civil Service is much maligned large scale shifting of government ordered under V.P. Singh were shifted, when P.V. Narasimha Rao became the Prime

Minister, he invested his trust in Naresh Chandra, Cabinet Secretary and A.N. Verma, Principal Secretary in PMO.

The administration in States had also witnessed number of cases where conflict arose as in Punjab, Pratap Singh Kaeron and R.P. Kapur, Lal Singh, Health Minister and A.K. Kundra, Health Secretary etc. Such cases of conflict are largely seen in other States like U.P., Haryana, Tamil Nadu etc. where civil servants are victimised and transferred to unimportant positions.

The C.M. Secretaries and P.M. Secretaries enjoys superior positions by those Civil Servants who occupy positions in their offices.

Prime Minister Narendra Modi feels that governance is all about delivery. So the Civil Servants have to shed their colonial attitude of Bara-Sahib and held accountable. Modi P.M. is transposing a model of Governance that is remarkable similar to the one he has in Gujarat. Hence, the traditional model of Minister-Secretary relationship has to be reviewed for better delivery system in the governance of the country.

A perusal of above analysis, we find that different models being operated such as Political Neutrality Model, Committed Civil Service Model of Indira Gandhi and Modi Model of Governance.

In all these models the Civil Servants in India fall in three different categories. The First, include absolutely devoted Civil Servants, who would do their work under Ministers directions efficiently and honestly. The Second category, comprises those who firm their behaviour according to the forecast of the day. If the Ministers are socially motivated and honest, they would abide by the prescribed rules and regulations and conduct themselves in a manner worthy of Civil Servants. The Third, one includes "incorrigibles" who are unscrupulous unworthy whatever be the level and measure of Minister-Civil Servant morality. They are the black sheep of any organisation.

6

Politician Civil Servant Relationship: Some Key Issues

— S.K. Singh

In a democratic polity power vests with the people which is exercised by their elected representatives having mandate to govern them for a specific term. The civil service, by virtue of knowledge, experience, expertise and sane understanding of public affairs assists these elected representatives in formulating public policy and is singly responsible to implement such policies. Parliamentary democracies are normally characterised by a permanent civil service which assists the political executive in the discharge of their mandated functions. Since India has adopted the British model of parliamentary democracy it has all the accrual advantages of an independent, permanent and impartial civil service viz.:

> "A credible recruitment by an impartial agency providing defence against patronage, nepotism and corruption. It provides continuity, develops expertise and institutional memory for effective policy-making which has today become a complex exercise requiring in depth knowledge and expertise in public affairs. Political executive may took to short-term political gains while it is more likely to assess long-term social payoffs of public policy. It helps ensure uniformity and acts as unifying force in a vast and culturally diverse nation. It is likely to evolve an ethical basis for its functioning."

A healthy and sound working relationship between political and permanent executive is very critical for good governance in a democratic polity. While the principles governing roles and responsibilities of the two have been well defined in Political Theory, in actual practice, this division (distinction) of responsibilities becomes blurred quite often with both sides encroaching upon the spheres of other. In a democracy, the political executive (the ministers) are responsible to the people through legislature and therefore the permanent executive (the civil service) has to be accountable to the ministers. However, the civil service is responsible not only to the government of the day (Political Executive) but also to the Constitution of the land to which it has taken an oath of loyalty. At the same time implementing the policies of the duly elected government (political executive) is a core function of civil service.

In India, the Constitution clearly lays down the roles and responsibilities of the three organs of government, the Legislature, Executive and Judiciary. However there is interface of legislature and executive at the level of Council of Ministers, which is collectively responsible to legislature. The Executive Powers of the Union and States vest in the President or Governors (Art. 53 and 154) directly or through officers subordinate to them, these officers constitute the permanent civil service governed by Part XIV of the Constitution.

The Political Executive is headed by the President or Governor who is required to act according to "**aid and advice of his Council of Ministers**" (Art 73 and 163). The work is allocated to the Ministers as per Government of India (allocation of business) Rules and the manner in which officers are required to "aid and advise" in the exercise of executive functions is governed by the Government of India (Transaction of Business) Rules. This clearly means that the officers are though subordinate to the President or Governor, they carry out the orders of the Council of Ministers in accordance with the rules frame thereof. The Rules of Business do provide for the Civil Servant to advise the Minister about the course of action proposed and submit to him a note which tells him about the propriety or legality of orders and suggest that either such order not be given or be appropriately modified.

"The relations between a minister and his secretary is organic as the minister has the people's mandate to govern and the secretary has an equivalent Constitutional mandate to advise the minister. Once secretary's advice has been suitably considered, he is bound to implement it unless the minister passes an illegal order. The minister has to support the secretary in implementation of his orders. Once a law is framed and rules and regulations are approved, they apply to everyone be it the member of the political executive or permanent civil service. A civil servant is duty bound to implement the above without bias, fear or favour and with utmost honesty. It is precisely this area where difference of opinion often occurs between the political executive (minister) and permanent executive (civil servant)".

Post-Independence India Scenario

The British legacy which the country inherited from the past civil service allowed the administration to function well with minimum glitches, negligent internal bickering and outside pressures and pulls. In the aftermath of independence relations between ministers and civil servants were characterised by mutual respect and understanding of each other's respective roles with neither encroaching upon others domain. Both the Prime Minister Pt. Nehru and the Home Minister Sardar Patel nursed the civil services with great care and affection since they were thoroughly convinced that the bureaucracy that evolved under the British constituted a vital and dependable machinery to push through various reforms that an infant nation desperately needed. They also ensured that the civil services were kept insulated from the day-to-day politics to play the key role in maintaining social stability thereby providing the right ambience for development. Overall the culture that respected the average civil servant got rooted despite a few aberrations. A clear distinction between the policy-making role of the minister and implementation role of the civil servant had come to be well established. Normally the civil servant could argue against the minister's decision without being humiliated or penalised. Once the minister made up his mind after discussions he has the last word and the civil servant (secretary) had no option but to implement the decision in right earnest. The system was endowed with everything that promoted candour and honesty.

In subsequent years the scene began changing for the worse. While some civil servants did not render objective and impartial advice to the political executive, on the other hand some ministers often began to resent the advice that did not fit in with their short-term political interests. Further a tendency of some ministers to focus more on routine matters (transfers and postings) than policy making. Similarly some civil servants learnt the art of manoeuvring for favours in return for pliability in their decision-making. This trend was further accentuated by rising materialism and acquisitiveness and decline in values across the board. As a result the political neutrality, the hallmark of the civil service in the pre-independence and just thereafter in India, was gradually eroded and politicisation of civil service became phenomenal. The watershed in the infamous history of Indian Administration was most probably the imposition of Emergency in the country in 1975. The ensued arbitrariness led to dilution of many well established traditional institutions and the civil service just caved in without any protest. Since then the floodgates remained open and no concerted efforts have been initiated ever to stop tinkering with the civil service. The casualty has been the fearlessness and objectivity of the civil service.

The 'Hindu' wrote "barring a few, ministers both at the Centre and States have steamrolled the bureaucracy so much that a fear psychosis now envelops the whole civil service. The Judiciary has generally been remiss in undoing the damage because of its stand that it cannot step in where routine administrative matters are involved like transfers, suspensions etc. and an act of injustice done to a civil servant does not constitute any infringement of Fundamental Rights embodied in the Constitution. The Administrative Tribunals have offered some redress, but it is not enough to remove the fear that grips the majority of civil servants. This explains the rot."

In the current situation an IAS or IPS can hardly muster enough courage to say 'NO' to minister's fiat. Blind obedience is expected even when the direction is totally illegal. The minister now demands instantaneous action, and any delay by any officer is fraught with grave consequences like inspired physical assault or dubious departmental inquiry.

The relationship between the political and permanent executive remained the grey area even in the early post-independence era. Perhaps the first such instance became public in the aftermath of L.I. C. Mundhra case. The relations between the Finance Minister T. T. Krishnamachari and his Secretary went sour with the outcome of the actions taken in purchasing the shares of Haridas Mundhra's company by the LIC which earned heavy losses. Both the Finance Minister and his Secretary H.M. Patel tried to blame each other for the decision. To examine the issues involved and to settle accountability Chhagla Commission of inquiry was constituted. Justice M. C. Chhagla went into the whole gamut of case and penned down the responsibility of secretary's actions on the minister concerned. Ever since then it is now well established that ministers must own the responsibility of actions of their secretaries. This became the landmark judgment of the Chhagla Commission in respect of ministerial responsibility in India.

In this regard quite a few cases of friction/misunderstanding or mistrust have come up since then where the civil servants were ill-treated/ignored and chided like the cases of K. Hanumantaiya and B. C. Ganguly, Guljari Lal Nanda and L.P. Singh, Rajiv Gandhi and A.P. Venkateshwaran, and Sri Niwas Shastri, Ram Jeth Malani and Kiran Agarwal to name a few at the Centre. At the State level the examples are: Bir Bahadur Singh and A.P. Pant, Mayawati and Rai Singh (this Rai Singh was the same civil servant who sat along with the chief minister Mayawati on the chair while his ministers sat on the floor along with the other party workers.

Friction Areas

The possible areas of friction and discontent in the realm of relations between the minister (the political executive) and the secretary (the permanent executive) can possibly arise in the following domains.

Civil Service Neutrality

In the Constituent Assembly Sardar Ballabh Bhai Patel supported the continuance of pre-independence civil service structure in the following words:

"It needs hardly to be emphasised that an efficient, disciplined and contented civil service assured of its prospects as a result of diligent and honest work is a sine-quo-non of sound administration under democratic regime even more than under authoritarian rule. The Service must be above party and we should ensure that political considerations, either in its recruitment or in its discipline and control are reduced to the minimum, if not eliminated altogether".

Unfortunately, this vision of civil service neutrality no longer prevails. Change of guards specially at the state government level very often leads to wholesale transfer of civil servants. The incoming political party invariably wants its men at the key posts thereby convincingly accepting the political allegiance of the civil service. Even in the change of portfolios of the ministers this swapping of the civil servants is not uncommon. The caste also plays a very significant role in mitigating the neutrality of the civil service. There have been reported instances of ministers demanding their own caste person as their secretary. The instances of civil servants being politically aligned openly abound and some of them unscrupulously make it known to people for obvious reasons. To buttress the point the example of one Principal Secretary of Social Welfare Department in U.P. at the time of Mayawati's Chief Ministership used to be seated along with the Chief Minister on the chair while his Minister (who was quite senior in the party and age) was seated on the floor among the other party workers. Hence political neutrality is no longer remains an accepted norms as so many civil servants are identified with certain political outfit. Common perception views the civil servants as normal human beings who cultivate and seek political patronage for obtaining rewarding positions.

Political neutrality of civil service should not be confused with programme neutrality. At the policy formulation level, the role of civil servant is to render free and frank advice without any political consideration or self prospects. After the Policy/ Programme is approved by the government civil servant is duty bound to faithfully implement it. Not carrying out this mandated task in the right spirit certainly amounts to misconduct attracting disciplinary action.

Advisory Role of the Civil Servant in Policy Making

The neat distinction of the traditional Public Administration scholars——that Politicians make policy and Civil Servants implement it——was always theoretical rather than real. The modern governments have had the way of eroding whatever truth there existed in this distinction. Today the implementation failures of policy are often the biggest and most significant political problems a government has to face e,g. In case of the United States war in Iraq and the Hurricane Katrina. Here three basic questions seemed pertinent to be answered.

Where does the policy stop and implementation begins? What is the responsibility of the civil servant towards the political executive and vice versa? Who should be held accountable ultimately?

These questions can best be illustrated by the two examples given below of the USA and Great Britain. These questions came to the fore on both sides of the Atlantic in 2006—in Great Britain and the USA—both being the great pioneers of the democratic polity. In Britain Home Office was rocked by turmoil over immigration and engaged in finger pointing between politicians and civil servants while in Washington the Military and Intelligence establishment took off after Bush administration terrified lest political leadership in Iran repeated the disaster of Iraq. In Great Britain the Prime Minister Tony Blair fired Home Secretary Charles Clarke after over thousand illegal migrants convicted of heinous crimes were let back into the society instead of being deported. The new Home Secretary Jack Ried took on the civil service vowing not to defend indefensible and firing people who would not improve. The Head of the Civil Service Association fought back accusing politicians of laziness and incompetence stating that Reid's tactics were specially bad because civil servants are not allowed to fight back. Their contention was that civil servants have been doing their best to clear the backlog of immigration system for years but the Blair government, specially his wife Cherrie who lobbied hard for passage of human rights law made deportation very difficult. Another battle raised in Washington between the Secretary of Defence Donald Rumsfield and military Generals (a group of retired Generals) demanding his resignation in respect of his conduct in Iraq War. It was called " the worst breach in civil military relations since Harry Truman dismissed General Douglas MacArther". The Generals cited quite a few instances of wrong decisions, they felt, from the initial failure on the WMD (weapons of mass destruction), micro-mismanagement of war, and disbanding of Iraq army. In all these instances it is really very difficult to draw a line between policy and administration. Indeed the two remain inexorably linked. The battle between the Defence Secretary and Generals and other Pentagon officers continued spilling in public with military officers desperate to avoid Iraq like situation in Iran. In both the cases the trust and cooperation between the civil and military officers and political executive broke down. The civil servants felt that there advice is not heeded while the political executives felt that permanent executive undermined them with poor performance and disloyalty. Here both can be said to be "right as well as wrong."

"It is the accepted principle that rendering, policy advice to Political Executive has been the most important staff function of the civil servant since the beginning of the organised civil service. After a policy is approved by the elected government, it is the duty of the civil servant to implement it in right earnest whether he/ she agrees with it or not. It is unfortunate that senior civil servants often get bogged down in routine administrative matters and are unable to contribute adequately to this crucial function. If a policy being formulated is perceived by the civil servant to be against public interest, his responsibility is to convince the political executive (the minister) about the adverse implications of such policy. However, if the political executive (minister) does not agree with such advice, the civil servant can do nothing tangible except putting his views clearly on record. The other institutional mechanism would hold the political executive accountable in case of failure or malfunction of that policy/ programme."

Statutory Role of the Civil Servant

Civil servants are required to discharge statutory functions under various enactments which may sometimes be of quazi-judicial nature like executive magistrate under Cr. PC, Assessing Officer under I.T. Act etc. It is increasingly been observed that seniors both in civil service and elected representatives including minister tend to interfere in such statutory functions. In such situations both the junior officer discharging statutory functions and the seniors bringing undue pressure on him need to be held responsible for miscarriage of functions. It is but not very easy to fix the responsibility on either of the two because the pressures for undue favours is more often than not brought in the form of unwritten direction/instruction. The person succumbing to such pressures is certainly going to be hauled up who has no evidence of the pressure being brought on him. Further it is not uncommon to come across the instances of such willful actions by the civil servants for furtherance of their own interests and mutual benefits. There exist the common perception that matters could be handled in one's favour by seeking the audience of a civil servant who is quite 'close' to the minister concerned. Such cases have been reportedly found in plenty at the Union and State Government level.

Discharge of Delegated Functions by the Civil Servant

It has been observed an increasing tendency in government departments to centralise authority and also to interfere in decision making of subordinate functionaries. Such centralisation generally leads to inefficiencies and poor service delivery. This tendency emerges probably of the common perception that decentralisation and delegation of authority to field functionaries leads to more corruption and abuse of power which has proved true many a times. The perception seems to emerge in the background of centralisation wave in the name of coordination and equitable observance of the provisions of the enactments, programmes/schemes. It is somewhat ironical that such an idea is being propagated and observed in a democratic country which has aggressively adopted the decentralisation of powers and functions at the grass-root level.

The charges being leveled at the doors of the delegated functionaries are not quite substantiated empirically to have an uniform generalisation. Of course, there is no denying the fact that such functionaries are more prone to and amenable to pressures of the seniors in the civil service hierarchy. Quite a few examples can be explored easily in this regard. The upright and unbending civil servants have been chided, sermonised and penalised even in quite few cases.

Appointment/Recruitment and Placement of the Civil Servant

The Indian Constitution provides for centralised recruitment agencies for the Union and States and Union Public Service Commission and State Public Service Commissions have been formed in this behalf. Besides, a large number of posts are filled by direct recruitment done by different departments both at the Centre and State levels. The UPSC has fairly done its job impartially while it cannot be said with certainty in respect of State PSCs. There have been widespread outcries, agitations, litigations by many aspirants of these PSCs, and the judiciary has to intervene quite often. To minimise complaints of favourtism, repotism, corruption and abuse of power following principles may help a great deal.

1. Well defined merit-based procedure for recruitment to all government jobs.
2. Wide publicity and open competition for recruitment to all posts.

3. Minimisation if not elimination of discretion in recruitment process.
4. Selection primarily on the basis of written exams or on the basis of performance in existing exams with minimum weightage to interview.

The great concern today in all democratic governments, specially in developing countries is that the recruitment process into the civil service is highly influenced by political and administrative leadership squarely. As the resultant fallout it is not only the society that is loser but also the political and administrative leaders needing the services of capable officers to achieve the mandated goals of their ministries. Further the preponderance of transfers from the states at the commanding heights of civil service many with doubtful competence. When the senior echelons of civil service is dominated by the officers other than the brightest and best ministers and permanent secretaries cannot function at their best as the capacity of higher civil servants to support them in carrying out their functions is largely impaired. It becomes more miserable for the system if the incompetence is led at the top the permanent secretary who is appointed on political consideration rather than on merit and competence. The net result definitely is that such officers are incapable of meeting the expectations of the high office while advising impartially without fear or favour. This glaring incompetence may result in friction between a dynamic minister and top bureaucrat. While ministers get fired for under-performance, the civil servant escapes under the cloak of 'ministerial responsibility.'

Postings and Transfers of the Civil Servants

The National Commission to Review the Working of the Constitution observed:

> "Arbitrary and questionable methods of appointment, promotion and transfers of officers by political superiors also led to corrosion of the moral basis of its independence. It has strengthened the temptation in service to collusive practice with politicians to avoid the inconvenience of transfer and to gain advantages by ingratiating themselves to political masters. They would do the politicians bidding rather than adhere to rules. Lest the situation becomes

more vicious, it is necessary that a better arrangement be conceived under the Constitution. The question of appointments, transfers and placements is not to be left to the discretion of politicians or administrative bosses, but be entrusted to independent and autonomous Boards".

Arbitrary and motivated transfers of civil servants which belie the public interest and good governance have become the matter of great concern specially in some states.

Frequent transfers postings and placements of the civil servants including permanent secretaries is also a contributing factor to the impairment of relations between political and permanent executive. Further, frequent cabinet changes or relocation of portfolios of ministers does result in the incumbent not staying long enough in their positions to understand fully the dynamics of public service. The resultant effect is that they are denied the opportunity of acquiring broader knowledge and experience to build enduring relationship with permanent secretaries to enable them to implement the policies/programmes of the government effectively. The placements/ postings are done on the basis other than merit. Serious charges of corruption have been leveled by a senior civil servant in the beginning of September, 2016, in a big north Indian state. It was alleged that the posting as a District Magistrate requires the incumbent to shell out ₹ 70 lakh, otherwise he is left rotting at the insignificant positions at Headquarters.

The empirical evidence gathered so far clearly depicts that the 'Transfer Industry' is flourishing progressively in the states of the Indian Union with a ever increasing nexus and clout of politicians, senior civil servants and criminals. It has been recorded and published that the average tenure of a District Magistrate in a north Indian state is around one year while the minimum tenure ranges for few days. Another case may be cited of a whistle blower civil servant being transferred for more than 44 times in his 22 years of service in another state. The State Government of another north Indian State transferred more than 44 IAS and IPS officers in a single day in March, 2016. The wholesale transfer of civil servants is routinely effected with the change of guards at the political helm of the state. The 'Bureaucracy on Wheels', 'Transfer and Posting Industry', and the like are some of the epithets that seems to justify the common perception about the prevailing scenario in the country.

Other Factors Affecting the Relations

The Forum of the Heads of the African Public Services held in Tanzania in 2005 after a thorough deliberations and critical analysis identified the following mitigating factors working as impediment/ deterrent in harmonious relations between politician and civil servant in any democratic polity.

1. Varied social and political backgrounds and multiple expectations of the ministers generally create frictions.
2. Overwhelming unofficial vs. official demands of the ministers to the civil servants expecting fulfillment/compliance lead to strained relations.
3. Non-sharing of information with the minister and failed briefing by the concerned officers lead to speculations.
4. Misuse of discretionary powers by the ministers and also by the civil servants and resort to double standards lead to conflict.
5. Financial resources crunch which affect programme implementation also leads to blame game between the two.
6. Personality and leadership styles of both actors either as a team player, a commander, an ideologue, a manager and an agent do bring moments of clash instead of assimilation and cohesion.
7. Competencies that the ministers bring on the job require civil servants to match up with, which most often that do not go down well with the stereotype bureaucracy and hence chances of one upmanship."

It is now universally recognised that good governance begins with establishing the quality relationship between political and bureaucratic leaders irrespective of the form of got in a democracy. The following statement amply signifies this position.

"The metaphorical ship of state has one tiller but two pairs of hands that give it direction, one belonging to party politician in elective positions or appointed political leaders and other to higher civil servants led by permanent secretaries".— Richard Rose

Forum also dwelt upon the ways and means to smoothen and harmonise the relations between the politician and civil servants and suggested under mentioned measures for improvement.

1. It is always better to devise a good strategy to manage the friction in the relationship rather than leave it to chance. (time lapse)
2. Always efforts be made to harmonise the relationship between the two in policy-making as a strategic imperative for strengthening and enriching the public services with knowledge and competencies from other sources. (outsourcing)
3. It is better for the civil servants to align themselves with complete loyalty with the agenda of their ministers and also of other political leaders to give effect and concrete shape to the government policies and programmes.
4. There is also the need to earn the respect of their ministers by the senior civil servants (Principal Secretary/Secretary to ministers by):

"Demonstrating administrative competence, Speaking the truth only, Developing the best talents to handle emerging core concerns, Avoiding negative gossips. Avoiding reinforcing negative opinions and perception which may tend to damage the system."

From the Political Executive perspectives the following may be suggested to improve the relationship.

It is imperative on the part of the political executive to properly understand the administrative nauche and recognise its professional nature. They must also avoid interference as far as possible in service matters e.g. postings, transfers, promotions. Further no request for deviation or departure from declared and approved policies should be heeded from whatever mightier source they might be originating. They must always remain prepared to act ethically with resolve without fear or favour. Further more they must lead from the front to demonstrate the competence which may act as example for the officers of the Ministry.

On the part of bureaucrat the following may essentially go a long way in improving the relationship between the two.

A sincere and honest attempt to find out what the political executive wants and make necessary adjustment in policies and procedures to suit his wishes. Readiness to fall in line with his political chief in all matters, unless strong grounds indicate a different course of action. Willingness to act professionally and ethically at all times.

Political and Permanent Executive in Governance

Civil servants advise ministers on policies and brief and support them generally in the functioning of the government on a daily basis. This thrusts on the civil servants the responsibility seek and explore the ways to improve the support they have to give to the ministers in the aftermath of changes in the Constitution, the government and the ministries. The main objective in seeking improved support to ministers is the better policy formulation where ministers need to know expected consequences of different policy options. Both the ministers and civil servants have certain defined roles in explaining the proposed new policies to the people. Thus, changes intended to support ministers are complementing programmes designed to improve service delivery system. It is more urgently needed in the regional and local government to help civil service and politician work in tandem more effectively for the common good of common man.

The need for reforms becomes inevitable when ministers complain about their civil servants and the advice they tender or when civil servants maintain that the ministers do not listen to their advice. Further, when ministers are inadequately briefed or make policy announcements which later are found impractical or when civil servants act contrary to a government policy. OR when ministers hold public meetings without civil servant being present to follow up decisions/ announcements taken/made therein. The evidence for need is anecdotal but plentiful given voice by ministers and civil servants in many countries familiar to diplomats and consulates. The problem is much discussed in some newly established multi-party democracies may reflect greater need for reforms and the greater need for freedom of speech.

The improvement and modification may surely be needed in structure, working practices and attitudes of the civil servants to provide information as effectively as possible to help ministers take decisions both individually and collectively. The help comes from papers (and information provided otherwise) and from people including the civil servants. The articulation of needs is part of every reform process and with experience the needs become more clearly defined. It may definitely help if the ministers and civil servants clarify their different responsibilities precisely.

Structural Changes

Many viable patterns of staffing to support ministers exist in the world e.g. in France, ministers have a small cabinet, in the United States, a management team to support them that they choose themselves, in Britain one or more private secretary for the purpose and in some countries, ministers have one or two typists as their "private offices". If the support is inadequate ministers do not have the requisite briefs or do not have them in time and officials do not know the minister's diary or requirements. The job description for those working closely with ministers may vary greatly. In addition, there is need for clear structure and collective responsibilities of ministers in the Cabinet or Council of Ministers and the Cabinet committees. The Cabinet secretariat has to provide briefs, relevant papers and records and follow up decisions and report progress.

Change in Working Practices

Ministers need briefs and submissions to save their time and effort that often means recommendation (or for a meeting the points to make) followed by defensive briefing on objections to be raised, arguments and background follow up. If the recommendation is acceptable the ministers need no further reading. This is the pattern already in vogue in many countries. Ministers and civil servants in all countries work with increasingly educated and informed public. Good Governance and sustainable development will depend on consulting the people (for the ministers re-election). Ministers may wish to announce new policies, but they will get the credit if their civil servants keep the people informed and answer question quickly and courteously in this regard. If officials help announce policies specially those hurting some sections of populace, ministers may face less criticism for decisions dictated by outside constraints.

Attitudinal Changes

Relationship between ministers and civil servants may be marred by suspicion and mistrust. Minister may suspect civil servants of continued loyalty to an earlier regime or despise the work ethics and practices developed by them on one hand and the civil servants on the other may think ministers motivated by short-term political interest or being naive about the problems of government. Either group may think the other being corrupt. If civil servants find difficulties with proposed policies, their objections to it may be thought to be political rather than technical. They may indeed be "prejudicial against new policies and new ways of working". Civil servants need to understand and accept new political priorities and show total loyalty to the government of the day. But minister's political future and good of the nation depends on civil servants offering honest and courageous advice. Ministers need to know what they may not want to hear.

Ministers and civil servants working together may help build a national consensus on matters about which most people agree or which offer very little room for manoeuvring government decision may become the subject for political controversy even where governing party would have to do the same. The problem is exacerbated in countries having an executive President, by the need to distinguish loyalty to the President as head of the state from opposition to the President's policy. Where controversy leads to public disenchantment with politics, there is special value in seeking a national consensus on core issues such as security, drugs, terrorism, development, health and education etc. Where relationship has deteriorated badly, some positive interventions needed for improvement. Definitely the advantages will accrue if the ministers and civil servants work together to consult and inform public. Additionally, further contribution may be made by occasional short-term ministerial seminars aimed at briefing ministers on national interest by bringing two-third ministers and a few of their civil servants together with professionals, leaders from private sector, trade unions, voluntary organisations and others.

Aid Donor Countries have appeared more interested in reforms of the Civil Services to improve services delivery to the public than to improve policy advice system to ministers. This reflects the perceived priorities of Donor Countries or Donor's fears that often lead them to interfere in internal policies and politics. However, some Aid Funded Projects have been reported to help ministers in promoting better cooperation between civil servants and politicians at the local government level. It is for ministers in each country to decide what priority they will give to reforming the structure, work practices and attitudes that determine the support they receive from the civil service.

Collaboration and Partnership

The collaboration and partnership of the political and permanent executive is very essential for proper administration of the state and achievement of strategic national priorities for development. To this end it is vital for both of them to maintain cordial relations to continue to render service to the people for the effectuation and sustenance of social contract that binds the governed and governors together.

Ministers must ensure that they have good working relationship with their higher civil servants personified in the Permanent Secretary, and secure their trust and confidence in the performance of their duties at all times with a view to harness their collective strength and capacity for the delivery of public good. As individuals with different background, orientation and experience, they must not allow these differences to undermine the need for collaboration complementary and synergy of actions towards fulfilling a common purpose of value addition to lives of citizenry. Thus, they can be exemplars of service excellence, probity and integrity in public office which are hallmark of worthy legacy that they are required to bequeath in office.

References

1. "Constitution of India—Bare Act", Eastern Book Company, Lucknow, 2015.
2. Elaine C. Kamarck, "Civil Servants and Politicians—a Not so Civil Relationship" in Management Insights, July19, 2006: www.governihg.com
3. "Ministers and Civil Servants: Characteristics, Roles and Relationships" in www.
4. R. K. Raghavan, "The Ministers Versus the Civil Servants." The Hindu, New Delhi, Feb. 11, 2011.
5. Ama Pepple, "Relationship between Higher Civil Servants and Political Masters"—"Vanguard"Aug. 6, 2012, Nigeria == www. vanguardngr.com
6. Denis Osborne, "Ministers and Civil Servants in the Governance Process"-DPMN Bulletin—Dec. 22, 2015, WWW.DPMF.ORG

7. "Relations between Political Executives and Civil Servants in Public Administration in India" (Survey Report)—O and M Division Cabinet Secretariat, Government of India, New Delhi: arc.gov.in——10th report.
8. C.Neuhold, "Civil Servants and Politics: a Delicate Balance": www.palgrave.com
9. "Relationship between the Political Executive and Permanent Civil Service"-July 24, 2013: https/bhargawp wordpress.com
10. Alexander Stevenson, "Fourways to Fix Ruptures between Politicians and Civil Servants", "Sept,12,2013: www.the guardian.com
11. Emanuel S. E. Leigh, "Political Parties and Civil Servants"—Standard Times, March 19, 2016: www.the guardian.com—Sept. 12, 2013.
12. BBC, "Higher Bitesize Modern studies: Decision making in:www.bbc.co.uk
13. M. Wright, "Ministers and Civil Servants: Relations and Responsibilities"——pa.oxfordjournals.org
14. V. Subramanium, "Evolution of Minister Civil Servant relations in India": www.tandfoline.com
15. "Let's Define the Roles of Ministers and Civil Servants Once": www.the guardian.com—Dec. 16, 2013.
16. Wikipedia, "Minister for Civil Service."
17. "Civil Servant Ministerial Relationship": www.slideshow.net
18. "Neutrality in Indian Civil Service": iasmaker.com—Jan.14, 2015.
19. "Civil Service Neutrality": www.insightsonindia.com
20. S. K. Singh, "Civil Service in U. P.: Perspectives and Challenges" in Indian Administration: Ideas and Issues ed. P. S. Bhatnagar, Mangal Publishers and Distributers, Jaipur 2002.
21. S. K. Singh, "Postings and Transfers in a Coalition" in Public Administration and Coalition in India ed. S. N. Singh, Bharat Book Centre, Lucknow, 2003.
22. Vaishali Saxena, "Bureaucracy on Wheels", Aalekh Publishers, Jaipur, 2003.
23. "Working with Ministers-Civil Service Learning": https:# civilservicelearning.civilsevice.govt.uk
24. "Civil Servants and Politics": www.ipa.ie
25. "Why and How Civil Servants be Subjected": www.academia.edu
26. "Challenges of Civil Service": www.academia.edu
27. "Administration Civil Service and Bureaucracy": www.academia.edu
28. Times of India, Lucknow.

7

Core Concerns in Indian Civil Service

— S.N. Singh

The roots of modern Indian administration are generally traced back to the days when the British have been ruling the country. The British governed India for about two hundred years. We, thus, inherited an administrative system from the British which allegedly based itself on the concept of "rationality". During the period under the British Raj there appears to be the primacy of rules and regulations over personal bias and other extraneous factors, particularly after the transfer of power to the Crown. The administration during those days was ably supported by the bureaucratic structure which was one of the best of its time and often termed as the "Steel frame". It was an administrative system which, by and large, based itself on the concept of neutrality as political or partisan factors had little influence on the decision-making and the governing process. After independence, the administrative system, apart from the continuity element, considerable changes were effected for the future governance in view of the parliamentary democracy adopted by India. The changes were initially effected in the nomenclature, but more and forceable changes were anticipated in the civil service system for an efficient and effective governance. The working of the administrative system for the last six decades or so shows gaps in the provision of law and the performances which seems to have affected the system adversely. This further led to inefficiency and corruption in public life. These are serious issues which need to be addressed rationally. The present paper makes an attempt to briefly examine the question relating to selection of civil servants, their training and then the relation between the politician and the civil servants which have undergone considerable changes and to see as to how far it has affected the credibility of Indian administration.

Recruitment

Since India opted for a closed career system for its civil services, there would be a sort of consensus on the fact that recruitment occupies the most important place in our public administration system. The integrity and the credibility of the government and its administration would much depend upon the quality of its work force. It is an oft repeated fact that a single wrong recruitment can cast a long-term damage on the public system. In view of its importance, every care has to be taken to have a sound system recruitment in terms of method as well as the machinery. The modern civil service is, in a way, a continuation of the British civil service in India which was popularly known as the "Steel frame" the ICS which formed this work force. However, it can now be noted that in its long evolution, the civil service in India has progressed from what essentially was an elitist service to a service that is now representative of Indian social order.[1] How far this change has helped the cause of the general mass of the people may be a matter of opinion. At the same time we note the change in different spheres of our civil service organisation and its functional priorities.

In order to ensure an objective and unbiased recruitment, the agency has to be independent of the Executive. In view of this and rightly so, a Public Service Commission was constituted to conduct the Indian Civil Service (ICS) Examination in India from 1926 on behalf of the British Civil Service Commission. After independence, the new Service called Indian Administrative Service (IAS), Indian Police Service (IPS), and Indian Foreign Service (IFS) were established. In the year 1950, with the Constitution coming into force, the Union Public Service Commission came into being for the said purpose. The UPSC has been successfully discharging its obligation as per the Constitutional provisions. An overview of the functioning of the UPSC over the years shows, many positives and little can be said against this constitutional body so far.

There are other aspects of recruitment which need appraisal in our context. These aspects are concerned with educational qualification, age limit, number of attempts and the like which need to be addressed for broader public cause. In this context, the first Administrative Reform Commission[2] had recommended quite a few measures then. For example, its recommendation about the increase in age from 26 years to 28 years is considered an important change suggested to include large number of aspirants from the rural sector who otherwise don't get adequate opportunity to appear in the examination for no fault of their. The ARC further recommended for the inclusion of Engineering and Medical subjects in the list of subjects for the Civil Service Examination to make the Service professional. There were quite a few other recommendations, but we would confine our observation on these two major recommendations as they had affected the civil service system to a large extent. Before making any observation on these aspects, we would like to mention here that these recommendations were accepted by the then government and subsequent examination of the civil service included these subjects in the list of subjects for the said examination.

The increase in age was advocated to accommodate probables from the rural areas who generally do not have access to higher education. This increase in age changed the compulsion of the Service wherein more mature people started coming to join the Service. On the one hand it can be appreciated that now people in their early and late thirties became part of the elite Service, on the other, it became difficult to instill any change in their attitude towards life and attitude. There has been a visible difference in the overall attitude of the officers who are fresh and others who come after serving in other professions lower than this.[3] It may not be easy to convince people who have their own fixed notions about ethics and values of public service. It is, therefore, argued that increase in age might have served one purpose but it affected the other purpose. One is, however, not arguing that simply because of increase in age the changes we observe have taken place. But it may be one of the factors contributing for lack of proper attitude and values for public service. It is a question that needs to be reassessed in the contemporary scenario.

The inclusion of subjects like medical and engineering in the civil service examination has also been a subject of debate over the years. In the decades following the acceptance of these recommendations there has been a marked change in the nature of the civil service. We now find more and more people with medical and engineering background entering the service. How far the service or the society in general has benefitted from such professionals is again a matter of debate.[4] Since the civil service continues to be a generalist service and their placement and promotion is guided by various factors where educational background is hardly an issue, little purpose could therefore, be served.

The number of applicants for the civil service examination has been rising making it difficult to have a scientific selection. In order to make the selection more rational and realistic, the Committee on Recruitment Policy and Selection Methods, namely the Kothari Committee, which gave its Report in 1966, recommended for a new scheme of examination for the All-India and Central Service. It recommended for a three sequential stages: (i) Preliminary Examination (Objective Type) for selecting the candidates for the Main Examination (ii) Main Examination (Written Examination followed by an interview for selecting candidates for entry into the civil service and (iii) Post Training Test at the end of the Foundation Course at the Academy, including an interview by a Board constituted by the UPSC.

The system of recruitment suggested by the Kothari Committee was an improvement on the earlier selection method. Consequent upon the acceptance of the recommendations by the Government of India, a new system of examination was introduced by the UPSC in the year 1979. Almost a decade later in the year 1989 this scheme was revisited by the Committee to review the scheme of Civil Service Examination (the Satish Chandra Committee), which recommended for the continuance of the structure while introducing a Compulsory Essay Paper in the Main Examination. This was again followed by another Committee which examined the issue of age and qualification required for entry into the civil service. These recommendations and issues connected with recruitment remained in active consideration of the government. Since these issues were important and their magnitude was also a concern, the Government of India appointed the Second Administrative Reforms Commission (The Moilly Commission) in the year 2005 to enquire into various issues connected with administration including personnel administration. The Commission examined the prevailing system of recruitment and came forward with quite a few recommendations. Consequent upon the acceptance of the recommendations there is going to be a change in the selection process.

The new scheme of examination has proposed only one paper of General Studies comprising of various segments connected with Polity, Economic, Public Administration. It has proposed for the abolition of subjects examination which will be there only in the Mains. Those who qualify the Main Examination will be put through an Interview/ Personality Test. These recommendations provide for some changes in the scheme of recruitment of higher civil service in India.

It can, therefore, be observed that during the last sixty years or so the recruitment system has undergone several changes. Various Committees and Commissions which have gone into the question of recruitment have addressed themselves about who should enter the civil service, at what age and with what qualification. There is still a debate on the pattern of civil service examination wherein some suggestions have come about lowering the age and following the pattern of the Army or the ENA in France. There is still no final word and we continue to chop and change without addressing the serious concern of governance.

Training

Training occupies an important place in personnel administration for obvious reasons. It plays an important role in keeping the contemporary framework under control. It helps in improving the managerial skill and attitude for increasing the efficiency of the work force. In a way training is considered a lasting investment in human force for long-term return. It complements a person's education by updating the knowledge, including skill and values. It also promotes team spirit and in general increases the value of an individual for his / her organisation and consequently society.[5] Training, therefore, is high on the agenda of the government as no government would like to have an untrained and unskilled work force.

After having noted the importance of training for the civil servants, it may be pertinent to briefly look into the training scenario in the country. In this context we find that there are separate training institutes and models for different services in the country. The training for the IAS and other all-India services alongwith the Central Services provide different training models. During the last few decades we observe several policy interventions in the training of civil servants in India. It may be particularly important to note the formation of a

National Training Policy in the year 1996. It is not that training was not on the agenda of the earlier governments, but the importance attached to training in earlier period kept changing. The Training Policy to focused on the following:

(a) **Responsiveness:** to the challenges democratic needs and expectations of the citizen and organisational and technological development.

(b) **Commitment:** to democratic values and concept of partnership and participation in decision making.

(c) **Awareness:** of technological, economic and social development.

(d) **Accountability:** to ensure high performance in every professional field and cost-effective methods of delivery.

With the growing role of technology in the governing process training has become all the more necessary to make the work force aware and capable for future needs. After the 1990s, developments, there has been additional pressure on the civil service to change its mode of functioning. The new LPG models demanded new approach and attitude from our civil service in order to compete in the global market. The traditional hierarchical system involves considerable delay in the decision-making which affects the policy intervention at various levels. The training modules have, therefore, to be such which cater to the future needs not only of India but of global scenario as well in order to compete with developed economies. This is being seen after the new government has taken over since 2014 under the Prime Ministership of Narendra Modi. There seems to be a departure from the policies in the UPA government in some respects, but we have to wait for the results to show on the ground level. But the new government of the NDA anticipating the expansion of the Indian economy which would not be possible without a properly trained and equipped civil services.

The Politician – Civil Servant Relationship:

The question of politician – civil servant relationship has been one of the core concern in Indian administration as much depends on the feasibility of their relationship. One is termed as the political executive while the other is the permanent executive and both have to address the issues connected with public and its welfare. These two constitute the two important wheels of the government and administration. The efficiency and the effectiveness of the government, often would depend upon their relation. This becomes more pertinent in a parliamentary system of government wherein there are specific roles, defined for these bodies. The policy formation as well as policy intervention calls for a kind of relationship that can help good governance in broader societal concerns.

An overview of the relationship between these two important components in government during the last six decades or so would provide varied information which would make it difficult to form any specific opinion. During the initial years of our parliamentary system, both sides were represented by men of high morality and integrity. The politicians then belonged to those categories of people who fought for India's freedom from foreign rule and therefore, there was a sense of commitment towards the people and the society at large. They were more worried about the public good rather than their own partisan and personal good. So also in the bureaucracy, we had great civil servants who made their presence in the administrative scenario. Once this class was out from the public view, changes started appearing on the administrative scenario. Since the Indian administration opted for a rule-bound rational bureaucracy, it was expected that civil servants who constitute the core will be non-partisan and would care for public cause in their work performance. Since they were selected by an independent agency on the basis of merit, it was expected a similar behaviour in their performance and not get impressed by specific group of people or the principles.

During the last few decades there has been a marked decline in administrative ethics and consequently we notice an increase in corruption in public life. The cases of corruption and misuse of office for personal gain have reached serious proportion causing damage to public delivery system. The cases regarding 'living beyond means' have become quite common. In many states the Lokayouktas have been kept quite busy in examining such cases. There is apparently a nexus between the politicians and civil servants engaging themselves in corrupt practices. It has affected the governance considerably. For example, we find corruption charges against the politicians including ministers as well as the civil servants and some officers have been sentenced to imprisons. In Uttar Pradesh, the NRHM scam was so big that several category of people have been involved and have been put behind the bar. It is an unfortunate situation wherein the politician and civil servant relationship is affected by corrupt means to help each other and serve their mutual interest causing serious damage to public exchequer and public life.

We observe another trend in our civil service, particularly at the State level, wherein civil servants are identified with the politician. It will be in public domain that 'X' civil servant is associated with 'Y' politician. There could be quite a few such officers whose names have been associated with different politicians. In a parliamentary system of governance, the civil servant has to be neutral to any political ideology, political party or political person. It is because of the neutrality concept the civil service maintains the continuity and the link between the outgoing and the incoming governments. In the absence of this neutrality there has been problems in the governance. We often notice, at least we can say for the state of U.P., that large number of transfers take place when there is change in the colour of the party in the government. We have particularly observed this for the last couple of decades wherein the government alternated between the Bahujan Samaj Party and the Samajwadi Party. This clearly indicates the fact that there is a group of civil servant and a group of politician which foots this bill. This also affects the governance and ultimately the issues connected with the general mass of people get ignored and neglected. The political and civil servant combines to serve the vested interest rather than the public interest.

It can, therefore, be observed that efficiency and effectiveness of public administration and the delivery of goods and services and the good governance would continue to depend on the issues raised in the paper. They need to be addressed at the policy level of our governance to serve the desired purpose.

Notes

1. Second Administrative Commission, Truth Report, Government of India, New Delhi, 2008, p. 76.
2. First Administrative Reform Commission, Report on Personnel Administration, Government of India, New Delhi, 1970.

3. During my tenure at the LBSNAA, Mussoorie between 1980-84 such situations have been observed.
4. I would like to recollect one incident here. During the Bharat Darshan of the 1980-81 batch of the civil service probations, we were in Goa to attend the Tea hosted by the then Lt. Governor Sri Jagmohan. We were introduced to him alongwith the probationers. One of the probationer was a medical graduate, this prompted the Governor to ask the probation as to why he joined to IAS. He answered that to do public service and on this he was countered that this you can do in the medical profession too. In a sense he was questioning the merit of allowing the medical professional in the civil services.
5. Second Administrative Reforms Commission, op.cit., p. 123.

8

Issues in Relations Between Politics and Civil Services in India

— U. B. Singh

Introduction

India is a constitutional democracy. Its functioning mainly depends upon four pillars – Legislature, Executive, Judiciary, and Free Press. The founding fathers had the foresight to create the necessary institutional framework for the country's governance. These effective and efficient institutions form the backbone of a successful development and governance process. Each one of these pillars has been assigned its role. First three of these are associated with the governance of the State (Pandey: 3066). For the governance of the country and delivering goods to public at large, the government roughly depends on two general processes: 'the process of politics', which consists of activities of the elected representatives of the people; and 'the process of administration', which consists of the activities of civil servants (CS: 2011). Civil Service refers to the body of government officials who are employed in civil administration that are neither political nor judicial. One of the basic elements of Indian governance architecture is the concept of an impartial, honest, efficient and fearless civil service, which forms the permanent structure and backbone of our administration system. Theoretically, the administrative machinery is subordinate to the elective body i.e. the Council of Ministers.

The institution of civil services in India is the oldest institution. Over the period the role of civil services has changed depending on the agenda of the governance of that particular period. During British period, enforcement of law and order and collection of revenue was the main concern of civil servants. In independent India, when the government has acquired the role of Welfare State, civil services act as an important tool for implementing national and state policies of welfare and planned development (Mishra: 2010). Once known as the 'steel frame' undesirable political pressure on it increased continuously. This has affected the quality, competence and commitment of the civil servants. It has been observed that there has been a growing realisation among the civil servants to maintain the 'status quo' in administration.

Interestingly, in polity, the country has travelled from one-party dominance to coalition governments over the years. Many a times, these coalitions were seen as 'marriage of convenience' with no clear political philosophy, sometimes a group of contradictions. These situations were bound to affect the administration. Managing the contradiction has been a challenge not to the political parties in power but also the civil servants.

In this backdrop, the paper makes effort to identify the grey areas in the relationship between the politics and civil services. The paper traces, in brief, the historical perspective of civil service and the changing facets of politics in the country as well.

Civil Service in India: Origin and Characteristics

The public administration system in India has a long history. Hence, the concept of civil service was prevalent in India from ancient times. In the earlier era the civil servants performed the role of servants of the king. The Mauryan administration employed civil servants in the name of '*adhyakshas*' and '*rajukas*'. During the medieval period they became State Servants, who helped in the development of land revenue system during the Moghul period. The East India Company had a civil service to carry out their commercial functions. Later on, during the British rule they started as servants to the Crown, and aligned themselves with their British masters. Gradually they started becoming 'Public Servants' (Pandey: 3066). The British Government set up the civil services, primarily with the objective of strengthening the British administration in India. In this period the role of civil services was to further the British interest and its role was totally regulatory.

Hence, after Independence public opinion was generally hostile to them in view of its identification with foreign rule.

The present civil service of India is mainly based on the pattern of the former Indian Civil Service of British India which was divided into two categories - covenanted and uncovenanted. The covenanted civil service consisted of only white British civil servants occupying the higher posts in the government. The uncovenanted civil service was solely introduced to facilitate the entry of Indians at the lower rung of the administration. With the passing of the Government of India Act, 1919, the Imperial Services headed by the Secretary of State for India, were split into two – All India Services and Central Services (Wiki). The present modern civil service was formed after the partition of India in 1947. The values of integrity, impartiality and merit remained the guiding principles of Indian civil service and over the period it has been evolved as an efficient and professional organisation. It is therefore that civil services are considered as the most important element of our administrative system that has the responsibility to fulfill the development objectives of the welfare state.

After the coming into force of the Constitution, the founding fathers wisely provided, by making provisions in Part XIV of the Constitution, for apolitical and independent civil services, with requisite protection for service matters. The members of civil service serve at the pleasure of the President of India and the Constitution protects them from politically motivated or vindictive action (Constitution of India).

It is therefore the neutrality and anonymity of civil servants that have been recognised as important to maintain in our system, which is full with diversities. This was emphasised by Sardar Patel in a letter to the Prime Minister (as quoted by Latasinha):

> "I need hardly emphasise, that an efficient, disciplined and contended (civil) service, assured of its prospects as a result of diligent and honest work, is a sine qua non of sound administration, under a democratic regime, even more than under an authoritarian rule. The (civil) service must be above party and we should ensure that political consideration, either in its recruitment or its discipline and control, are reduced to the minimum, if not eliminated altogether."

Changing Political Scenario in India

The Independent India has experienced a unique multi-party system dominated by one party for long. Over the years, the country has travelled from single party rule to coalition governments at both central and provincial levels. The last few decades have witnessed the emergence of strong local political parties, mostly centred on a charismatic individual personality or dominated or controlled by a single family. Thus, ruling government in such situations has to deal with conflicting interests arising out of different political aspirations. Different ruling dispensations try to mould policies to their advantage.

Interestingly, a good number of bureaucrats enter into politics generally after reaching very high positions in the government. They have many years of experience, expertise, loyal subordinates left behind. Many of them give up a bureaucratic career in favour of a political one. They have the extensive webs of personal relationships and the rich experience of governance. Many of them are very talented, but their role has to be fundamentally different from that played by politicians. Further, politicians get deeply involved in micromanaging the policy process. That, after all the so-called policy tribes that are made up of politicians with specialised knowledge, or at least intense interest, in a particular set of policy issues—do when they use their power to get policy outcomes desired by various sectoral interests that support and fund them (Curtis: 2002). Even the political parties themselves have become bureaucratised (WB).

In our system, the ultimate responsibility for running the administration rests with the elected representatives of the people which are the ministers. But the handful of ministers cannot be expected to deal personally with the manifold problems of modern administration. Thus, the ministers lay down the policy and it is for the civil servants to carry out this policy. The executive decisions are implemented by the civil servants. The responsibility of political chiefs becomes formal, as they are forced to listen to the advice of the civil servants, which can dig and present data in a matter as they consider fit. The service role in relation to the minister is that of influence and not of power. The First Administrative Reforms Commission of India (1966) dwelt the issue of relationship comprehensively and observed that:

> "*Secretaries and other civil servants need to show greater sensitivity to and a better appreciation of the Minister's difficulties, and to discriminate between minor adjustments on the one hand, and acts of political and other forms of accommodation compromising basic principles or likely to have substantial or lasting repercussions on efficiency and morale of the services, on the other.*"

Changing Public Attitudes

The issue of bureaucrat versus politician is important today not because bureaucrats have had all the power but because fundamental social change, shifting popular values, basic structural changes in the political system, and new social needs have undermined a policymaking system that functioned well for many years in the past. Today, attitudes are very different. Most urban dwellers no longer have close ties to countryside. Consequently, the idea that money should be taken from people in the cities and spent on public works in the countryside, now enrages the public where a couple of decades ago they applauded it (Curtis:2002). Now, the urban habitants and managers (consisting of political elites, civil servants and effluent class of society) demand share in economy proportionate to their contribution to national economy. This has led increasing the complexity of development paradigm as well as administrative culture in the country.

Factors Affecting Relations between Politics and Civil Service

Although legal measures provide for neutrality of services, there are also structural arrangements that facilitate the separation between politics and administration both substantively and procedurally. However, neutrality does not mean that high-ranking civil servants cannot or should not be involved in articulating public policy. The secretary of the ministry is a permanent civil servant who heads the ministry's administration and acts as the chief advisor to the minister. He is thereby involved in discussing and often influencing political matters that relate to the ministry. Indeed, senior officials are professionally and morally obliged to provide their political leaders with policy alternatives based on sound arguments, relevant precedents, and sustainability in the context of changing political environments. It is essential that they do so, however, from a non-partisan position.

Usually, a thin line is drawn between the secretary's advisory capacity and his active involvement in promoting the interests of the ruling dispensation in policy formulation and implementation.

For political scientists the relationship between politics and bureaucracy has been an important topic. The father of modern political sociology, Max Weber, identified the struggle between bureaucrats who commanded technical expertise and popularly elected politicians who were accountable to the public for the government's policies as potentially one of the most serious challenges to the effective functioning of the democratic political party systems. Weber wrote that skillful bureaucrats do not try to compete openly with politicians for power. They pay lip service to the principle of politician control over the decision-making system and exercise their power by explaining that for technical reasons something the politicians want to do is not feasible or that something the politicians do not want to do is absolutely necessary. And they can even sabotage a lot of government policy simply by stalling the implementation of policies of which they do not approve (Curtis: 2002)). Weber and others were more occupied with outlining how the relationship should be, rather than trying to describe it. Reading Weber, one sees that it is not possible to distinguish empirically between good and bad values, opening up for political conflict and procedural arrangements to reach decisions in situations with diverging interests. Political behaviour should be characterised by passion and a willingness to fight for one's beliefs, whereas administrative behaviour should be characterised by neutrality, impartiality and not including personal feelings and emotions. (Gerth and Mills:1946).

Much of modern research about the relationship between politics and administration has focused on deviations from the Weberian ideal. One of the first to attack Weber's distinction between values and facts was Herbert Simon. He argued that under conditions of uncertainty it would be impossible to distinguish clearly between facts and values, and that choosing certain means would in it have implications for values and goals. In short, he argued that there always would be a "grey zone" between purely ethical and purely factual decisions, causing uncertainty on whether a decision should be located in the political or the administrative sphere. A second attack was set in against the Wilsonian ideal that different tasks should be allocated to the political and the administrative spheres, i.e. that politicians should concentrate on strategic and principled tasks, while more "technical" tasks should be delegated to the administration (Jacobsen, 2001). One of the strong voices against this attempt to make a clear distinction between political and administrative tasks was Mosher (1982) who argued strongly that it was impossible to analyse public tasks only in technical (factual) terms. If politics were about the distribution of scarce resources, almost every public task including the use of discretion would fall under the politics.

Another type of critique against the clear distinction between politics and administration focused on the idea that politicians and administrators had responsibilities for different phases in the public decision processes. Politicians should be in charge of taking initiatives by setting the agenda, making formal decisions and controlling these decisions, while administrators should assist in the preparation of decisions as well as in implementing political decisions. Although Finer (1941) and Friedrich (1940) disagreed in many ways, both of them took as a starting point from a notion that politics could not be separated into different phases, but rather that the different phases were tightly connected, and concluding that politics was "a continuous process" (Friedrich, 1941). It therefore seems more plausible that there is a political and an administrative sphere, and that these spheres can be distinguished both by factual/ethical decisions, principled/technical tasks and preparation and implementation versus initiative, deciding and controlling. In many instances, however, the line between these spheres becomes more or less blurred, resulting in a zone that may be coined as being both administrative and political (Svara, 1998).

Given the importance and universal nature of the relationship of political leaders to bureaucracy, academics have focused considerable attention on this issue. One of the most durable of doctrines is the need to create a clear separation between political and administrative responsibilities. Politicians should act as sovereign representatives of political values and interests whereas bureaucrats are subordinate policy executors, whose major concern is efficiency. However, there is mounting evidence, both theoretical and empirical, that this doctrine is far too simplistic and just does not hold up in practice. However, in reality the respective role conceptions and interaction patterns between politicians and administrators are more complex and differentiated (Page, 2003).

In India, during the long period of one-party dominance, the relationship between bureaucrat and politician cannot be explained in terms of a zero-sum game in which the bureaucrats had all the power and the politicians had none. Political leaders, not bureaucrats, set the framework for domestic and foreign policy. When bureaucrats say today that they need strong political leadership in order to work effectively, they are not dissembling. The bureaucracy is in reality a complex of largely independent, often competing ministries and departments, each with its own policy preferences and goals and none with the ability to establish overarching policy. That is the job of political leaders. It is the failing of political leadership that is responsible for so many of the problems that the country currently finds itself facing.

India is a democratic republic and thus it also needs political accountability. For achieving the political accountability, bureaucrats have to be accountable to political leaders. Sometimes, this is termed as committed bureaucracy. There is no single or simple formula for striking the right balance between bureaucrat and politician. The electoral process has proved to be a powerful constraint on bureaucratic power. Political parties and incumbent candidates wanting to win reelection invariably force their policy preferences on the bureaucracy whenever they have believed that doing so was necessary for their own political survival(Das:1998). In this regard views of the First Administrative Reforms Commission of India deserve a mention. The Commission recommended that "*The official relationship of the Secretary to the Minister should be one of loyalty and that of the Minister to Secretary one of confidence.*"

In a simple way, the distinction between politics and administration can be viewed as a continuum ranging from a total and clear distinction between politics and administration to a situation where there is no distinction between the two spheres. In the situation there is a sphere where politics and administration is difficult, if not impossible, to distinguish from each other. Most likely, this is the most common situation in most political-administrative systems (Jacobsen, 1999).

Policies are chosen and implemented by both elected representatives (politicians) and non-elected bureaucrats. The basic notion that politicians choose policies and bureaucrats execute them is overly simple. The boundaries between decision and execution are a grey area and in many cases bureaucrats do much more than executing. Many observers believe that as economies become more complex and the need for expertise in making public policy become more pronounced, the bureaucrats' control of information and technical knowledge would give them the upper hand over politicians who are mostly generalists and whose time in office is uncertain (Paipanandikar, 1971). The First Administrative Reforms Commission of India observed that:

> "*Minister should try to develop a climate of fearlessness and fair play among the senior officers and encourage them to give frank and impartial advice. They should give the Secretaries the necessary guidance in carrying out their policies and orders.*" The Commission further added.

Summing Up

The paper may be concluded with the remark that today, politics and administration is seen as two overlapping spheres. The conventional wisdom is that policy-making in the government is a system of bureaucratic dominance in which politicians have little. It would involve reducing the power of the bureaucracy and increasing that of the politicians. In practical terms, this notion implies that administrators most probably are important political actors (WB). An overlapping between politics and administration also opens up for the possibility that there may be both conflict and co-operation between politicians and administrators. The observations made by the First Administrative Reforms Commission of India that *"Ministers should not intervene in the day-to-day administration except in cases of grave injustice, serious default or maladministration on the part of civil servants.......*" should form the basis of relationship between political masters and the civil servants, 'Loyalty' and 'confidence' should be the focal points to maintain a healthy relationship between two important pillar institutions (political masters and civil servants) of our democracy.

References

- Aberbach, Joel, et al.(eds.)(1981): *Bureaucrats and Politicians in Western Democracies,* Cambridge, Mass., Harvard University Press.

- Beteille, Andre (2000): *Antinomies of Society : Essays on Ideologies and Institutions,* Delhi, Oxford University Press.
- Bendix, R. (1964): *Nation-Building and Citizenship,* Berkley, University of California Press.
- Civil Service (CS): The British Library, 8 June 2011, Retrieved on 14 August 2015.
- Civil Services in India: Wikipedia, retrieved on December 7, 2015.
- Civil services/bureaucracy in Government of India: Latasinha's Weblog, Word Press. com weblog, retrieved on 8/12/2015.
- Constitution of India, Thirty sixth edition(2014): Lucknow, Eastern Book Co.
- Curtis, Gerald L.(2002): *Politicians and Bureaucrats: What's Wrong and What's to Be Done, Policymaking in Japan: Defining the Role of Politicians,* (ed.)Gerald L. Curtis, Tokyo: Japan Centre for International Exchange, pp. 1-17.
- Das, S.K. (1998): *Civil Service Reform and Structural Adjustment,* Oxford University Press.
- Government of India, Department of Administrative Reforms and Public Grievances (8 June 2011), "The civil service system", Retrieved on 11 October 2011.
- Finer, H. (1941): *Administrative responsibility in Democratic Government,* Public Administration Review, Vol. 1, pp. 335-350.
- Friedrich, C.J. (1940): *Public Policy and the Nature of Administrative Responsibility; in* Friedrich, C.J. and Mason, E.S. (eds): *Public Policy,* Cambridge, Harvard University Press.
- Gerth, H.H. and Mills, C.W. (1946): *From Max Weber Essays in Sociology,* New York, Oxford University Press.
- Government of India: First Administrative Reforms Commission of India (1966) as quoted by the Second Administrative Reforms Commission of India in its Thirteenth Report entitled as Organisational Structure of Government of India (2009).
- Hagen, T.P. and Sorensen, R. (1997): *Kommunal organisering,* Oslo, Tano-Aschehoug.
- *Indian Civil Services Examination Handbook/Probity in Governance, Retrieved on 7/12/2015.*
- Jacobsen, D.I. (1999): *Trust in Political-Administrative relations: The Case of Local Authorities in Norway and Tanzania,* World Development, Vol. 27, pp. 839-853.
- Jacobsen, Dag Ingvar (2001): *Are the relations between Politicians and Administrators at the local level determined by the degree of Central Government Regulations? Paper presented at ECPR Joint Sessions of*

Workshops, Grenoble, April Workshop No. 21: "Local Autonomy and Local Democracy.

- Misra, P.K.(2010): "The Role of civil services in India (Standard Note: DOPT/Government of India)" , Department of Personnel and Training, Government of India, Retrieved 2011-08-27.
- Mosher, F.C.(1982): *Democracy and the Public Service.* New York, Oxford University Press.
- Page, E. (2003): *Localism and centralism in Europe.* New York, Oxford University Press.
- Paipandikar V.A. (1971): *Bureaucracy in India – An Empirical Study,* IJPA, XVII(2), April-June, 1971, p. 187.
- Pandey, Sanjay Kumar, *Changing Role of Indian Civil Services in the context of Globalisation,3066, retrieved on 7/12/2015.*
- *Perrow, C. (1986): Complex Organisations. A Critical Essay.* New York, Random House.
- *Peters, G.B. (1978): The Politics of Bureaucracy.* New York, Longman.
- *PM Modi tightens screws, gives babudom a new rush hour, The Times of India, Sep 2, 2014, Retrieved 17-09-2014.*
- Sabharwal, Meghna and Berman, Evan M.(2013): *Public Administration in South Asia: India, Bangladesh, and Pakistan, Public Administration and Public Policy.*
- Satish, M.(2004): *Civil Service Reforms, Hyderabad, Centre for Good Governance.*
- Saxena, N.C.(2012): *Administrative Reforms for Better Governance, Perspective on Governance and Development-4, National Social Watch,* New Delhi, Daanish Books.
- Simon, H.A. (1976): *Administrative Behavior,* New York, Free Press.
- Svara, J.H. (1998): *The Politics-Administration Dichotomy as Aberration.* Public Administration Review, Vol .58, No. 1, pp. 51-58.
- Wilson, W. (1887/1992): *The Study of Administration, in Shafritz,* J.M. and Hyde, A.C. (1992)(eds): *Classics of Public Administration Pacific Grove,* CA, Brooks/Cole Publishing Co.
- World Bank (2001): *Civil Services Rationalisation in India.*

9

Political Neutrality of Civil Servants in India: Multiple Perspectives and Issues

— *Abhinav Sharma*

There is a pronounced lack of balance in the relationships between the public, the civic, and the private sectors, resulting in a lack of balance in the relationships between the politicians, civil servants and the people. In theory, politicians who represent the people are to translate popular needs into public policies, and civil servants are to implement them. This was laid down as a result of politics-administration dichotomy. In practice, subordinate/delegated legislation has resulted in enhancement of powers of civil servants. Politicians try to help, by fair means or foul, all those who, in some way or the other, can contribute to their electoral fortunes. Experiences of administrators often indicate that politicians actively interfere, for personal or sectarian gains, even in such unimportant details of administration as transfer of messengers. Aberbach (1981) highlighted that politicians' responsiveness to society's demand and bureaucratic advice that is rooted in experience and analysis creates situation of tussle between the two.

The Concept of Neutrality: Multiple Perspectives

Neutral competence refers to expert analysis, carried by professional civil servants, enjoying an unclear degree of independence from political bosses (Aberbach *et.al.,* 1981). The need for political neutrality of civil servants arose when politicisation was seen as eroding their competence. Forest (2009) laid down certain parameters for the notion of competency. He was of the view, that it has three dimensions: application of existing or development of new legislation; well versed in the techniques of human resources management, long-term planning, performance evaluation and the like; lastly, one who is political –not partisan, but political. By political he meant an ability to communicate the social aspiration of the people to the law-makers for channelisation as policy decisions.

Another conceptual tool that can be used for understanding neutrality is recognition and loyalty. If we go by the background of civil servants, they have sufficient loyalty as citizens to inspire civil participation, to collaborate for common good. The concept of loyalty in the nineteenth and twentieth century revolved around the context that political masters have been given the mandate and civil servants have to accepted it by simply executing the policy decisions. Now, things have changed. Forest (2009) opines that the senior civil servants have to deal with –loyalty to civil society, to the leadership provided by an experienced and competent public service, to political leaders that are elected, and to the broader democratic institutions that bind countries together in common purpose.

Nunes (1976) was of the view that the notion of neutrality may be operative in situations where the ideological differences between the competing functions of the political elite are minimal. Further, if there is a common set of values between politicians and civil servants then the issue of neutrality shall never arise. There is also an issue of social difference which separates the civil service from the masses whom it governs and seeks to mobilise. Though, the notion of representative bureaucracy was tried, but the dominance of middle class and a fast expanding army of technocrats along with booming special advisors have made an impact on political neutrality.

In the words of Bhattacharya (2003), "Under Parliamentary system of government, the superiority of the minister and the subordination of the secretary are axiomatic". This call for another aspect- ministerial responsibility, related with accountability. Traditionally speaking, the doctrine of ministerial responsibility means that civil servants are not subject to external or direct accountability for their roles or functions they perform. It rests on the understanding that civil servants are accountable to ministers, who directly and exclusively accountable to Parliament. But, in today's governance there is fluidity in organisational boundaries along with the need to constantly re-balance independence and interdependence in devising ways to navigate multiple forms of accountability (Roy, 2008). We are living in a networked age where civil society, Non-Governmental Organisations, and private players have been dealing with public services. This has resulted in collaborative ventures; thereby top to bottom (vertical) accountability has to be seen with horizontal one.

Rohr and Vile (1998, 2003) has adopted the constitutional approach which asserts that public administrators operate in the service not merely of the government of the day, but of the polity's sovereign which is designated in different countries as the state, the Crown, the Constitution, or the people. The civil servants may be politically neutral but as citizens they have their political inclinations. But, as a part of the government they must avoid uttering either political sympathies or antipathies. Kernaghan (1986, 2002) was of the view that partisan politics should be separated from the administration of government policies and programmes. Similar views were given by Paul Appleby, who said that policy neutrality has to be seen different from political neutrality. Once a policy or programme has been approved by the elected government, it is the duty of the civil servant to faithfully and enthusiastically see its implementation (Second Administrative Reforms Commission, 2008).

In order to summarise the multiple perspective on political neutrality, let us quote Dunsire (1973):

> We, the masses, need a category of people in public office who will be on "short term" tenure, so that the quality of their stewardship of office can be frequently assessed, and innovation made possible; a class of person who can get rid of without violence to our consciences or theirs. But we need also a category of public officer on "long term" tenure, so that there can be assurance of development of skills and expertise, experience and specialisation; and in respect of these person it is better that we should never be put in the position of wishing to get rid of them. So it is clear that this "long term" tenure class must be inhibited from taking sides in matters on which we are likely to be divided amongst ourselves,

and that on such a matter, sides should be taken only by the "short term people."

Role Confusion

There is confusion about the duties of politicians and administrators, conflict between public interest and private interest. Unwarranted interference by politicians in the daily activities of administrators is one of the greatest enemies of administrative efficiency. It results in blurring of the line of demarcation between policy formulation and execution. As long as the administrators conform to the policy laid down by political leaders, he must enjoy substantial freedom in carrying out his daily tasks. The political executive derives its power from the people through a mechanism of periodic elections, and exercises power by virtue of the Constitutional position. The permanent executive is selected on the basis of merit and derives powers from both the administrative positions and the technical expertise.

Traditionally speaking, the expected role of a politician was to formulate sound policies to convert the electoral policies into action. They were seen to make decision on important matters that affected the public interest. Further, being representative of the people, would also supervise the implementation of policies. Even, the framework against which an administration should perform duties was determined by them. The power to appoint and remove the higher level of civil servants lies in the hands of political leadership of the country; this affects the very nature of political neutrality. Politicians also tend to intervene in administration for the redressal of legitimate public grievances. On the other hand, an administrator is thought to implement policies and decisions of the elected government. But, they have to provide information, facts, and ethical judgements needed in policy makings. Their main responsibility is to maintain continuity of administration. They have also to direct and supervise the work of subordinates. Ministers are concerned with the public acceptability of policy, civil servants with its administrative rationality (James, 2010). Political appointees provide the energy and political support to run the government, and latter provide continuity, expertise and institutional machinery (Korten, 2009).

Issues: Indian Context

We have been following the Westminster model of political neutrality that has ensuing principles:

1. Both, the politicians and civil servants should uphold the constitutional principles and Parliamentary laws;
2. A minister has the ultimate prerogative;
3. A civil servant should execute faithfully all policies and decisions of the minister;
4. A civil servant enjoys full freedom to express himself frankly without fear in tendering advice;
5. A civil servant should observe the principles of neutrality, impartiality and anonymity.

When there was a dominance of a single party both at the Centre and at States, the political neutrality was not questioned and most of the above mentioned were adhered to. Further, the earliest leadership of our country after independence pursued a policy of non-interference in the day-to-day administrative affairs and gave space to civil servants. It was only when the non-Congress governments started to gain political power and an issue of 'commitment' crop up, then political neutrality of civil servants became a burning issue. The role differentiation between a Minister and a Secretary was not always possible due to certain misgivings because of their shared responsibilities. If it was the Life Insurance Scandal of 1957 or the confrontation between Home Minister and his Secretary in 1966 created a flutter in the government.

Different Historical Role

Historically speaking, the portfolio system in India was introduced in 1861, but it was only after the Government of India Act, 1935 the party politics gained credibility. Meanwhile, the civil service based on the 'Macaulay model' was deeply entrenched in securing the interests of the British Empire. The civil servants were simply seen as carrying out orders given by higher authorities, i.e. a politics-administration dichotomy. They must carry out orders irrespective of who is doing the ordering (Burra, 2010). At the same time they are to stay aloof from what might be termed direct political activity. All this helped in the continuation of Indian Civil Service even after independence.

But with the advent of 1990s and the new economic policy, the government started to hire the services of the consultants as special advisors. They began to encroach upon the area of civil servants. This made them jittery and insecure; they thought there relevance and importance as adviser was in danger.

Different Social Background

Prior to independence it was extremely difficult to become a civil servant because of closed system. It was a 'club' where English educated Indians or British middle class were able to make entry. Also they were far away from the political decisions that were in the hands of the British Crown. But, majority of nationalist leaders were educated in Western education and some of them had either direct or indirect contact with the civil servants. Thus, when we became independent, there was much compatibility in the social background of political leaders and administrators. It was only when that representativeness of civil services was questioned then differences became more clear. The issues of regionalism, casteism, and communalism began to affect the politician-civil servant relationship. Therefore, social differences began to affect the political neutrality of civil servants. If a minister belonged a different social class other than his/her secretary there would be a feeling of distrust. A first timer becoming a minister would be seen as a stooge in the hands of an experienced administrator. On the other hand an experienced and important political leader would like to undermine the Constitutional position of the civil servants.

Difference in Professional Commitment

Professionalism is an overarching value that determines how activities will be carried out. Though both politicians and civil servants have to serve society and advance public interest to secure sound and democratic governance, they have difference in professional commitment. But, it is difficult to define professionalism in politics and administration. Comparatively speaking because of code of conduct enacted through legislation, recognised associations, adequate training, and a guided career make civil servants professionals. Nonetheless, politicians engaged themselves in politics for life time, take membership of political parties, follow their constitution, and rewarded for positive political fallout.

A civil servant needs to be well versed in the technicalities of policy process- formulation, implementation, monitoring, and evaluation. The rich experience gained for example by an Indian Administrative Service officer since working at the district till called upon by the Centre prepares them for factual analysis and assessment of results. On the other hand, very few politicians are able to get hold of 'proper' power centre. They have to struggle to make their way for 'political career'. In order to have an easy and better advancement, the political leaders at times try to create pressures on the administrators for the benefit of their 'constituent' (or vote banks). This results in confrontation of professional commitments of politicians and civil servants.

Difference in Mental Ability and Outlook

According to Pierre (1999),...On one hand, there is 'politicisation of bureaucracy'; policy-makers have increasingly come to realise that the bureaucracy is a source of tremendous executive powers and capabilities which require strong political control to ensure that they serve the objectives formulated by policy makers. On the other hand there is 'bureaucratisation of politics' due to its higher degree of continuity and specialised expertise. There is paucity of times for the political leadership due to short tenure within which it has to fulfill their electoral promises. This results in non-encouragement of free, frank and impartial advice from the civil servants. There has been a case of the attitude of the ministers to blame civil servants for their failures. On the other hand, there has been an increase in the habit of civil servants to criticise the ministers and their policies in social and private circles.

There is a clear cut emergence of personal affiliation. Whether they are serving or retired, the civil servants have joined political parties and switched their careers. Recently, the number of administrators who have joined politics have escalated. This has affected the traditional notion that a bureaucrat is to be averse from party politics. Even, many of the blood relations have become ministers, Members of Parliament, legislative assemblies, and local bodies. Though, the recruitment is somewhat difficult to 'manage', but political power with regards to service conditions- promotion, transfer and postings, and disciplinary proceedings- have been misused. Nepotism and favouritism is still being practiced by overlooking seniority and merit, more so with 'bossism'. With the change of power, the political leadership tries to assess the loyalty of the senior bureaucrats. Meanwhile, the civil servants do not want their discretionary power curtailed because of the whims and fancies of their 'political masters'.

There have been suggestions and practices, both from the politicians, administrators, and other experts on the concept of political neutrality. Sardar Patel talked of free, frank, and impartial advice by the administrators. M.C. Chagla Commission, 1957 wanted that the Ministers should be constitutionally responsible for the actions of their secretaries. The Second Administrative Reforms Commission focused on making the civil servants sensitive towards the difficulties and problems of the ministers. In one of its judgements, the Supreme Court of India said that there has to be written communication which is recordable so that the decisions could be analyses and responsibilities fixed. All these denote to one aspect that the relationship between the bureaucrat and the political executive is of complementarity. Now politicians and civil servants are one amongst the players, other being civil society, Non-Governmental Organisations, think tanks (National and International) affecting policy decisions. Both must understand that in the 'constellation of governance' they are stars in their own capacities, thus have to focus on public interest and be SMART-Simple, Moral, Accountable, Responsive, and Transparent.

References

1. Peters, B.G., Pierre, J. (ed.) (2004), Politicisation of the Civil Service in Comparative Perspective: The Quest for Control (London: Routledge).
2. Putnam, R.D., Aberbach, J.D., Rockman, B.A. (1981), Bureaucrats and Politicians in Western Democracies (Cambridge: Harvard University Press).
3. Peters, B.G. (2009), Politics of Bureaucracy: An Introduction to Comparative Public Administration (London: Routledge).
4. Joshi, R.C., "Bureaucrats and Politicians Relationship", *The Indian Journal of Public Administration,* January –March, 1976, p. 19.
5. Ray, J.K. (1981), Administrators in a Mixed Polity (Delhi: Macmillan).
6. Ray, J.K., (2001), "Politicians, Civil Servants and the People", in *India in Search of Good Governance* (Calcutta: K.P. Bagchi & Company).
7. Chakrabarty, B., Bhattacharya, M. (ed.) (2003), " Bureaucracy and Politics", in *Public Administration: A Reader* (New Delhi: Oxford University Press).

8. Neuhold, C., Vanhoonacker, S., Verhey, L. (ed.) (2013), Civil Servants and Politics: A Delicate Balance (Basingstoke: Palgrave Macmillan).

9. Second Administrative Reforms Commission (2008), Chapter 15, "Relations between the Political Executive and Civil Servants", pp. 272-281.

10. Overeem, P., "The Value of the Dichotomy, Politics, Administration, and the Political Neutrality of Administrators", *Administrative Theory and Praxis,* Vol. 27, No. 2 (Jun., 2005), pp. 311-329 (www.jstor.org/stable/25610729, accessed: 29-10-2015).

11. Roy, J., "Beyond Westminster governance: Bringing politics and public service into networked era", *Canadian Public Administration,* Vol. 51, No. 4 (December 2008), pp. 541-568.

12. Nunes, F.E., "The Nonsense of Neutrality", *Social and Economic Studies,* Vol. 25, No. 4 (December 1976), pp. 347-366 (www.jstor.org/stable/27861626, accessed, 07 on 12-2015).

13. Forrest, P. (2009), Keynote address, Political Neutrality of the Civil Service: A Rorschach Test for Democratic Maturity, *Political Neutrality in the Civil Service: From Theory to Reality,* Kiev, Ukraine, 3-5 September, 2009.

14. Burra, A., "The Indian Civil Service and the nationalist movement: neutrality, politics, and continuity", *Commonwealth and Comparative Politics,* Vol. 48, No. 4 (2010), pp. 404-432 (www.dx.doi.org/10.1080/14662043.2010. 522032, accessed on 23-08-2015).

10

Bureaucracy and Democracy

— K.K. Srivastava

Prelude

A healthy relationship between politics and administration is inherent in the concept of democracy, more so parliamentary system of government. Expanding functions of the government and newer frontiers of public sphere demanded a change in the existing role of administration. Bureaucracy could not be contained with traditionally understood confines. Similarly, politics in the country since independence has developed as a full time job and an earning profession. Most of the politicians either have no other activity or seek gains through politics. They are not specialists in any specific field and become alien to the environment. Initially this somewhat aloof position was a cementing force for the relationship between administrators and politicians. But similarity of situations and dissimilarity of specialisation had the potential to create conflict. First, the nature of power sharing, then the developing composition of interest groups and finally the profit maxim and attractions of office could not sustain the harmony needed to sustain the integrity of the system.

The dyarchy under reforms of 1919 and then Provincial Autonomy under the Act of 1935 created conditions of conflict between the elected representatives and the permanent Civil Servants. Disharmony of loyalty hurts a system. It creates a mindset that perpetuates itself even after the equations have changed. This was expressed by Philip Woodruff in the following words: Dyarchy was meant to be a bridge from authoritarian to popular government. The district officer was too often forced to consider not how much he could hand over but how much he cling to. Provincial Autonomy under the Act of 1935 created conditions under which conflict arose from transfer of specified functions to people's representatives without effective dilution of the authority of the critical functionaries such as district magistrates, the secretaries and Governor.

There was some difference in the perception of how this inheritance had to be adjusted in changed circumstances. Despite sharp clashes two all-India services, for instance, were continued because of the sheer weight of pressure from Sardar Patel. Efforts for the desired harmonisation between the Central and the State administrative relations brought in a potent conflict between political class and civil services. As different ruling parties appeared at the Centre and in the States the cleavage grew further. Relations between political masters and civil servants have seen open confrontation. It grew with time but the seeds had been sown in the initial years.

Nothing in Weber's list of bureaucratic principles mentions "government by the people". Instead, bureaucracy is government by experts obeying their superiors. Decisions are made on the basis of training, analysis, and authority, not on the basis of opinion polls or votes. The realisation that an establishment of bureaucrats makes most laws and decides most legal cases makes many people wonder whether a system with a large bureaucracy can really be democratic. There is evidence that bureaucrats themselves are aware of inconsistency between the guiding principles of bureaucratic and the ideals of democracy.

Bureaucracy

Although we often use the term bureaucracy as a pejorative (He's just a mindless bureaucrat or She's going to give us some bureaucratic resistance"), the term actually refers to a distinctive form of organisation.

The famous German sociologist Max Weber set forth the concept of the bureaucracy 1922. His work was an attempt to describe what he believed to be the basic features of a form of organisation that would eventually exist in all modern societies. In fact, Weber argued that bureaucracy was an essential part of modern life. He identified several core principles of this new form of organisation.

- Bureaucrats function within fixed jurisdiction and are responsible for specific tasks. This enables them to develop expertise in particular areas, and it also makes bureaucracy accountable, by establishing which individuals are responsible for which concerns.
- They exercise authority within a firm system of hierarchy. Subordinates are clearly under the control of their superiors, a fact known by subordinate and superior alike. This strengthens accountability, because each official knows which person he or she is expected to obey.
- Civil servants operate each function on the basis of written rules. Consistency of treatment and efficiency are improved when bureaucrats are required to keep detailed official records of their actions and when specific rules apply to specific cases. Without a system of written rules, two welfare claimants with identical circumstances would receive different treatment, for example. Written rules ensure that the working of bureaucracy do depend on the personality or opinions of individual bureaucrats.
- Bureaucrats assume their positions through expert training. Thus, bureaucrats should not normally be appointed on the basis of political patronage or through nepotism.

Weber's model was an ideal that the bureaucracies of even the most modern nations fail to achieve fully.

Yet, Weber's model is worth considering for three reasons. First, even though bureaucratic principles are not perfectly realised anywhere, they are achieved to some degree everywhere. Second, Weber's model identifies those characteristics of bureaucratic that can make them effective agents of public policy. Third and finally, Weber model is characterised of having both negative and positive consequences.

Bureaucrats are public officials who acquire their positions on the basis of their qualifications and skills and who are primarily responsible for the implementation of public policy.

Bureaucracy Resists Democratic Control

Many administrative actions, decisions, and policies are based on scientific data, careful and elaborate studies, and highly technical issues. When a political leader questions a bureaucratic decision, officers are usually in a poor position to evaluate whether or not the answer given by the bureaucrat is sound. The politician is a generalist; he or she knows a little about a great many issues. In contrast, either is usually a specialist with detailed knowledge of subject matter that may be highly technical, there is a basic trade-off between the extent to which a bureaucracy develops useful expertise and the extent to which it remains politically dependent on elected legislators. When legislators need an agency to acquire a broad range of expertise, they generally grant it a great deal of administrative independence, thus making political control more difficult.

Bureaucracy Compatible with Democracy

Bureaucracy or bureaucratic power can be accommodated within democratic principles in several ways. Considering them helps as appreciate the long standing tension that has existed between bureaucracy and democracy.

Politics/Administration Dichotomy

One approach is to deny the existence of the problem by invoking the politics/administration dichotomy. This is the simple idea that policies are made by politicians and that civil servants merely carry out, or administer those policies. If functional power of civil servant is applied to the mundane tasks of implementing the policy choices made by political leaders, then we can be made to feel much more comfortable about the existence of bureaucratic power. Perhaps "there is no Democratic way to pick up the garbage", that sentiment is an expression of politics/ administration dichotomy. It suggests that civil servants make decisions on the basis of objective managerial considerations while steering clear of political matters. To the extent that is true, the reality of bureaucratic power need not threaten democracy. Nevertheless, this dichotomy cannot resolve our concerns about civil servants power in a democracy. Because vast majority of decisions – even so many decisions involving basic policy choices actually made by them.

Technical Responsibility

Carl Friedrich stated in his essay titled "Public Policy and the Nature of Administrative Responsibility" in 1946 that civil servants make basic policy choices and, moreover, that they make so many of them, involving so much technical knowledge, that it is impossible for politicians to oversee officials effectively. Instead of concluding that democratic values are hopelessly lost, however, Friendrich suggested that bureaucrats are effectively controlled and made to act responsible by the force of their own standards and sense of professionalism. He called that force Technical Responsibility.

Civil servants normally feel the force of the standards used to evaluate performance in their respective fields. For example, an environmental engineer considering a new pollution standard may not be effectively controlled by public opinion (since the public is not able to evaluate the decision independently), but the bureaucrat's desire to maintain his professional standards leads to generally sound and responsible decisions. Civil servants make more decisions on the basis of what sound professional practice demands than on the basis of public preferences. Yet, it take little imaginations to think of cases in which officials make decisions opposed by the public but nonetheless sound in technical terms. Thus, was critically examined by Herman Finer in 'Administrative Responsibility in Democratic Government', that bureaucrats may be skillful because of having professional standards and technical responsibility; but if their doing things are against the wishes of people means non-democratic actions.

An Expanded Role for Citizens

It is often suggested that bureaucrats will be more innovative, flexible, and responsive to public needs if they are forced to listen to the public as they make decisions. Governments therefore require that public hearings be held before new bureaucratic rules and regulations are passed into law. The bureaucrats are not normally required to abide by the wishes expressed at those hearings, but at least they are exposed to the complaints and ideas presented. Evidence suggests that public hearings lead officials to consider problem from different perspectives as they encounter factors that had not occurred to them before such hearings and the hearings thereby affect actual decisions.

Unfortunately, most public hearings required by law in most developed or developing countries have little effect. The general public is normally not able to explore the high-tech issues involved in most bureaucratic decisions, and people's concerns are often met with such statements as, "oh, we have considered that, and your idea cannot be adopted because of...". Moreover, many ideas at public hearings are contradictory. Thus, although it is difficult to be against the idea of citizen participatory, the ability of participations to remove concerns about bureaucracy in a democracy is limited.

Strengthened Political Supervision

Popular democracy is featured by wishes and sweet will of the citizens in the form of elections. These elected representatives are enabling to oversee the bureaucracy more effectively. Though, the technical nature of many bureaucratic decisions, coupled with the vast number of bureaucrats and programmes normally makes it impossible for politicians to exert rigorous control. Nevertheless, steps can be taken to strengthen political supervision, thus impressing the surveillance and monitoring of bureaucratic activity by both legislatures and chief executives.

Reorganising the bureaucracy may also be strengthening the hand of politicians in dealing with bureaucrats. Usually, reorganising (taking programmes and officials from one agency and giving them to another or to a new agency) is advocated as an efficiency measure. Much duplication and waste are eliminated through effective reorganisation. Nevertheless, reorganisation also helps to disrupt the iron triangles that inevitably develop and that make bureaucrats so difficult to control. For example, during the final years of the Soviet Union, Mikhail Gorbachev made great efforts at reorganisation largely in an attempt to counter the tremendous power of Soviet bureaucracy. Similarly, Richard Nixon initiated a failing attempt at a fundamental reorganisation in the early 1970, for the same reason.

Accountability

Political commitment was taken to a high pedestal in relations between the political and administrative class, since the days of Smt Indira Gandhi. This has now become part of the governing culture, irrespective of party affiliation of the government of the day. This is meant to imply that as and when there is a conflict between the political and the administrative interpretation of law or the rule the political must prevail. There can be no objection to this provided the transaction is transparent. The problem appears when the officials are made to own the interpretation and not only to obey it. The next step is implementation. Administration is denied the choice in this sphere too. In revenue work, the selection of beneficiaries for surplus land or preference in grant, in development the executing agency, in allocation and release of government grants to aided institutions and for a host of other matters politics appear dominant. Once a senior bureaucrat pleaded with a senior Central Minister to lay down criteria for foreign deputation, he completely declined this argument was the well-worn cliché that "every case has to be decided on merit". So far, so good. The problem appears when the going gets rough. The official is the convenient scape goat. A foreign journalist once wrote in late twentieth century that if scape goats were for eating, India would not go hungry. The hunger for scape goats has only intensified with the passage of time. This the crux of the issue in accountability.

In this context goals of the system, the structure of command in the system and the location of accountability need to be examined. Under all circumstances, the goal has to be the service to the mass of population and satisfaction to the electorate as a whole. The goals must not be vague. They are reflected in the laws framed by the legislature and sustained by judiciary. They are operated according to rules framed under the authority of legislature. In India there is much derision attached to the rule-bound administration. It is asserted the administration should be innovative and result bound rather than rule oriented. The authority to change rules is with the political sphere but that authority is rarely used in cases of conflict. The embarrassment of changing the rules which apply uniformly to all cases is expected to be by passed by suitable interpretation of rules from case to case. This is the route to substitute the rule of law by rule of individuals. This is what distorts the goals. It is a misconceived notion that the political class alone the repository of the public interest since it represents the public will. By that taken, the judiciary would lose the authority to quash laws made by legislature and the action taken in the public interest. Public interest can have varying interpretations and administration cannot be derived a role that is due by virtue of the pool of experience and expertise at its command. If the public will is what has to be reflected through the functioning of administration, then the political class has to reflect a unity of purpose with administration in its harmonisation of diverse signals.

In conclusion, none of the methods of reconciling bureaucracy with democracy seems entirely satisfying. Even with technical responsibility, citizen participation, and strengthened political supervision, bureaucrats will inevitably have tremendous power in all modern societies. Dealing with this problem in an enduring challenge for all modern political leaders, democratic or otherwise.

References

- Philip Woodruff, The Guardians, Jonathan Cape Thirty Bedford Square, London, 1954.
- Henry, Nicholas, Administrative and Public Affairs, Prentice Hall, 2007.
- Heady Ferrel, Public Administration: A Comparative Perspective CRC Publishers, 2001.
- Hwang, Sung-Don, Bureaucracy Verses Democracy in the Minds of Bureaucrats, New York, Peter Lang, 2000.
- Herman Finer, "Administrative Responsibility in Democratic Government", Public Administration Review (Summ.....1941).
- Max Weber, Essays in Sociology, ed. H.Gerth and C. Wright Mills (New York: Oxford University Press, 1946).
- R.P. Naronha, A Tale Told by an Idiot, New Delhi, Vikas Publishing House Pvt. Ltd., 1976.

11

Politician Civil Servant Relationship: Legacy and Contemporary Concerns

— ***S.S. Chauhan***

India is a democracy with parliamentary system of governance. A public official (Secretary) in a parliamentary democracy, as in India, is accountable directly to the political executive (Minister) and indirectly through him to the parliament and the people. A good relationship between the politicians and the civil servant is key to the success of good governance. The relationship between the minister and secretary is based upon mutual confidence and trust, therefore former is expected to provide the overall leadership and direction. A.D. Gorwala in his report on administrative reforms discussed the question of relationship between the Minister and Secretary. He pointed out Secretary should not be an amicable yes man to carry out the whims of the Minister, but should be able to provide free and frank advice on policy formulation based on an objective examination of administrative issues involved. The Secretary and his senior officers have a right to express their views fully and frankly as in the words of Sardar Patel on the role of civil servants

> *"Today, my Secretary can write a note opposed to my views. I have given that freedom to all my Secretaries. I told them, 'if you do not give your honest opinion for fear that it will displease your Minister, please then you had better go. I will bring another Secretary'. I will never be displeased over a frank expression of opinion…".*

In the initial years after Independence relations between Ministers and Civil Servants were characterised by mutual respect and understanding of each other's respective roles with neither encroaching upon the other's domain. However, in subsequent years, matters started changing for the worse while some civil servant did not render objective and impartial advice to their Ministers, often some Ministers began to resent advice that did not fit in with short-term political interests. There was also a tendency for some Ministers at the Union and the State levels to focus more on routine administrative matters such as transfer in preference to policy making. At the same time, some civil servants learnt the art of 'manoeuvering' for favours in return for pliability in their decision making. This trend was further accentuated by rising materialism and acquisitiveness in society as well as decline in values across the board. As a result 'political neutrality' which was the hallmark of the civil service in the pre-independence era as well as in the period right after Independence was gradually eroded. These trends led to the phenomenon of politicisation of the civil service in India.

Now a question arises here why the relationship between politicians and civil servants has been deteriorating over a period of time. It is now relevant to take a relook at this issue in the context of the general expectation of change required in administration.

Points of Distinction

Pfiffner enumerates the points of distinction between politician and civil servants under ten points as follows:

	Politicians	Civil Servants
1.	Amateur	Professional
2.	Non-technical	Technical
3.	Partisan	Non-partisan
4.	Temporary	Permanent
5.	More Public Contacts	Fewer Public Contacts
6.	More Legislative Contacts	Fewer Legislative Contacts
7.	More Policy Formulating	Less Policy Formulating
8.	More decision	More advisory
9.	More coordination	More performance
10.	Influenced by technical opinion	Influenced by technical data collected from study and research

Another major difference between them is that the civil servants like IAS, IPS officers are highly educated officials having no criminal record before coming to power while majority of the politicians are not very much educated and they may have even criminal background. Another contributing factor to this situation has been the coming to power of different parties in many states. The differences between the political executives (Ministers) and the Permanent Executives (Civil Servants) arises not due to any great ideological differences or due to the refusal of the civil servants to accept the final policy decisions of the political executives, but due to the allergy of the political executives to any civil servants advice (based on uniformity of treatment of individuals and claims) that is, counter to the decision that they want to take (based on sensing public demands and making these is to popularity promises).

Causes of Rift

1. The frequent changes in the portfolios of the Ministers do not provide adequate time to both the minister and the civil servants to develop proper trust and understanding, which are ingredients of happy relationship between the two.
2. Some of the officers are in the habit of criticism individual minister or their respective policies in private and in social circles. When the ministers come to know about those officers they also react and it is the officers who are the sufferers.
3. Ministers do not often appreciate the value of independent advice when the same has been impalatable to them, they rather think that civil servants are putting hurdles. Some of them have irrational attitudes, when some case is put before them for decision they would, write, "I do not agree", without stating any reason for disagreement. In such circumstances mutual cooperation and understanding cannot be inculcated.
4. Both the Secretary and Minister lack proper understanding of their respective roles. It has been noted that the Ministers sometimes interfere even in petty matters of day-to-day administration of the department while the Secretaries on their part put through 'half baked' proposals before the Ministers or such letters or correspondence having important

nature are not brought to the notice of the Ministers. Such tendencies never can provide sound backing to the growth of better relation. The Secretary must present full facts before the Minister and the Minister must have the last word.

5. Ministers are in the habit of giving an impression to the politicians, legislators and others that they are prepared to do a certain thing but they are helpless because the officers of their departments are putting unfavourable notes. Not only that, the Ministers are person to have sometimes shown the files to the politicians to prove that they are innocent and that only the officers are to blame for a particular thing.
6. It is also complained that in some States the group politics has filtered down to the civil service. As a result of this, certain officials becoming identified with some ministers and become instruments in their hands for the retention of political power. Such tendency is harmful for administration as such officials cannot loyal to their successors.

Political Interference in Administration

Political interference in administration has become very common nowadays. It has taken two forms, first tampering with rules and regulations and second, distribution of patronage, appointments on key and important positions, transfers and plump postings. Politicians do not like to observe rules and regulations if they came in the way of their interest. Everyday politicians telephone directly to the lower level officials to get some work done, without going through the proper channel, the Secretary of the department and officials who develop access to the Ministry don't care for superiors in the hierarchy. Thus, in every ministry/department a coterie of convenient officials have been formed by the minister to safeguard and watch their interests. Such collusion of politician and administration is harmful for the public as well as for the administration. The civil servant who insists for rules and regulations have to face remote transfer or unimportant positions and several other kinds of harassment. Writings of some retired civil servants proved how they were forced to resign or harassed beyond imagination. Nabagopal Das, who had resigned from the ICS, said about his Bengal experience "...(there) functioned an administration in which decisions were taken by only one man

(Dr B.C. Roy, Chief Minister), who would often impatiently brush aside advice given by senior officers. I do not deny that, in a problem State like West Bengal, a certain degree of firmness was both necessary and desirable, but I have always held that even the most well meaning dictator cannot rise above his predilection and prejudices and these latter need not necessarily be always for the common good. It was not, therefore, to be wondered that the Chief Minister and I often clashed. The climax came in 1958 when, as Special Secretary, Home Department incharge of anti-corruption and the enforcement of special laws, I started submitting reports on corruption and other malpractices in high places and desired action be taken against certain individuals. A gentle hint was given to me that I should 'go slow' with these inquiries. I was even promised a better assignment if only I would be a little more accommodating. Unfortunately, I was far too pig-headed to listen to such counsel. The result was a virtual deadlock causing considerable mental agony and worry to me.

N. Baki in his paper 'In Bihar – The State of my selection' narrated his experiences how he was pressurised and harassed by the Minister in the Bihar government headed by Dr Krishna Sinha. The harassment was so acute that he had resigned on 16 March 1959, stating that "my spirit was not in harmony with the official environment of my life."

Nowadays there are many more episode of politicians civil servants relationship is focusing how in most of the cases politicians are misusing their power. In November 2015, Narendra Modi government gave marching orders to L.C. Goyal, Union Home Secretary, and names Rajiv Mehrishi as new Home Secretary. Mr Goyal was appointed as the Chairman of the relatively low profile Indian Trade Promotion Organisation. Mr Goyal's departure comes amid reports of serious differences with home minister Rajnath Singh over his 'style of functioning' where Home Minister's authority was challenged and decisions were not implemented to his satisfaction (Asian Age, 21-11-15).

In Uttar Pradesh in 2015 when former Chief Minister Mulayam Singh Yadav threatened Mr Amitabh Thakur, an IG rank officer, and Mr Thakur leak the audio in social media. Then he was suspended and a false rape case had been slapped against him.

In another episode, Mr Azam Khan, UP's Urban Development Minister accused a senior bureaucrat Mr Pravir Kumar, Principal Secretary, Health, as 'Anti-Muslim'. Even Chief Minister Akhilesh Yadav himself praising the health department for undertaking several medicare measures. Mostly officers didn't want to work with Mr Khan due to his bad behaviour of openly criticism the officer.

In 2011, several officers of IAS cadre of West Bengal met with State Chief Secretary Samar Ghosh to lodge their protest against the manner in which the Chief Minister Mamta Banerjee was humiliating them in meetings in presence of Junior Officers. In the wordings of a senior bureaucrat 'As the Chief Minister, she can always express her displeasure about any officer in a private meeting with the officer concerned. But the kind of dressing down senior officers are receiving in presence of junior officers is insulting and demoralising. The Chief Minister attitude really dis-heartened us. She should sit with the officers to know the ground reality. But instead she is humiliating senior officers in large gatherings. This will not take the State anywhere.'

Similarly, in Maharashtra, the situation is not so cordial between politician and civil servants. The article of Kiran Tare in Sunday Standard, published on 31st May, 2015, reflects the picture as – "*We are jokingly called a community of migrants because of our frequent transfers but now we have become a nomadic tribe*", says a senior IAS official from Maharashtra. His comment reflects the current state of mind of the State's Bureaucrats; they are not sure whether they will be allowed to work in a free and fair atmosphere.

A cold war between ministers and bureaucrats has led to a p...... lable sense of loss in the Maharashtra government within seven months of it coming to power. Several ministers have complained to chief minister Devendra Fadnavis against the Secretaries of their respective departments. The ministers allege that the *babus* refuse to follow their instructions. On the other hand, the bureaucrats complain that their ministers are too demanding.

The row intensified when food and civil supplies minister Girish Bapat raised the issue of a minister's supremacy at a cabinet meeting "who is superior in the government, a Minister or a Secretary? The administration does not follow the minister's instructions. They don't have to face the people's ire". Bapat reportedly said at the closed door meetings. Other ministers such as Eknath Khadse, Diwakar Raote, Prakash Mehta and Girish Mahahan echoed Bapat. They got furious when Chief Secretary Swadheen Kshatriya advised them to take decision after due consultation with the Secretaries. They felt that the advice was an encroachment on their constitutional rights. Sensing a possible confrontation and a subsequent rift, Fadnavis transferred the bureaucrats against whom the ministers had grudges.

Like Maharashtra the IAS officers in Andhra Pradesh have virtually raised a banner of revolt after the arrest of two senior IAS officers and two more were named in charge sheet filld by the CBI. The State's top bureaucracy is protesting that they are being made answerable whereas the ministers and the Cabinet are let off and not answerable. The IAS officers association in the State has come out in the open to protest against the manner in which CBI is investigating.

> "we are deeply disappointed over the manner in which the investigation is being carried out by the CBI without following established procedure conclusions are being arrived at without any bases and the investigation being used to furnish the image of the IAS", said S. Bhale Rao, President IAS officers association.
>
> "the business rule says the minister is responsible for the working of the department. It does not say the Secretary is responsible. Whatever the scams in the mining or industries department, the entire cabinet is responsible. We are asking why officers are being made answerable" said Madhav Rao, former Chief Secretary of Andhra Pradesh.

Suggestions

Now a big question arises here how a good relationship could be regulated between the two. The ARC has given some suggestions in this regards.

1. Both the Minister and the Civil Servant should clearly and sympathetically appreciate the role of the other, and attempt at a maximum accommodation of each other's view.
2. On the part of the Minister there should be –
   (a) a proper understanding of the administrative functions and recognition of its professional nature.

(b) as little interference as possible in service matters, e.g. Postings, transfers, promotions etc. Discouraging officers of the department to see him personally for redress of service grievances.

(c) no requests for departures from declared and approved policies to suit individual cases either as a result of political considerations, or other consideration, which can not be reduced to general principles of actions.

3. Similarly on the part of the services it asserts.

(a) there must be a sincere and honest attempt to find out what the political head wants and make the necessary adjustments in policies and procedures to suit his wishes.

(b) a readiness to fall in with his political chief in all matters, unless strong grounds indicate a different cause. In such a case he should politely indicate his dissent and if he is overruled in writing he should willingly carryout his orders.

(c) and finally the civil servants should not criticise his political boss publicly as some civil servants do this.

Besides the ARC's views there are some points if followed and then definitely we can change the type of politics of our country.

1. No person should be given party ticket, if he has criminal records, in any circumstances.
2. In a government any decision making power should not lie completely in the hands of politicians. They must get approval from bureaucrats before taking any decision.
3. The politician should not given power to suspend Bureaucrats neither they should be given power to order bureaucrats blindly. Instead there must be special department for it which would deal with matters regarding suspension and transfer of bureaucrats.
4. The tenure of bureaucrats should be fixed i.e. it should be at least three years and if he is being transferred there should be valid reasons for that.
5. There must be some criteria to become a politician. There must be some age limit like between 30-70 years and not

above that. Similarly, politicians should be highly educated i.e. Post Graduate and they should have the knowledge of the constitution, because they are protector of the Constitution.

6. The civil servants must observe neutrality in the implementation of policies and programmes of the party in power. They should not be biased but should be ready to cooperate if some new party come in power. They should not identify themselves with the political programmes of a particular party.

The above suggestions even today are relevant and there should be followed properly. As the relationship between the political and permanent executives has grown in to complexity. Therefore, it is necessary that both the Minister and Secretary should try to know and understand their respective fields and must not try to dominate each other. If some controversy arises that should be solved through discussions, mutual trust and confidence. In a democratic setup like ours they should go hand-in-hand in service of the country. They should work together while keeping in view their respective status and dignity. It is desired that they should be sincere, dedicated committed towards their roles and should not evade responsibility.

References

1. Indian Administration – Hoshiar Singh.
2. Relation between Politicians and Bureaucrats in the functioning of Government – Siddhartha Agarwal.
3. Maharashtra Stalemate and a State of Cold War – Kiran Tare, the Sunday Standard, Mumbai, 31st May, 2015.
4. Mulayam vs. IPS Officers: U.P. top cop taken to task, bureaucrats Fume – Deccan Chronicle, 14 July 2015.
5. Azam Khan accuses senior bureaucrat of being anti Muslim – Atiq Khan, The Hindu, August 28, 2013.
6. Rajiv Maharishi replaces L.C. Goyal at North Block – Asian Age, November 22, 2015.

12

Politician–Civil Servant Relationship: A Critical Analysis

— *Nimish Gupta*

Introduction

In a democracy, power vests with the people. This power is exercised through its elected representatives who have the mandate to govern them for a specific period. The civil services by virtue of its knowledge, experience and understanding of public affairs assist the elected representatives in formulating policy and are responsible for implementing these policies. Parliamentary democracies are usually characterised by a permanent civil service which assists the political executive. Under the Presidential form of government (like in the US), the higher echelons of the civil services are, in contrast, appointed by the government of the day (spoils system). India has adopted the British model.

A healthy working relationship between Ministers and civil servants is critical for good governance. While the principles governing the roles and responsibilities of ministers and civil servants are well defined in political theory, in the actual working of this relationship this division of responsibility becomes blurred with both sides often encroaching upon the other's sphere of responsibility. In any democracy, ministers are responsible to the people through Parliament and therefore the civil servants have to be accountable to the minister. However, an impartial civil servant is responsible not only to the government of the day but to the Constitution of the land to which they have taken an oath of loyalty. At the same time, implementing the policies of the duly elected government is a core function of civil servants. That is why the division of responsibility between the civil servants and ministers needs to be more clearly defined. A framework in which responsibility and accountability is well defined would be useful.

Constitutional Framework

The Indian Constitution provides for separation of powers between the legislature, executive and judiciary with well-defined roles and responsibilities for each one of them. Since India is a parliamentary democracy, there is an interface between the legislature and the executive at the level of the Council of Ministers, which is collectively responsible to the legislature. The Constitution separates the executive into two parts. In terms of Articles 53 and 154, the executive power of the Union and the States vests in the President or Governor directly or through officers subordinate to him. These officers constitute the permanent civil service and are governed by Part XIV of the Constitution.

The other part of the executive is the 'political'. The President or Governor is required to act according to the aid and advice of his Council of Ministers, appointed under Articles 73 and 163 of the Constitution. Because the advice is normally binding, such advice for the officers becomes an order which they must obey under Articles 77 and 166 respectively. The President and Governor frame rules for the conduct of business in the government. Work is allocated among ministers as per the Government of India (Allocation of Business) Rules and the manner in which the officers are required to help the President or Governor to exercise his executive functions is governed by the Government of India (Transaction of Business) Rules. What this means is that though officers are subordinate to the President or Governor, they carry out the orders of the Council of Ministers in accordance with the rules framed in this behalf. The Rules of Business of Government do provide for the Secretary to the Government to advise his Minister about the course of action proposed in a particular matter and to submit to him a note which tells him about the propriety or legality of his orders and suggest that either such orders not be given or that they be suitably modified. The relationship between the Secretary and the Minister is organic. The Minister has the mandate of the people to govern, but the Secretary has an equivalent constitutional mandate to advise the Minister. Once his advice has been suitably considered, unless the Minister passes an illegal order, the Secretary is bound to implement it. The Minister, on his part, is required to support the Secretary who is implementing his order. Once a law is framed or rules and regulations are approved, they apply to everyone, whether a member of the political executive or of the permanent civil service. A civil servant is required to implement the orders of government without bias, with honesty and without fear or favour. It is precisely in this area that a degree of a difference of opinion begins to emerge between the political executive and the civil servants.

Areas of Friction

The areas of potential conflict in the relationship between the political executive and the permanent civil service can be identified as follows:

1. The concept of neutrality.
2. Advisory role of civil servants in policy making.
3. Statutory role of the civil servants.
4. Discharge of delegated functions.
5. Appointments/Recruitment to the civil services.
6. Transfers and postings of civil servants.

This happens because there is no system of specifying of accountability, thus making the relationship between the political executive and the permanent civil servants only issue sensitive.

This underscores the criticality of defining the relationship between the minister and the civil servant more objectively. This is possible only if we put the relationship in an output-outcome framework. Outputs or key results are specific services that the civil servants produce and deliver, and therefore, the civil servants should be held to account for the delivery of key results, which becomes the basis for evaluation of their performance. Outcome is the success in achieving social goals and the political executive decides what outputs should be included so that the desired outcomes or social goals can be achieved. In such a scheme, the political executive becomes accountable to the legislature and the electorate for the outcome. The political executive is judged on the basis of whether it has chosen the right outputs to achieve social goals. If this is done, the relationship between the political executive and permanent civil service would have been objectively defined.

Another area which has tension in the relationship is the arbitrary transfer and posting of civil servants at the behest of ministers and other political leaders particularly in the states. Robert Wade, in his study of Andhra Pradesh, has shown how the process works. As Wade says, "The transfer is the politicians' basic weapon of control over the bureaucracy and thus the lever for surplus-extraction from the clients of the bureaucracy. With the transfer weapon not only can the politicians raise money by direct sale; they can also remove someone who is not being responsive enough to their monetary demands or to their request for favours to those from whom they get money and electoral support-in particular, the contractors. One is thus led to visualise a special circuit of transactions, in which the bureaucracy acquires the control of funds....then passes a portion to MLAs and especially ministers, who in turn use the funds for distributing short-term material inducements in exchange for electoral support. These funds, it should be noticed, do flow through the public domain; but they are neither open to public scrutiny nor available for public expenditure programmes."

In fact, the process of transfers of civil servants is perceived to be so lucrative that it is popularly known as the transfer industry. N.N. Vohra, a retired civil servant, has commented that:

Ethics in Governance Relationship between the Political Executive and the Permanent Civil Service, "Transfers of government functionaries have in many States, virtually assumed the status of an industry. Officials at all levels are repeatedly shifted from station to station in utter disregard of the tenure policies or any concern about the disruption of public services delivery and the adverse effect on the implementation of development programmes." In Mohsina Begum's case, the Allahabad High Court lamented that 'whenever a new government is formed, there is a tidal wave of transfers of government servants on the basis of caste or community or monetary considerations' leading to 'total demoralisation of the bureaucracy and its division on caste and communal basis, besides spread of corruption' and breakdown of all norms of administration'.

H.D. Shourie of Common Cause had filed a Public Interest Litigation in the Supreme Court asking for a direction for framing of rules governing the process of transfer of civil servants. But the Supreme Court refused to do so on the ground that, we don't consider it necessary to entertain this writ petition...since the guidelines for taking such administrative decisions are well settled and it is obvious that all administrative decisions should satisfy the rule of non-arbitrariness and be honest and fair. Individual cases in which the decision making process is vitiated for any such reason can always be challenged in a suitable manner.

Role of Pay Commission

The Fifth Pay Commission was driven to make some adverse observations about the 'transfer industry'. The Commission declared: There is a definite feeling that the instrument of transfer is widely misused in this country, particularly by politicians in power, to subjugate the government employees. Transfer is also used as an instrument of punishment....Demands have, therefore, been made that no transfer before the expiry of three years in a post, should be made appealable, particularly if it has been made at the behest of politicians.

The Fifth Pay Commission made several recommendations about evolving detailed, clear, and transparent transfer policies. First, the Commission recommended that detailed guidelines should be formulated and publicised by each department as part of a comprehensive transfer policy, so that arbitrariness in transfers is eliminated altogether, and transfers are effected in as transparent a manner as possible.

Second, in order to ensure administrative continuity and stability to incumbents, frequent transfers should be discouraged, and a minimum tenure for each posting of officers should be predetermined, and it should normally be three to five years, except in cases where longer tenures are justified on functional grounds, like continued availability of certain specialised skills. In the case of sensitive posts, where opportunities exist for developing vested interests, the tenure should be defined for a shorter period, which may be two to three years.

Third, any premature transfer before the completion of the prescribed tenure should be based on sound administrative grounds, which should be spelt out in the transfer order itself. The civil servant should be given the right to appeal against such an order if he feels aggrieved, and a provision for a summary procedure to deal with such a situation should be made within each department. In case of emergency, when such an order is made in the exigencies of public interest and has to be implemented at once, representation against the transfer order should be dealt with by an authority superior to the officer ordering the transfer after personal discussion, if possible, on the same day.

Fourth, the instrument of transfer should not be allowed to be misused either by bureaucrats themselves or by politicians in power. It should not be used as a means of punishment by circumventing the procedure laid down for disciplinary proceedings.

The issue was raised by many persons in every public hearing and press conference held by the Commission. Amongst the many letters/ comments received by the Commission on this matter, is a detailed one written by Lokayukta of Karnataka. He says: Over the years, my experience as a Lawyer, Judge and now as Lokayukta has made me feel that the policy of the government in regard to transfer of its officers requires serious re-consideration. I had several occasions to meet various officers both of State and Central Government and in the course of my discussion with them, I found there is lot of discontentment amongst them in regard to the transfer policies of their respective governments.

Lack of Proper Policy

The common complaint seems to be that there is no proper policy at all and transfers are effected at the whims and fancies of the decision-making authority which is mostly influenced by the pressure from the politicians' various hues. Such transfers are likely to have serious adverse effect on the efficiency of the government itself. Even otherwise, to have an independent attitude and peace of mind, a government servant must have some assured tenure in any post to which he is posted before he is transferred. Transfers based on the recommendations of persons who are not connected with the government in any way, which includes elected representatives, would certainly lead to corruption and undue favours being shown in favour of such beneficiaries.

At the same time, transfers though shown for administrative reasons, quiet often seem to be the outcome of someone's personal grievance, amounting to punishment. Such occasions will certainly have adverse effect on the performance of the government. There is a talk amongst the public that transfers to certain powerful posts are being made for collateral considerations which involves corruption. It is in this background I think it appropriate to write to you, requesting the Administrative Reforms Commission, to make suitable recommendations in regard to the transfer policies, both in the Central and at the State Government levels.

One suggestion I could make in this regard, which may at the outset may seem to be rather rigid, is to leave the transfer to bureaucracy itself without there being any interference whatsoever by the ministry. In my opinion, in so far as the statewide transfer is concerned, the same should be done on the recommendations of a Committee consisting of the Chief Secretary of the State, next senior-most Secretary and the Secretary of the Department in which the transfer is sought to be effected. If this Committee is directed to perform its functions transparently, it will be open to the ministry to oversee the complaints on the actions of the Committee and remedial actions could be taken. This would certainly take away the public perception that transfers are being done on political or collateral considerations. Similarly, in regard to transfer of officers at Divisional and District levels, the same should be effected through a Committee headed by the seniormost officer of that Division or the District, and next senior officer of the department in which the transfer is sought to be effected. Lastly and most importantly, there should be minimum of three years' fixed duration for the officers' stay in a particular post, which should not be normally reduced or enlarged except for good reasons to be recorded in writing.

The National Commission to Review the Working of the Constitution has also commented on this. The Commission said:

> The questions of personnel policy including placements, promotions, transfers and fast-tract advancements on the basis of forward-looking career management policies and techniques should

be managed by autonomous Personnel Boards for assisting the high level political authorities in making key decisions. Such Civil Service Boards should be constituted under statutory provisions. They should be expected to function like the UPSC. The sanctity of parliamentary legislation under Article 309 is needed to counteract the publicly known trends of the play of unhealthy and destabilising influences in the management of public services in general and higher civil services in particular.

The Draft Public Services Bill, 2006 moots the idea of constituting a Central Public Services Authority for good governance. In terms of Article 19(e) of the Bill, the Authority has been charged with the responsibility of ensuring that: "the transfers and postings of public servants are undertaken in a fair and objective manner and the tenure of the public servant in a post is appropriately determined and is maintained consistent with the need to maintain continuity, and the requirements of good governance". However, the recommendations of the Authority in these matters cannot be mandatory, but only advisory.

Another likely area of conflict between the minister and the officers is the influence exercised by the minister in the day-to-day functioning of subordinate officers. Efficient running of activities of a ministry or department requires delegation of powers and functions to the various levels of bureaucracy. Once this delegation has been done, the bureaucracy should be allowed to discharge its duties, of course as per the delegated authority. It has often been observed that ministers issue instructions, formal or informal, to influence the decisions of the subordinate bureaucracy. It has also been observed that officers, instead of taking decisions on their own, look up to the ministers for informal instructions. Several states have created an institution of 'District In-charge Minister' to review the development activities in the district. There have been instances when District Ministers have exceeded their brief and issued instructions on issues which come totally within the officer's domain. These practices are unhealthy as they can have a propensity to check an officer's initiative and impinge on the authority delegated to him. It could lead to decisions which are not in public interest and also demoralised a conscientious civil servant. It is necessary to spell out the relationship between the political executive and the bureaucracy in a comprehensive manner. The Commission would suggest the details of the institutional and legal framework required to build a healthy relationship between the political executive and the bureaucracy in its forthcoming Report on Civil Services Reforms.

Recommendations

(a) There is a need to safeguard the political neutrality and impartiality of the civil services. The onus for this lies equally on the political executive and the civil services. This aspect should be included in the Code of Ethics for Ministers as well as the Code of Conduct for Public Servants.

(b) The Commission would like to reiterate its recommendation made in its Report on "Ethics in Governance" while examining the definition of corruption under the Prevention of Corruption Act, 1988, wherein it has been recommended that "abuse of authority unduly favouring or harming someone" and "obstruction of justice" should be classified as an offence under the Act.

(c) It is essential to lay down certain norms for recruitment in government to avoid complaints of favouritism, nepotism, corruption and abuse of power. These norms are:

  (i) Well-defined procedure for recruitment to all government jobs.

  (ii) Wide publicity and open competition for recruitment to all posts.

  (iii) Minimisation, if not elimination, of discretion in the recruitment process.

  (iv) Selection primarily on the basis of written examination or on the basis of performance in existing public/board/ university examination with minimum weight to interview.

References

1. Relationship Between Political Executive and Civil Servants, Article published in Arc.gov.in in its 10th Report, p. 272.
2. Relationship Between Political Executive and Permanent Civil Servants, bhargawp. wordpress.com.

3. 'Political Executive and Bureaucracy: Administrative System in India', op.cit. pp. 372-381 and Laxmikanth, p. 495.
4. 'Political Executive and Bureaucracy: Administrative System in India'.
5. 'The Dichotomy of Politics and Public Administration: Lessons from premial debate', International Association for Political Science Students, 30 June, 2014. Laxmikanth, pp. 494-495.

13

India's Politics and Administration: A Growing Concern

— *Noor Fatima Ansari*

In a democracy, power vests with the people. This power is exercised through its elected representatives who have the mandate to govern them for a specific period. The civil services by virtue of its knowledge, experience and understanding of public affairs assist the elected representatives in formulating policy and are responsible for implementing these policies. Parliamentary democracies are usually characterised by a permanent civil service which assists the political executive.

A healthy working relationship between ministers and civil servants is critical for good governance. While the principles governing the roles and responsibilities of ministers and civil servants are well-defined in political theory, in the actual working of this relationship this division of responsibility becomes blurred with both sides often encroaching upon the other's sphere of responsibility. If any democracy, ministers are responsible to the people through Parliament and therefore the civil servants have to be accountable to the minister. However, an impartial civil service is responsible not only to the government of the day but to the constitution of the land to which they have taken an oath of loyalty. At the same time, implementing the policies of the duly elected government is a core function of civil servants. That is why the division of responsibility between the civil servants and ministers needs to be more clearly defined. A framework in which responsibility and accountability is well-defined would be useful.

The Indian constitution provides for separation of powers between the legislature, executive and judiciary with well-defined roles and responsibilities for each one of them. Since India is a parliamentary democracy. There is an interface between the legislature and the executive at the level of the Council of Ministers, which is collectively responsible to the legislature. In terms of Articles 53 and 154, the executive power of the Union and the States vests in the President or Governor directly or through officers subordinates to him. These officers constitute the permanent civil service and are governed by Part XIV of the Constitution.

The other part of the executive is the 'political'. The President or Governor is required to act according to the aid and advice of his/her Council of Ministers, appointed under Articles 73 and 163 of the Constitution. The President and Governor frame rules for the conduct of business in the government. Work is allocated among ministers as per the Government of India (Allocation of Business) Rules and the manner in which the officers are required to help the President or Governor to exercise his/her executive functions is governed by the Government of India (Transaction of Business) Rules. What this means is that though officers are subordinate to the President or Governor, they carry out the orders of the Council of Ministers in accordance with the rules framed in this behalf. A civil servant is required to implement the orders of government without bias, with honesty and without fear and favour. It is precisely in this area that a degree of a difference of opinion often occurs between the political executive and the civil servants.

When we are talking about democracy, we have to bear in mind the unique features that our country exhibits that cause any number of problems in the exercise of democracy. It is not as simple as the books on political science would tell us but extremely complex. Unlike the countries that boast of democracy like England, France or the United States, we are a multi-ethnic, multi-religious, multi-linguistic nation with a huge population and an uneven development of economy. Our democracy is an open democracy where the rule of law prevails and freedoms are exercised without any interference. This multi-ethnic, multi-religious nature of our polity makes it incumbent on us to be secular. Secularism is the foundation on which the modern and scientific society can be built. Intelligent and discerning participation in the election is therefore at once a right and duty cast on every free Indian. It is also necessary to be vigilant against any exercise of coercion, threat or undue influence or bride by the powerful and unscruplous men that throng in the party circles for tickets. In addition to these practices is the invocation of religion and caste feeling to prevent the voting. All these have made nonsense of our elections.

The representatives who have come to power in such process are not real representatives of the people and the people have their inherent right to rebel against such unrepresentative nature of this bogus leadership. Gandhiji has demonstrated this truth in his actions against the government. People have a right for civil disobedience when the rulers have lost their legitimacy to rule. Hence, it is essential that the elections ought to be conducted on fair lines wherein the issues are posed before the people and there in no resort to violence, rowdyism and communal passion.

Questioning the intelligence of the electorate is a very sensitive issue. We cannot blame the electorate for the ills that the political system has become a victim. The society has not become free from the vestiges of the old villages do not hesitate in using unscrupulous methods of intimidation. Money, liquor and other things flow like water, but I withdraw that expression since water has become a rare commodity. Human blood is the cheapest commodity. Money that has to be spent on elections is assuming astronomical dimensions and in this game it is impossible for an ordinary honest man to contest and win even though the law is not against him. Impersonation, booth-capturing, preventing people from going to the polls, tampering with the ballot boxes have all become so common.

Since large quantities of money are needed for fighting the elections, collection of funds becomes a regular occupation of some leaders who hold high offices for this capacity of theirs. Political pundits argue that these things are necessary in politics and there is no use criticising them. Collection of so-called party funds is a very convenient alibi for enhancing personal wealth. We do not have to mention about such dynamic men. Industrialists and businessmen enter into contract with these politicians on a quid pro quo. Licences and permits are the reward for munificent party funds. Price are allowed to shoot up as a reward for liberal help of funds. It has become a common practice for the prices to go sky rocketing every time an election is over.

India is a land of contradictions. It is a rich country of poor people. It is a highly advanced country with a back-breaking backwardness. A land that produced a Buddha, the great acharyas, the sufis and Swami Vivekananda and Gandhi who preached love and tolerance suffers from the wound of communal intolerance which is festering. The process of elections does not end with election. As the saying goes eternal vigilance is the price of liberty.

In the development of these national maladies, the part played or misplayed by the civil services in not insignificant. It is today neither steel nor is it a frame. Drawing fabulous salaries with permanency of tenure protected constitutionally, their responsibility to the nation and its taxpayers is even higher than that of any other wing of government, political executive or members of the legislature or even judiciary. With every irresponsible recommendation of the pay commission, which seems to be oblivious to the growth of inflation by their favouring just the salaried sections of the government, their neglect of their legitimate duty to be responsive to the people is getting eroded.

Their negative attitude, the undue delay in disposing the so called files that gather dust and cobwebs, their ignorance of science and technology, the rapid needs of the present world process are the standing impediment to sustained development. Their insensitivity to the way in which other parts of the developing world function are the stumbling blocks. They protest against any introduction of computers and other time saving devices which make corruption difficult. The constant threat of either strike or other tactics have already done a great deal of damage to the country. The tragedy is that the so called leftists oppose developments of technology like the old Luddites who tried to destroy machines for fear of losing their jobs. Scientists get frustrated and many a young scientist wants to leave the country in utter frustration mainly because of bureaucratic attitude. The salaries of the civil services particularly the favoured IAS personnel increases geometrically while efficiency moves in arithmetic progression. As days progressed this once reputed service learnt to dance to the tune of the political masters since that is the safest way to avoid inconvenient postings. Otherwise they join one faction of the casteist politicians to thwart the machinations of the other casteist politicians.

The less said about the academic profession, the better. At the entry point itself there is a premium on non-academic qualifications. Even after entry, devotion to the profession has become very dubious. One has to address oneself to the question as to how the nation can produce able scientists, and other professionals unless the quality of education is not strictly maintained and positive efforts made to raise the levels of underprivileged sections with special efforts.

To plead that no other sector is doing its duty is irrelevant since it is the administrative and the teaching communities that have to play the role of leaders of thought and action. They have to stand firm in their commitment to service, knowledge and progress as otherwise in this highly competitive world and the engulfing globalisation process we will be lost. These are days of knowledge when more than at any other time knowledge is power.

The days of dominant leadership that could command the legitimacy in the whole country are no more available since the very nature of the heterogeneity and the largeness of the territory don't permit of such leadership, as was available during the independence struggle and immediately after. The leadership has to learn the art of the possible coalitions and smoothen their angularities. This may have uncertainties in politics and their implementation. This circumstance should not become an alibi to the administration to stop their work. Already the caste orientation has become an excuse for administrative lethargy. The civil services should once again recapture their spirit of neutrality and independence of judgement in implementation of agreed political policies by the coalition partners.

Since coalition is not a United Front there will be a great deal of clash of interests among the political partners, and it is the duty of the administrators to so advise the political leaders as to bring about consensus among them to eliminate frictions and co-ordinate their different activities and create confidence in the people.

The framers of our constitution in their wisdom and foresight did not contemplate many of the developments that could take place in the country. While they thought that in the states there might arise a need for the centre to take over due to various reasons, their forethought did not extend to such possibilities at the centre. There was no thought about the possibility of hung parliament at the centre. Now there is an urgent need for providing to avoid hung parliament and securing certainty for the executing during the term. There is also the need for preventing disturbance of proceedings and making the freedom of speech and parliamentary privileges a sheer nonsense. This indirectly enabled the bureaucrats to imperceptibly increase their powers and decrease their accountability and responsibility to the people at large.

In a democracy, the ultimate executive authority for all purposes lies with the political executive which is accountable to the people through Parliament. However, like in any large organisation, government also has to function through a hierarchy of functionaries to carry out defined tasks at different levels and in different locations. This necessitates on practical considerations the delegation of authority and responsibility to the civil servants at different levels in government. Such delegation is in line with the principles of subsidiarity which helps to take government closer to the people. The principles of sound management demand that authority and responsibility should go hand-in-hand.

It has been observed that there is an increasing tendency in government departments to centralise authority and also after having first delegated authority downwards, to interfere in decision-making of the subordinate functionaries. This is an unfortunate trend and it is for those holding leadership position in government both in the political executive and in the civil services to correct it since such centralisation leads to inefficiencies and poor service delivery. It is also for the legislature to correct this trend by means of legislative enactment in certain critical areas as has been done for local bodies through constitutional amendments (73rd and 74th) followed by State laws.

The Constitution of Indian provides for an independent Union Public Service Commission (UPSC) and State Public Service Commissions (PSCs). It lays down that it shall be the duty of the Union and the State Public Service Commissions to conduct examinations, for appointments to the services of the Union and the services of the States respectively. The Commission feels that it is essential to lay down certain principles/norms for such recruitments to avoid complaints of favouritism, nepotism, corruption and abuse of power that have often characterised these recruitment exercises. So, civil servants having the merits of intelligence and sound character have become more and more significant for a successful public administration.

The intelligentsia once led the country for liberty, democracy, secularism and economic betterment. They have once against to play their legitimate part in restoring the country's lost ideals. But yet in a small way we have to do our bit in this gigantic task of lifting this country from the morass in which it has stuck.

In the midst of all these dark clouds there is a silver lining. The protest movements of citizens, the civil rights movement, the citizens associations that are springing up, the high level of intelligence among the youth today are all factors on which our hope is posited. If this is encouraged, we will be able to march with confidence into the future.

References

1. Appleby, P., 1949, Policy and Administration, Tuscaloosa: University of Alabama Press.
2. Fredrickson, H.G., 1976, "The Lineage of New Public Administration and Society, Volume 8: 149-175.
3. Golembiewski, R.T., 1977, Public Administration as a Developing Discipline, New York: Marcel Dekker.
4. Goodnow, F.J., 1900, Politics and Administration: A Study in Government, New York: Russell and Russell.
5. Waldo, D., 1987, "Politics and Administration: On Thinking about a Complex Relationship". In a Centennial History of the American Administrative, ed. Chandler R.C. New York: The Free Press.
6. Wilson, W. 1887, "The Study of Administration", Political Science Quarterly, Reprinted in 1997 in Classics of Public Administration, 2d ed. Shafrutz, J, and Hydl, A, Chicago : Dorsey press.

14

Emerging Concerns about Politicians-Civil Servants' Relationship

— *Stuti Saxena*

Abstract

Drawing evidence from the online resources available with the Department of Administrative Reforms and Public Grievances (DARPG), the paper seeks to underscore the emerging issues and concerns regarding the relationship between politicians and civil servants. Specifically, the paper draws qualitative evidence from the textual evidence available in light of the views exchanged on Civil Services Day for select years. Briefly touching upon the extant academic literature regarding the politicians-civil servants' relationship; the paper discusses the qualitative findings derived from online resources (http://darpg.gov.in/relatedlinks/civil-services-day) and concludes with directions for future research. The paper's originality lies in the methodology adopted in the paper wherein online resources from a credible governmental portal have been tapped for generating qualitative evidence.

Key words: *Politicians; Civil servants; Department of Administrative Reforms and Public Grievances (DARPG); Civil Services Day, India.*

Introduction

Confronting a dichotomy based on the classical politico-administrative divisions, it has been alleged that while some democracies have witnessed an extension of the functioning of civil servants in terms of exercising their authority in to; there are other democracies where the politicians are at the helm of policy-making and civil servants remain confined to being implementers of policy (Hacek, 2006). Politically-informed decisions on recruitment, promotion and dismissal of civil servants negatively impacts the quality of personnel in the civil service besides tarnishing the image of civil service system in the country (Pierre and Peters, 2003). In principle, four approaches have been forwarded for analysing the trends in politicians-civil servants' relationship. The first approach is the determinist or historical hypothesis according to which it has been assumed that the historically developed pattern of strong law-based civil service systems would re-emerge after the stabilisation of the political situation in a country. This approach finds most relevance in Central and East European governance systems. The second approach is known as integration approach which assumes that reforms in public administration would follow in European countries with EU cooperation. The third approach pertains to the reform dynamic approach according to which politicians pay attention to reforming the civil service by infusing quality in the same. Finally, the fourth hypothesis is known as "influence of traditions" hypothesis which concerns the collapse of bureaucratic machinery which would, in turn, impede policy reforms. The last approach is yet to be witnessed in actual sense of the word. Nevertheless, these approaches signify the crucial link between politicians and civil servants in effecting policy reforms in a country.

This paper seeks to underscore the emerging concerns via the relationship governing the politicians and civil servants in the Indian context. Section 2 shall be a brief on the literature review of politicians-civil servants' relationship; Section 3 shall be a discussion on the qualitative evidence drawn from the online resources of Department of Administrative Reforms and Public Grievances (DARPG) and Section 4 shall encapsulate concluding remarks and directions for future research.

Literature review: Politicians-civil servants' relationship

While India has adopted the British Parliamentary model, there is a clear emphasis upon the principle of "democratic accountability" according to which the Members of Parliament (MPs) are assisted by the civil servants and the latter are permanent and politically impartial. Thus, ministers remain accountable to the Parliament and civil servants are accountable to ministers. According to the Administrative Reforms Commission (10th report, Chapter 15), the advantages of having an independent, permanent and impartial civil service are as follows:

(a) There is no patronage, nepotism and corruption in civil service system.

(b) With a permanent civil service system, there is continuity and efficiency in policy making.

(c) A permanent and impartial civil service has inclinations towards social reforms but a political executive may have inclinations for short-term political gains.

(d) A permanent civil service helps to ensure uniformity in public administration.

(e) There is an ethical basis for the functioning of a permanent civil service.

The report of Administrative Reforms Commission also pointed out the need for having a healthy relationship between ministers and civil servants for ensuring "good governance". Ideally, the relationship between politician and civil servant is "organic" given that the minister has the constitutional mandate to govern but the civil servant is required to advice the minister besides implementing a policy decision. Since a civil servant is required to implement government orders honestly without prejudice, fear or favour, there are bound to be differences in opinion between the executive and the civil servants.

While initial years of institutionalisation of civil service system proved to be healthy for the running of Parliamentary democracy in India showing mutual respect and understanding between ministers and civil servants; there was a marked degradation of relationship between the two owing to growing materialisation, compromise of ethical values and acquisitiveness in society with the result that the phenomenon of "politicisation of civil service" gathered pace in the country.

Politicians and civil servants have an "uneasy relationship" (Aberbach, Putnam and Rockman, 1972). Extant literature identifies the following areas of conflict between the political executive and the civil servant in the country:

(a) *The concept of neutrality:* Neutrality in civil service implies that political considerations are reduced to the minimum or eliminated in spheres of recruitment, discipline and control besides other matters. However, the emerging trend is that of increasing political interference in civil service. This was reiterated elsewhere that at the time of policy formulation, the civil servants should render free and frank advice which should not be coloured by political considerations.

(b) *Advisory role of civil servants in policy making:* At the time of policy-making, the civil servant is expected to offer frank and factual information to the political heads. Given the quantum of routine administrative duties, civil servants are required to contribute to expanding their learning about the sectoral problems. Thus, the bureaucrats are required to provide advice on policies, implement the decisions arrived at the political level and remain accountable to elected officials (Gains, 2009).

(c) *Statutory role of the civil servants:* While there are statutory provisions governing the functions of the civil servants, it has been witnessed that political representatives are interfering in the statutory functions of the civil servants as well. Thus, there have been cases of "abuse of authority unduly favouring or harming someone" besides "obstruction of justice".

(d) *Discharge of delegated functions:* In civil service system, delegation of authority is ensured wherein the civil servants are accorded authority and responsibility at different levels in government. However, there is a growing trend of centralisation of authority there are instances of inefficiencies and poor delivery of public services. Further, there is corruption and abuse of power.

(e) *Appointments/recruitment to the civil services:* While the statutory provisions provide for appointment and recruitment of civil servants through an independent Union Public Service Commission (UPSC) and State Public Service Commission (SPSC), there are chances of corruption and instances where merit is superseded and there is favouritism, nepotism and abuse of power.

(f) *Transfers and postings of civil servants:* Transfers and postings of civil servants are being done arbitrarily thereby leading to a corrosion of the moral basis of civil service. Collusive practices are being witnessed wherein the civil servants adopt questionable practices and collude with politicians to gain undue favours.

Specifically, the relationship between politicians and civil servants has undergone two waves of change. In the first wave, researchers observed that civil servant was a permanent official who survived successive governments and functioned as a primary advisor to the government (Roberts, 1987; Aucoin, 1995; Campbell and Wilson, 1995; Halligan, 2001). The second wave of politician-civil servant relationship may be witnessed in 2010s when giving advice was not merely the work of the civil servants and civil service was no more a permanent service and the apolitical or impartial service rendered by the civil servants could be dented by political infractions over time (Boston *et al.,* 1996; Haligan, 2001; Aucoin, 2012).

Qualitative Evidence from Online Resources of Department of Administrative and Public Grievances (DARPG)

This section draws qualitative evidence from select online resources available at the website of Department of Administrative and Public Grievances (DARPG), Government of India (http://darpg.gov.in/). Specifically, the online resources available at the link (http://darpg.gov.in/relatedlinks/civil-services-day) have been referred for the present purpose. These online resources pertain to the speeches and discussions held on account of Civil Services Day in India which is commemorated on April 21 every year. The prime purpose of referring secondary data from the aforesaid source is to underscore the emerging trends, issues and challenges in the politician-civil servants' relationship.

In the function of Civil Services Day in 2011, the relationship between politicians and civil servants was discussed across diverse parameters. Firstly, even though administration falls under the purview of the political executive, it has been seen that the bureaucracy is becoming subservient to the political masters.

In 2012, the "background papers" meant for panel discussions were held covering three themes: "Security for the marginalised: Vision for a caring India"; "Civil services in the 21st century: Responding to emerging challenges" and "Information revolution: Challenges of an open society". The forum discussed the issue of corruption in civil services which is a consequence of a strong nexus between the politicians and the civil servants. Political leaders work for their opportunistic gains and manoeuver decisions and actions which impact the overall systemic performance. At the same time, with the frequent change in political leadership, a strong working relationship between the politicians and civil servants is starkly lacking. Thus, there is lack of motivation on the part of civil servants which hampers effectiveness of the civil servants and dampens the entire administrative machinery.

Marking the Civil Services Day of 2013, several concerns were raised regarding the relationship between politicians and civil servants. Firstly, it was pointed out that the norm of political neutrality was apparently disappearing from the system because civil servants evinced some kind of political involvement. Thus, civil servants seek to obtain from their political counterparts significant favours like favourable positions and other benefactions. Thirdly, in terms of the advisory role of the civil servants, it was being pointed out that their advice is not being followed by the politicians. Fourthly, appointments and recruitment to the civil services are rife with complaints and controversies given the increasing political influence. Finally, civil servants seek favourable spots during transfers and postings and such cases of arbitrary and motivated transfers are against public interest and good governance. Discussion regarding the relationship between politicians and civil servants assumed significance in the 2013 Civil Services Day celebrations. Panel discussions veered around "Civil Services-Fit for future", "Addressing the challenges of public services delivery" and "Rural economy with focus on employment". Vis-à-vis the theme on the relationship between the political executives and civil servants, it was explicitly laid down that "inadequately defined roles and responsibilities of the ministers and civil servants have led to many political complexities". It was pointed out that there should be a code of ethics for civil servants which would go a long way in maintaining political impartiality. Further, for ensuring that the tenets of "good governance" are being followed, there should be a healthy relationship between the politicians and civil servants. Further, the demarcation of responsibilities is only in principle and in reality, the zones of responsibilities of the ministers and civil servants are blurred and distorted. Civil services are perceived to be increasingly politicized in the eyes of people.

In the 2015 address of the Indian Premier to the civil servants on the eve of Civil Services Day, it was emphasised how accountability, responsibility and transparency are essential for good governance. Regarding the relationship between politicians and civil servants, the Indian Premier pointed out that the two sides are interwoven and political intervention is significant because politicians represent the voice of the common citizen. At the same time, he affirmed that excessive political interference may devastate the system. It is commonplace to observe that hierarchical structure in bureaucracy hinders accomplishment of work therefore it is essential that bureaucracy and politicians work in harmony for a people-friendly governance in the country.

Summarising this section, it may be pointed out that there is an uncomfortable relationship between the politician and civil servants in Indian civil service system. The relationship is based on mutual benefits, undue advantages and opportunism rather than trust and public service. Therefore, the challenges in terms of maintaining an accountable civil service while retaining an efficient and citizen-centric political system.

Conclusion and Future Research Pointers

This paper sought to underline the politician-civil servants' relationship in the midst of changing politico-administrative trends in the country. The paper based itself on secondary data in the form of online resources available with the Administrative and Public Grievances (DARPG), Government of India (http://darpg.gov.in/). Based on the discussions and dialogue exchanged on the eve of the Civil Services Day of selected years, the paper brought to light the main challenges in the efficient functioning of the relationship between the civil servants and politicians. Further research may be conducted on the primary data collected from the civil servants and politicians to garner their perspectives regarding the erosion of values underlying their relationship. With emphasis upon New Public Management (NPM) in the West since the 1980s, it was postulated that politicians should be engaged in policy formulation and civil servants should be charged with the implementation of policies (Hood, 1995; Pollitt & Bouckaert, 2011). Further research may take up case studies in select departments to ascertain the veracity of such idealistic standpoints. Further, a comparative perspective may be drawn across diverse government systems in developed and developing countries to assess the efficacy and challenges governing politician-civil servants' relationship. Finally, it would be interesting to compare the politicians-civil servants' relationship in the pre-1990's and post-1990's era in India.

References

1. Aberbach, J. D., Putnam, R.D. and Rockman, B.A. (1981). *Bureaucrats and politicians in Western democracies*. Harvard University Press: Cambridge.
2. Aucoin, P. (1995). *The New Public Management in Canada in comparative perspective*. Institute for Research in Public Policy: Montreal.
3. Aucoin, P. (2012). New political governance in Westminster systems: Impartial public administration and management performance at risk. *Governance*, 25(2), 177-199.
4. Boston, J., Martin, J., Pallot, J. & Walsh, P. (1996) Public Management: The New Zealand Model. Oxford University Press: Auckland.
5. Campbell, C. and Wilson, G.K. (1995). *The end of Whitehall: Death of a paradigm?* Blackwell: Oxford.
6. Hacek, M. (2006). The relationship between civil servants and politicians in a post-communist country: A case of Slovenia. *Public Administration*, 84(1), 165-184.
7. Halligan, J. (2001). Politicians, bureaucrats and public sector reform in Australia and New Zealand.(In) B.G. Peters and J. Pierre (eds.) *Politicians, bureaucrats and administrative reform*. Routledge: London, 157-68.
8. Hood, C. (1995). The 'New Public Management' in the 1980s: Variations on a theme. *Accounting, Organisations and Society*, 20(2), 93-109.
9. Pierre, J. and Peters, B.G. (2003). *Handbook of Public Administration*. Sage: London.
10. Pollitt, C. and Bouckaert, G. (2011). *Public management reform. A comparative analysis: New Public Management, governance, and the Neo-Weberian State*. Oxford University Press: Oxford.

15

मन्त्री-लोकसेवक सम्बन्धः सैद्धांतिक एवं व्यवहारिक प्रचलन (उत्तर प्रदेश के विशेष सन्दर्भ में)

– नन्द लाल भारती, रामजीत

लोक प्रशासन के जनक वुडरो विल्सन ने 1887 में अवलोकन, विश्लेषण तथा तुलनात्मक अध्ययन के आधार पर जिस राजनीति-प्रशासन द्विभाजन पर बल दिया, उसे विल्सोनियम आह्वान कहा जाता है। जिसमें उन्होंने कहा कि ''एक संविधान का निर्माण सरल है पर इसे चलाना बड़ा कठिन है।'' उसे वेबर सहित परपंरावादी शास्त्रीय विचारकों ने पल्लवित एवं पुष्ठिपत किया। उस समय से लेकर अब तक वुडरो विल्सन से लेकर क्रिस्टाफेर हुड तक राजनीतिक कार्यपालिका एवं लोक सेवकों के मध्य सम्बन्धों को संतुलित करने की कोशिशि की जाती रही है। नवीन लोक प्रशासन के विद्वानों ने भी इस विभाजन को नकारते हुए इनके एकीकरण पर बल दिया। उनके अनुसार राजनीति (नीति-निर्माण) और प्रशासन में विभाजन अनुचित है। राजनीति और प्रशासन के मध्य सम्बन्ध शरीर और उसकी छाया की भांति हैं। इनके मध्य सम्बन्ध-विच्छेद सम्भव नहीं है। संसदीय शासन व्यवस्था में मंत्री तीन तरह से उत्तरदायी होते हैं।

प्रथम-व्यक्तिगत रूप से, द्वितीय-सामूहिक रूप से तथा तृतीय-विधिक रूप से। भारत में प्रत्येक मंत्री अनुच्छेद 75(2) के अन्तर्गत व्यक्तिगत रूप से राष्ट्रपति के प्रति तथा अनुच्छेद 75(3) के तहत् सामूहिक रूप से लोक सभा के प्रति उत्तरदायी होते हैं। भारत में ब्रिटेन की भांति मंत्री विधिक रूप से उत्तरदायी नहीं होता है, क्योंकि मंत्री सभी पत्रावलियों पर प्रतिहस्ताक्षर नहीं करता है। इसीलिए कहा जाता है कि संसद में जब मंत्री से प्रश्न पूछा जाता है तो दर्शक दीर्घा में बैठे सचिव का दिल धड़कता रहता है, क्योंकि प्रश्न का जवाब तो सचिव के द्वारा ही तैयार किया जाता है।

मंत्री-लोक सेवक सम्बन्धों में सैद्धांतिक एवं व्यवहारिक संतुलन बनाये रखने के लिए सचिव को राजनीतिक तटस्था तथा अनामता के सिद्धांत का भी पालन करना होता है। सचिव से यह भी आशा की जाती है कि वह शासन सचिव (Secretary to Government) की भांति कार्य करे न कि मंत्री के सचिव (Secretary to Minister) की तरह। इस प्रकार मंत्री-लोक सेवक सम्बन्ध राजनीतिक तटस्थता तथा अनामता के सिद्धांत पर भी निर्भर करता है। दूसरी तरफ श्रीमती इन्दिरा गांधी की प्रतिबद्ध नौकरशाही की अवधारणा ने भी मंत्री-लोक सेवक सम्बन्धों को प्रभावित किया है, क्योंकि नौकरशाही की प्रतिबद्धा को दो अर्थों में लिया जा सकता है। प्रथम-नीतियों एवं संवैधानिक आदर्शों के प्रति प्रतिबद्धता और द्वितीय-राजनीतिक दल एवं राजनेता के प्रतिबद्धता अर्थात् सत्तारूढ़ दल या मंत्री के प्रति प्रतिबद्धता।

प्रत्यायोजित विधान या हस्तान्तरित विधान के रूप में मंत्री को प्राप्त शक्तियाँ भी मंत्री-सचिव सम्बन्धों को कुछ हद तक प्रभावित किया है, जिसे लार्ड हीवर्ट ने नौकरशाही की ''नवीन निरंकुशता'' कहा है। अधीनस्थ विधान के रूप में मंत्री को संवैधानिक रूप से प्रदत्त इन शक्तियों का उपयोग व्यवहारों में लोक सेवकों द्वारा ही किया जाता है।

रैम्जे म्योर हस्तांरित विधान पर टिप्पणी करते हुए कहते हैं कि ''संसद ने अपनी वास्तविक शक्ति अधिकारी वर्ग के हाथ में सौंप दी है जो पर्दे की आड़ में अत्यधिक वास्तविक शक्ति प्रयुक्त करता है।'' प्रत्यायोजित विधान पर डोनोमोर समिति ने लिखा है कि, ''इस बात का भय है कि सेवक कहीं स्वामी न बन जायें।'' ऐसा भी कहा जाता है कि प्रत्यायोजित विधान संसद पर अधिकारी वर्ग की विजय है जबकि प्रो. सी.पी. भाम्बरी का मानना है कि ''हस्तांरित विधान की प्रक्रिया के विरूद्ध की जाने वाली आलोचनायें निराधार तथा निर्मूल हैं क्योंकि विधायिका एवं न्यायपालिका दोनों ही नौकरशाही की इस शाक्ति पर नियंत्रण रखते हैं।'' इतना ही नहीं मंत्री अपने अधीनस्थ सचिव का स्थानान्तरण, पदस्थापन एवं निलम्बन की संस्तुति कर अप्रत्यक्ष रूप से नियंत्रण रखते हुए उसे सीमाओं में रखता है। इस प्रकार मंत्री-सचिव सम्बन्धों के विवाद हेतु प्रदत्त विधान भी एक प्रमुख कारण रहा है।

प्रो. एस.आर. माहेश्वरी का मानना है कि, ''मंत्री एक पेशेवर राजनीतिज्ञ होता है और उसके उत्तरदायित्व राजनीतिक, जनप्रिय एवं संसदीय उत्तरदायित्वों के सम्मिश्रण है। वह उनकी उपेक्षा नहीं कर सकता, अगर करता है तो उसके भविष्य के सूर्य को ग्रहण लग जायेगा। अतः सचिव के व्यापक दायित्वों में एक दायित्व यह भी है कि वह देखे कि मंत्री की सार्वजनिक छवि बनी रहे।'' वह आगे इनके सम्बन्धों को स्पष्ट करते हुए कहते हैं कि, ''सचिव अपने मंत्री का प्रमुख सलाहकार है और उसे चाहिए कि वह यह सलाह बिना भय या लालच के दे। सचिव को चाहिए कि मंत्री उसके उत्तरदायित्व क्षेत्र में होने वाले महत्वपूर्ण घटना चक्र से सूचित करे तथा मंत्री के राजनीतिक एवं संसदीय दायित्वों के प्रति भी संवेदनशीलता प्रदर्शित करे, क्योंकि ये भी कम महत्वपूर्ण नहीं माने जा सकते।''

ब्रिटेन में लोक सेवा पर बने टामलिन आयोग (1929-31) के समक्ष सर वारेन फिशर ने मंत्री-सचिव सम्बन्धों की संक्षिप्त एवं सारगर्भित

व्याख्या करते हुए कहा था कि, ''नीति-निर्धारण एक मंत्री का प्रकार्य है और एक बार जब नीति बन जाती है तो यह लोक सेवक का निर्विवाद कर्तव्य है कि वह व्यक्तिगत रूप से चाहे उस नीति से सहमत हो या न हो, उसे पूरी निष्ठा, ऊर्जा तथा पूर्ण सद्भावना के साथ सम्पन्न करे।''

प्रेस्थस के अनुसार, ''लोकतंत्र में नौकरशाही निर्वाचित व्यवस्थापकों के वृहत् निर्देशन में कार्य करती है, जिसके लिए कि मुख्य कार्यकारी प्रमुख रूप से विधायिका के प्रति उत्तरदायी होता है, परन्तु नीति-निर्माण के विशिष्ट कार्य में लोक सेवक महत्वपूर्ण भूमिका निभाते हैं।''

हर्बट मोरिसन का विचार है कि, ''यदि मन्त्री को यह मालूम हो कि उसे क्या करना चाहिए और यदि वह प्रखर बुद्धि का है तो वह अपने सचिव और अन्य लोक सेवकों का सहयोग प्राप्त कर सकता है, किन्तु कमजोर मन्त्री अपने सचिव के विचारों से प्रभावित होकर उसके सामने झुकने लगता है।''

लॉस्की का कहना है कि, ''दोनों के सम्बन्ध वस्तुत: उनके व्यक्तित्व पर आधारित होते हैं। यदि मन्त्री का व्यक्तित्व प्रभावी है तो वह लोकसेवकों पर हावी रहता है, यदि मंत्री एक ढीला-ढाला व्यक्ति है तो उसे लोकसेवकों के इशारों पर चलना पड़ता है। अत: यह कहना अनुचित है कि प्रत्येक मन्त्री लोकसेवकों के हाथों का खिलौना होता है।''

प्रो. राब्सन का कथन है कि-''ये एक संयुक्त उद्यम के भागीदार होते हैं और विचार करने की बात यह है कि दोनों में से एक के बिना भी क्या होगा? यदि अधिकारी तत्व न हो तो प्रतिनिधि तत्व निरर्थक हो जायेगा, और अपने दृष्टिकोण को पूरा करने में वास्तव में प्रभावहीन होगा तथा प्रतिनिधि तत्व के बिना सरकारी प्रशासक लक्ष्यहीन होकर रह जायेगा।''

इस प्रकार किसी देश का संविधान और नीति-निर्माता मंत्रीगण कितने ही अच्छे और योग्य क्यों न हो, परन्तु बिना दक्ष लोक सेवकों के उस देश

का शासन सफल नहीं हो सकता। राज्य की नीतियाँ कितनी ही अच्छी क्यों न हों उसके अच्छे परिणाम तभी निकल सकते हैं। जब उन्हें लोक सेवकों द्वारा कुशलतापूर्वक निष्ठा के साथ क्रियान्वित किया जाये। वास्तविकता तो यह है कि मंत्री और लोकसेवक के पारस्परिक संबंधों को संचालित करने वाला कोई भी अपरिवर्तनीय मापदण्ड अथवा नियम बनाया नहीं जा सकता। बहुत कुछ इस बात पर निर्भर है कि उस देश में लोकतांत्रिक परम्परायें कैसी बनी है, और मंत्री तथा उसके स्थायी सचिव को परस्पर व्यवहार के एक निश्चित सांचे में बाँध देती हैं, जहाँ उनसे हटकर चलने की संभावना कम हो जाती है।

मंत्री-लोकसेवकों के सम्बन्ध को निर्धारित करने वाले तत्व

मंत्री-लोकसेवक सम्बन्धों को निर्धारित करने वाले तत्वों को पूर्णरूपेण समझना कठिन है, परन्तु अब तक हुए अध्ययनों के आधार पर जो तत्व उभर कर सामने आयें हैं। वे दर्शाते हैं कि मंत्री तथा लोकसेवक किन परिस्थितियों में शक्तिशाली हैं तथा किन परिस्थितियों में शक्तिहीन हैं तथा किन परिस्थितियों में एक-दूसरे पर निर्भर करते हैं। प्रोफेसर मोहित भट्टाचार्य के अनुसार, "मंत्री-लोक सेवक सम्बन्धों को प्रभावित करने वाले प्रमुख कारक संस्कृति, आयु, अनुभव, औपचारिक समझौता, इतिहास और परिवर्तन आदि हैं।" संक्षेप में यहां उन आयामों का विवेचन करना प्रासंगिक होगा जो इन सम्बन्धों को प्रभावित एवं परिवर्तित करते हैं:-

1. **राजनीतिक दल की प्रकृति**-मंत्री अपने राजनीतिक दल का एक प्रभावशाली नेता है, उसका नौकरशाही पर बहुत कुछ प्रभाव इस बात पर निर्भर होता है कि वह कहाँ तक सुगठित है तथा उसकी विचारधारा विभिन्न विषयों पर कहाँ तक सुस्पष्ट है तथा उसकी जनता के मध्य कितनी मान्यता है? वह विभिन्न दलों के सहयोग से सत्तारूढ़ हुआ है अथवा उसका विधान मण्डल में स्पष्ट बहुमत है?

2. **मंत्रिमण्डल में स्थिति**-यदि मंत्रिमण्डल में सम्बद्ध मंत्री की स्थिति प्रभावपूर्ण है तथा उसके पीछे राजनीतिक समर्थन विद्यमान है तो वह अपने सचिव तथा अन्य विभागीय अधिकारियों के समक्ष प्रभावशाली सिद्ध होगा, किन्तु इन सबसे पहले स्वयं प्रधानमंत्री की स्थिति का शक्तिशाली होना आवश्यक है।

3. **सामाजिक तथा राजनीतिक संस्कृति**-प्रायः मंत्री तथा लोकसेवकों के मध्य भेद की उनकी विभिन्न सामाजिक संस्कृतियों के कारण होते हैं। लोक सेवक औपनिवेशिक काल से ही समाज के उच्च वर्गों से सम्बद्ध रहते हैं। मंत्रियों तथा उनके दलीय साथियों का निर्वाचन जीतने सम्बन्धी आवश्यकताएँ, निर्वाचन प्रणाली, मतदाताओं की प्रकृति आदि घटक भी उक्त सम्बन्धों को सीमित करते हैं।

4. **लोक सेवकों के विश्वास, दृष्टिकोण तथा प्रस्थिति**-टॉब, कोठारी व रामाश्रय राय के अध्ययनों से पता चलता है कि राजनेताओं तथा नौकरशाही के मध्य न तो लक्ष्यों सम्बन्धी एकरूपता होती है और न ही वे एक-दूसरे के प्रति सद्भाव रखते हैं। नौकरशाही अभी भी पुरानी मान्यताओं पर आधारित है। प्रशासक समझते है कि वे उच्च शिक्षा प्राप्त वर्ग के प्रतिनिधि हैं तथा वे ही समग्र राष्ट्रीय दृष्टिकोण तथा जनहित को समझते हैं। उनका सामाजिक, आर्थिक एवं सांस्कृतिक स्तर भी दोनों के सम्बन्धों को प्रभावित करता है।

5. **वैयक्तिक विशेषताएं एवं लक्ष्य**-मंत्री एवं लोकसेवक के मध्य जाति, धर्म, भाषा, विचार एवं पृष्ठभूमि सम्बन्धी एकता, उनके मंत्री के साथ सम्बन्धों को प्रभावित करती है। भारतीय मंत्री यह प्रयास करते हैं कि किसी तरह अपने परिचित प्रशासकों को लाया जाये ताकि उन पर भरोसा किया जा सके। स्वयं लोक सेवक को अपने उद्देश्य उसको प्रेरित करते हैं। वह शीघ्र पदोन्नतियों, सेवानिवृत्ति के पश्चात् नियुक्तियों, आर्थिक

लाभ, स्वजनों की नियुक्तियों आदि की दृष्टि से मंत्री का अनुगामी बन जाये आदि।

6. नीति निर्माण का स्तर एवं अभिकरणों का प्रकार-मंत्री एवं लोकसेवकों के सम्बन्ध विभागीय नीति या निर्णय निर्माण के स्तरों पर भी निर्भर करते हैं। उच्च स्तर पर उनके सम्बन्ध बराबरी और सहयोग, मध्य स्तर पर आदेश अनुपालन तथा निम्न स्तर पर स्वामी-सेवक जैसे होते हैं।

प्रथम प्रशासनिक सुधर आयोग (1968) के अध्ययन दल ने मंत्री-लोकसेवक सम्बन्धों के सौहार्दपूर्ण नियमन के लिए निम्नलिखित सिद्धांत निर्धारित किये-

1. मंत्री को इस बात का विशेषाधिकार प्राप्त होता है कि नीति निर्धारण तथा प्रशासन, दोनों ही मामलों में उसका निर्णय अन्तिम हो। परन्तु व्यवहार में यह होना चाहिए कि नीति-निर्धारण के सम्बन्ध में उसे अपने सचिव से निकट सम्पर्क एवं सहयोग से कार्य करना चाहिए और प्रशासन का कार्य सामान्यतः पूरी तरफ से सचिव पर छोड़ देना चाहिए। किन्तु इसका अर्थ यह नहीं है कि नीति के क्रियान्वयन की प्रगति से परिचित रहने अथवा अपने मंत्रालय में अच्छे प्रशासन के विकास के दायित्व से मंत्री ने स्वयं को मुक्त कर लिया है। वास्तव में ये कार्य तो उसके अत्यंत महत्वपूर्ण कार्यों में से कुछ है, किन्तु ये कार्य अपने सचिव को अधिक क्रियाशील बनाने के लिए प्रोत्साहन देकर किये जाने चाहिए, न कि उसके कार्य में हस्तक्षेप करके।

2. यह तो सचिव का कर्तव्य है कि वह मांगे जाने पर मंत्री की सलाह दे, और जब भी वह आवश्यक समझे तब सलाह देना उसका अधिकार है। यह भी उसका कर्तव्य है कि वह यथासम्भव पूर्ण निष्ठा के साथ मंत्री के निर्णयों को लागू करे और उस सम्बन्ध मे हुई प्रगति से तथा महत्वपूर्ण घटनाक्रमों से उसे

(मंत्री को) अवगत कराये। यदि सचिवों में ऐसी प्रवृत्ति पायी जाती हो कि वे अपनी सलाह को ऐसा बाना पहनाने लगे जिससे कि उनके विचार से मंत्री चाहते हों तो ऐसी मनोवृत्ति दृढ़ता से हतोत्साहित किया जाना चाहिए।

3. जहाँ तक भी सम्भव हो सके, मंत्री तथा सचिव के बीच सभी महत्त्वपूर्ण मामलों पर हुए विचार-विनिमयों का न्यूनतम विवरण अवश्य रखा जाना चाहिए। यदि किसी महत्वपूर्ण मामले के सम्बन्ध में उनमें मत-भिन्नता पायी जाये तो सचिव के विचार तथा मंत्री के निर्णय, दोनों का ही विवरण रखा जाना चाहिए।

4. सचिवों को यह बात सदा दृष्टिगत रखनी चाहिए कि भारत सरकार के सचिवों के रूप में उनके क्या दायित्व है। वे मंत्रियों को जो भी सलाह दें, उसमें भारत सरकार के हितों को निश्चित रूप से सम्मिलित किया जाना चाहिए। यदि कोई मंत्री ऐसा आदेश जारी करता है, जिसे कि सचिव यह समझता हो कि भारत सरकार के दृष्टिकोण से लोकहित के विरूद्ध है, तो उसे यह अधिकार है और वस्तुतः उसका यह कर्तव्य है कि मंत्री परिषद के सचिव का ध्यान उस ओर आकर्षित करे, इस सम्बन्ध में ब्रिटेन में की जाने वाली कार्यवाही का उल्लेख उचित ही होगा। वहां यदि वित्तीय आधारों पर आपत्ति किये जाने के बावजूद यदि किसी स्थायी सचिव को आदेशों का पालन करने को बाध्य किया जाये तो उसे यह अधिकर होता है कि वह उस मामले से राजकोष तथा नियंत्रक तथा महालेखा परीक्षक को अवगत कराये।

5. मंत्रियों को इस बात की पूरी छूट देना वान्छनीय नहीं है कि वे अपने सचिवों का अपनी इच्छानुसार चयन करें, क्योंकि ऐसा हुआ तो योग्यता के बजाय जाति और क्षेत्र के आधार पर सचिवों

को चयन करने का रास्ता खुल सकता है। हां उन्हें यह छूट अवश्य होनी चाहिए कि मंत्री परिषदीय सचिव तथा कार्मिक वर्ग विभाग द्वारा तैयार की गयी नाम सूची में से अपने सचिव का चयन कर सके, किन्तु इस सम्बन्ध में अन्तिम निर्णय प्रधानमंत्री के हाथ में ही रहना चाहिए। मंत्रियों द्वारा इस विषय में प्रधानमंत्री द्वारा दिये गये निर्णयों को सही भावना से स्वीकार कर लेना चाहिए।

6. यदि सचिवों की नाम सूची सावधानी से तैयार की जाये तो साधारणतया: ऐसा प्रश्न ही उपस्थित नहीं होगा कि वे अपने सचिव को बदलना चाहें।

7. मंत्री के साथ सचिव के मतभेद उत्पन्न होने की स्थिति में उसके लिये अपील की संस्था बनाने का भी कोई प्रश्न नहीं है। प्रधानमंत्री तथा मंत्रिपरिषदीय सचिव को समय-समय पर मिलते रहना चाहिए, यदि इस पद्धति को अपनाया गया तो कोई भी सम्भावित कठिनाई अपने प्रारम्भिक चरण में ही प्रकाश में आ जायेगी और समाधान भी उसके प्रारम्भिक चरण में ही निकलना सम्भव हो जायेगा।

प्रशासनिक सुधार आयोग (1968) ने मंत्री तथा सचिव के बीच उचित सम्बन्धों की स्थापना के लिए अध्ययन दल की उपर्युक्त टिप्पणियों के आधार पर निम्नलिखित सिफारिशें प्रस्तुत की-

1. सभी प्रमुख निर्णय कारणों सहित संक्षिप्त रूप से लिखित में रखे जाने चाहिए, विशेष रूप से ऐसे निर्णय जिसमें कि सरकार की नीति स्पष्ट न हो अथवा जिनमें नीति से कुछ विचलन हुआ हो अथवा जहां किसी महत्वपूर्ण मसले पर मंत्री का सचिव से मतभेद हो।

2. मंत्री को चाहिए कि वरिष्ठ अधिकारियों में निर्भयता का उचित एवं न्यायपूर्ण व्यवहार का वातावरण उत्पन्न करें और उन्हें स्पष्ट तथा निष्पक्ष परामर्श देने को प्रोत्साहन दें। मंत्री को ये भी चाहिए कि वे अपनी नीतियों व आदेशों को लागू करने में अपने सचिवों को समुचित मार्गदर्शन करें।

3. प्रधानमंत्री को इस बात में विशेष रूचि लेनी चाहिए कि वे मंत्री-परिषदीय सचिव तथा केन्द्रीय कार्मिक अभिकरण की सहायता से इस बात पर रोक लगाये कि सिविल सेवकों में किसी भी मंत्री विशेष के प्रति कोई खास व्यक्तिगत लगाव उत्पन्न न हो।

4. सिविल सेवकों द्वारा किये गये भारी अन्याय, गम्भीर भूलों अथवा प्रशासन के मामलों को छोड़कर, मंत्रियों को दिन-प्रतिदिन के प्रशासन में हस्तक्षेप नहीं करना चाहिए। जब किसी नागरिक की शिकायत या प्रार्थना द्वारा किसी नियम, कार्य-विधि या किसी नीति के पुनर्विचार की मांग की जाये तो उस मांग की पूर्ति ऐसा पुनर्विचार करके की जानी चाहिए, ऐसे नहीं कि किसी व्यक्ति विशेष के मामले को सहूलियत देने के लिए नियमों को कुछ ढ़ीला कर दिया जाये।

5. सचिवों तथा अन्य सिविल सेवकों को चाहिए कि वे मंत्रियों की कठिनाईयों को अधिक अच्छी प्रकार समझें और उनके प्रति अधिक उदारता व संवेदनशीलता दिखायें और एक तरफ तो छोटे-छोटे समायोजनाओं तथा दूसरी तरफ ऐसे राजनीतिक तथा अन्य महत्वपूर्ण समायोजनओं के बीच भेद करें जिनमें मूल सिद्धांतों से समझौता किया गया हो अथवा जिनका सेवाओं की कार्य-कुशलता व मनोबल पर हानिकारक प्रभाव पड़ता हो।

6. सचिव को अपने मन्त्री के प्रति अधिकारिक सम्बन्ध निष्ठा का होना चाहिए और मन्त्री का अपने सचिव के प्रति सम्बन्ध विश्वास पर आधारित होना चाहिए।

मंत्री-लोकसेवकः ऐतिहासिक निर्णय एवं घटनाएं

भारत में मंत्री-सचिव सम्बन्धों की शुरूआत सर्वप्रथम सन् 1921 ई. से होती है, जबकि 1919 के मॉण्टेग्यू चेम्सफोर्ड सुधार एक्ट के अन्तर्गत पहली बार प्रान्तीय शासन में निर्वाचित मंत्रियों का प्रावधान किया गया। पहली बार भारत मे प्रशासनिक इतिहास मे 'सचिव' को अपने अनिपुण मंत्री के मातहत होकर कार्य करने की आदत डालनी पड़ी। यह एक नवीन प्रयोग था, जिसमें मंत्री-सचिव सम्बन्धों में तनाव पैदा होना स्वाभाविक था। सुधार जाँच समिति (1924) के समक्ष अनेक मंत्रियों ने शिकायत की कि उन्हें अपने सचिवों से पूर्ण सहयोग नहीं मिला। सी.वाई. चिन्तामणि, जो कि संयुक्त प्रान्तों में शिक्षा मंत्री थे, ने इसलिए त्याग पत्र दे दिया कि उनके सचिव ने उनकी उपेक्षा करते हुए गवर्नर से सीधे सम्पर्क स्थापित कर लिया। भारत शासन अधिनियम 1935 के अधीन उत्तरदायी शासन का गठन किया गया। फलस्वरूप एक सचिव के कार्य तीन प्रकार से प्रभावित हुए। प्रथम-मंत्री जो कि देश के सार्वजनिक जीवन से था, हो सकता है कि उसे कोई सरकारी अनुभव न हो और उसे अपने समय का बड़ा भाग राजनीतिक, संसदीय एवं सार्वजनिक दायित्वों के निर्वहन करने मे व्यतीत करना पड़े। द्वितीय-मंत्री वह शीघ्र परिवर्तित होने वाला व्यक्ति है, विशेषकर गवर्नर जनरल सदस्यों से तो और भी शीघ्र। तृतीय-लोक प्रशासन की मशीन जो सरकारी नीतियों के क्रियान्वयन के लिए उत्तरदायी है उसका अपना पृथक एवं स्वतंत्र अस्तित्व होता है। मंत्री का व्यवस्थापिका के प्रति उत्तरदायी का आशय है कि मंत्रालय के मंत्री के प्रति अभिभाज्य उत्तरदायित्व। यह विभागीय कार्यकुशलता एवं अनुशासन के लिए अत्यंत आवश्यक है, यही कारण है कि आज भी सचिवों के स्थानान्तरण,

निलम्बन एवं पदोन्नति में मंत्री की भूमिका काफी महत्वपूर्ण होती है। मैक्सवेल समिति (1937) की धारणा थी कि सचिव, विभाग का प्रशासनिक मुखिया है, जो कि मंत्री के अधीन रहकर मंत्री को प्रशासनिक परामर्श देगा। मंत्री को अन्य विशेषज्ञों से परामर्श लेने की छूट है, तथापि सभी ऐसे परामर्शों में उसे सचिव के साथ रहना चाहिए। मैक्सवेल समिति का मत यह था कि केवल महत्वपूर्ण नीति सम्बन्धी मसले ही मन्त्री की स्वीकृति के लिए प्रस्तुत किये जाने चाहिए और दिन-प्रतिदिन के सामान्य प्रशासनिक मसलों पर सचिव को ही निर्णय ले लेना चाहिए। स्वाधीनता प्राप्ति के बाद भी मंत्री-सचिव सम्बन्धों को लेकर मामले प्रकाश में आते रहे हैं। पाकिस्तान में तत्कालीन भारतीय हाई कमिश्नर श्री प्रकाश ने अपने संस्मरणों में लिखा है कि, 'उनके द्वारा लिए गये निर्णयों के क्रियान्वयन में उनका 'डिप्टी' जो कि आई.पी.एस. का सदस्य था, रोड़े अटकाता रहता था।' जवाहर लाल नेहरू जैसे व्यक्ति ने भी अपने प्रारम्भिक दिनों में महसूस किया था कि, 'सिविल सेवा के अधिकारी अपनी मर्जी से शासन चलाने की मंशा रखते थे न कि मंत्रियों की मंशा से।'

सरकारी अधिकारियों की एक उचित व्यवस्था देने के समर्थन में बोलते हुए सरदार पटेल ने संविधान सभा में कहा कि "आज मेरा सचिव मेरे विचारों के विरूद्ध नोट लिख सकता है, मैंने यह स्वतंत्रता अपने सभी सचिवों को दी है, मैंने उनको बता दिया है कि, 'यदि तुम अपना सच्चा मत इस ढंग से व्यक्त नहीं करते कि इससे तुम्हारा मंत्री नाराज हो जायेगा, तब अधिक अच्छा यही होगा कि तुम चले जाओ, मैं दूसरा सचिव ले आऊँगा।'"

न्यायमूर्ति एम.सी. छागला को सन् 1957 ई. में मुद्रा केस की जाँच पड़ताल करने के लिए नियुक्त किया गया था। उन्होंने सैद्धांतिक टिप्पणी करते हुए कहा कि, "संविधान की दृष्टि से सचिव के द्वारा किये गये कार्य के लिए मंत्री उत्तरदायी होता है। अपने अधीस्थ अधिकारियों द्वारा

किये गये कार्यो का उत्तरदायित्व मंत्री को लेना पड़ता है। वह उनकी आड़ में शरण नहीं ले सकता और न ही वह उनके कार्यो का परित्याग कर सकता है।'' अपनी सत्ता के क्षेत्र में मंत्री को पूर्ण स्वामितता प्राप्त होती हैं। इसके अनिवार्य निष्कर्ष के तौर पर उसे अपने अधीन अधिकारियों का पूर्ण उत्तरदायित्व लेना आवश्यक है। यह सच है कि इससे मंत्री पर बहुत बोझ बढ़ जायेगा, उसके अधीन कर्मचारियों को चाहिए कि वे उसी की नीति को प्रतिबिम्बित करें और उसे कादारी से लागू करें, यदि कोई अधीनस्थ कर्मचारी ऐसा करने में असफल रहता है, तो उसे भले ही दण्ड दिया जाये या पदच्युत किया जाय, परन्तु कितने प्रतिनिधिमूलक हो, उसके कार्य का उत्तरदायित्व मंत्री को ही लेना पड़ेगा। मंत्री को यह कहने की आज्ञा नहीं दी जा सकती कि उसके अधीनस्थ अधिकारी उसकी नीति को प्रतिबिम्बित नहीं करते या उन्होंने उसकी इच्छाओं अथवा निर्देशन के विपरीत कार्य किया।

स्वंत्रत भारत में मंत्री-सचिव संबंधों की दृष्टि से निम्नलिखित मामले अत्यंत रोचक व उल्लेखनीय रहे हैं-

टी.टी. कृष्णामाचारी तथा एच.एम. पटेल विवाद (1957), गुलजारी लाल नन्दा बनाम एल.पी. सिंह (1963), के. हनुमन्तैया तथा बी.सी. गांगुली विवाद (1971), प्रधानमंत्री राजीव गांधी और श्री श्रीनिवास शास्त्री, डॉ. बद्योपाध्याय तथा ए.पी. वेकंटेश्वर का मामला (1987), रामजेठमलानी तथा किरन अग्रवाल मतभेद (1998) आदि।

मंत्री और लोक सेवकों का सम्बन्ध स्वतंत्रता प्राप्ति के पश्चात् कुछ हद तक ठीक था। सन् 1967 ई. के चुनाव के बाद अस्थायी सरकार के गठन के साथ ही मंत्री-लोकसेवक सम्बन्ध में कटुता आने लगी। अस्थायित्व के कारण मंत्रियों के बारम्बार परिवर्तन होने अर्थात् एक मंत्रालय से एक मंत्री के जाने, दूसरे मंत्री के आने से निकट का सम्बन्ध स्थापित हो सकने के लिए पर्याप्त समय नहीं मिल पाता है। मंत्रीगण स्वतंत्र सलाह को

विशेष महत्त्व नहीं देते हैं, क्योंकि उनके विचार से प्रशासनिक अधिकारी कार्य सम्पादन में अड़ंगेबाजी करते हैं।

उत्तर प्रदेश में मंत्री-सचिव सम्बन्धों की दृष्टि से निम्नलिखित माामलें अत्यंत रोचक व उल्लेखनीय हैं।

1. मुख्यमंत्री वीर बहादुर सिंह तथा जगदीशचन्द्र पंत विवाद-मुख्यमंत्री वीर बहादुर सिंह ने विधायक भोपाल सिंह के पत्र पर शिक्षा सचिव जगदीश चन्द्र पंत को 30 सितम्बर सन् 1987 को एक आदेश दिया था। यह आदेश मेरठ के एक महिला विद्यालय का परीक्षा के केन्द्र को बदले जाने के लिए था। शिक्षा सचिव पंत इस आदेश को 2 मार्च, सन् 1988 तक दबाते रहे। तब भोपाल सिंह उनसे मिले और आदेश दबाये जाने का करण पूछा। पंत ने जवाब दिया कि 'यह संभव नहीं है'। इस पर भोपाल सिंह ने कहा कि "फिर आपने मुख्यमंत्री जी को सूचित क्यों नहीं किया।" इसी बात को लेकर एक दर्जन विधायकों व सचिवालय कर्तियों में जमकर झगड़ा हुआ था। नौकरशाही की खिलाफत की शुरूआत सन् 1984 ई. से ही हो गयी थी। सन् 1984 ई. में एक विधायक ने विधानसभा में दो दर्जन आई.ए.एस. अधिकारियों की सूची पेश करते हुए प्रश्न उठाया कि इन्हें 250 रू. से लेकर 400 रू. मात्रा तक कट पिट कर वेतन मिलता है। ऐसी स्थिति में ये कैसे शान-शौकत से जिंदगी बसर कर रहे हैं। विधायक ने सबूत के तौर पर इन अधिकारियों द्वारा आयकर विभाग में दाखिल हुए। वार्षिक रिटर्न की फोटो प्रति भी प्रस्तुत की थी। 24 जून 1988 ई. तक सरकार का नेतृत्व किया और केन्द्र में बुला लिये जाने के कारण उनकी जगह पर श्री नारायण दत्त तिवारी ने मुख्यमंत्री की कुर्सी सम्भाली। तिवारी ने इस प्रकरण पर जांच के आदेश दिये थे। उस जांच पर क्या हुआ आज तक किसी को पता नहीं।

2. मुख्यमंत्री विश्वनाथ प्रताप सिंह तथा मनोहर सुब्रह्मणियम विवाद-विश्वनाथ प्रताप सिंह मुख्यमंत्री थे और मनोहर सुब्रह्मणियम खाद्य

सचिव थे। वे मैले कुचैले कपड़े पहनकर साइकिल से सचिवालय आते थे। इसलिए उन्हें अत्यंत ईमानदार समझा जाता था। बाद में उन्हें भी धन खरीद मे प्रदेश सरकार के कई करोड़ रूपये का चूना लगाने का आरोप लगा, मामला काफी उछला, लेकिन आई.ए.एस. अफसरों ने **'क्लीन चिट'** देकर उन्हें आरोपों से मुक्त कर दिया।

3. एजाज रिजवी तथा प्रबन्ध निदेशक विवाद-एजाज रिजवी खाद्य मंत्री थे। अपने ही विभाग, आवश्यक वस्तु निगम के प्रबन्ध निदेशक से परेशान रहे। प्रबन्धक निदेशक ने अपने चहेतों को नियम कानून, त्यागकर महत्वपूर्ण पदों पर बिठा रखा था। जिनको खाद्य मंत्री पसंद नहीं करते थे। उन्हें नियम के विरूद्ध दूर-दराज के इलाकों में तैनात कर दिया गया था। परेशान कर्मचारियों ने मंत्री जी से गुहार लगाई, तो इस सम्बन्ध में एजाज रिजवी ने 29 अगस्त सन् 1991 ई. को प्रबन्ध निदेशक से आज्ञा मांगी। मगर उक्त अफसरों ने उसे तरजीह ही नहीं दी। दो महीने बाद पुनः एजाज रिजवी ने निगम को पत्र लिखा, जिसमें उन व्यक्तियों के सम्बन्ध में लिखा जो दस बारह सालों से एक स्थान पर जमे बैठे थे। खाद्य विभाग के राज्य मंत्री बाबूराम ने भी निगम के प्रबन्ध निदेशक को कड़े पत्र लिखे, परन्तु उनके कान पर जूं तक नहीं रेंगी।

4. गंगाभक्त सिंह तथा हरिशचन्द्र विवाद-गंगाभक्त सिंह कृषि मंत्री थे और हरिशचंद्र उद्यान सचिव। उद्यान सचिव हरिशचन्द्र ने गंगाभक्त सिंह को खूब छकाया। कृषि मंत्री इतने क्षुब्ध हो गये कि उन्होंने उद्यान सचिव पर लगे भ्रष्टाचार के आरोप की जाँच के सीधे आदेश कर दिये। उन्होंने उद्यान निदेशक डॉ. आर.डी. सिंह की जाँच जारी करवाने का फरमान जारी किया था। जबकि नियमतः गंगाभक्त सिंह को उद्यान सचिव के खिलाफ जाँच बिठाने की सिफारिश मुख्यमंत्री से करनी चाहिए थी। मगर हड़बड़ी में वे खुद ही आदेश दे बैठे। उसी सरकार में काबीना मंत्री रमापति शास्त्री से तो विधायक रामप्यारे आजाद ने यहाँ तक कह

डाला- ''मंत्री जी अगर आप नहीं सुनेंगे तो हम अफसर को भी नहीं बख्शेंगे। उसके दरवाजे का चक्कर लगाते-लगाते हम थक गये हैं। अब एक ही चारा है कि जैसे बने हमारा काम बनना चाहिए। इसके लिए उन्हें हाथ उठाने से भी संकोच नहीं होगा।'' इसके अतिरिक्त कल्याण सिंह के पहले मुख्यमंत्री काल में स्वास्थ्य मंत्री डॉ. दिनेश जौहरी भी नौकरशाहों की अड़ंगेबाजी से परेशान रहे। हालाँकि कल्याण सिंह ने डॉ. दिनेश जौहरी को मंत्रिमण्डल से निकाल दिया था। मगर वे जितने दिन कुर्सी पर रहे उनको यही शिकायत रही कि अफसर उनकी बात नहीं सुनते हैं। वे कई उदाहरण भी गिनाते थे। मसलन वे नेपाल में होने वाले आयुर्वेद सम्मेलन में इसलिए वे भाग नहीं ले पाये क्योंकि अधिकारियों की लापरवाही के कारण उनको वक्त रहते वहां जाने की अनुमति नहीं मिल पायी थी। सूचना विभाग से उनको सख्त शिकायत थी। उनका कहना था कि सूचना निदेशक की उदासीनता के कारण विभाग उनकी पत्रकारवार्ता की सूचना पत्रकारों को नहीं देता था। डॉ. दिनेश जौहरी नेपाल में स्वास्थ्य मंत्रियों के सम्मलेन में शामिल होने की अनुमति मुख्यमंत्री से मांगी तो उनका वह पत्र ही गुम हो गया। उन्होंने मुख्यमंत्री कल्याण सिंह को अफसरों के इस बर्ताव के सम्बन्ध में कई पत्र लिखे मगर अफसरों का कुछ नहीं बिगड़ा अलबत्ता दिनेश जौहरी से स्वास्थ्य मंत्री की कुर्सी छिन गयी।

5. कलराज मिश्र तथा रवीन्द्र सिंह विवाद-कल्याण सिंह के दूसरे मुख्यमंत्रित्व काल में कलराज मिश्र पर्यटन मंत्री थे और रवीन्द्र सिंह पर्यटन सचिव। वरिष्ठ मंत्री कलराज मिश्र ने अपनी प्रतिष्ठा का प्रश्न बनाकर एक आई.ए.एस. अफसर को उसके पद से हटाया। दरअसल रविन्द्र सिंह पर्यटन सचिव की हैसियत से निगम के पदेन अध्यक्ष भी थे। परम्परा के मुताबिक पर्यटन महानिदेशक के साथ निगम के प्रबन्ध निदेशक का दायित्व भी रवीन्द सिंह ही संभाले थे। निगम का अध्यक्ष पद पाने की लालसा में पर्यटन मंत्री कलराज मिश्र ने अपने एक विश्वास पात्र

भाजपा नेता दिनेश शर्मा को रवीन्द्र सिंह के मातहत उपाध्यक्ष के पद पर बिठा दिया। वैसे मर्यादा और परम्पराओं के मुताबिक अब तक राजनीतिज्ञों को नौकरशाहों से ऊपर का ओहदा दिया जाता था। पिछले पाँच सालों के दौरान नियमों की वजह से मुलायम सिंह यादव और मायावती की सरकारें इस पचड़े से दूर रहीं। कल्याण सिंह भी इस मामले में हाथ डालने से कतराते रहे। उपाध्यक्ष शर्मा रवीन्द्र सिंह जी की मातहती में थे। लिहाजा पहले कलराज मिश्र को निगम के अध्यक्ष पद का दायित्व सम्भालने सम्बन्धी प्रस्ताव पारित करवाया गया। तत्पश्चात् एक अन्य प्रस्ताव संचालक मंडल से पारित करवाया गया उसमें निगम के नियमों को संशोधित करते हुए शासन को किसी भी गैर सरकारी व्यक्ति अथवा प्रमुख सचिव पर्यटन को निदेशक रहते हुए अध्यक्ष नामित करने का अधिकार दे दिया गया। इतना ही नहीं रवीन्द्र सिंह की निगम के प्रबन्ध निदेशक पद से भी छुट्टी कर दी गयी ।

6. उत्तर प्रदेश परिवहन मंत्री एवं रोड़वेज महाप्रबन्धक विवाद-परिवहन निगम उत्तर प्रदेश के मंत्री और रोड़वेज के महाप्रबन्धक जो एक योग्य प्रशासक माने जाते थे, कुछ ही दिनों बाद मंत्री महोदय द्वारा इसलिए स्थान्तरित कर दिये गये कि डिपों में बस की कमी के कारण खरीददारी के प्रश्न पर दोनों में मतभेद हो गया। मंत्री महोदय नई बसों को खरीदना चाहते थे, जिसमें उन्हें सम्भवतः उचित लाभ मिलने की संभावना थी। नई बस को खरीदने के लिए महाप्रबन्धक महोदय ने यह सुझाव दिया कि हमारे पास गाड़ियाँ प्रचुर मात्रा में उपलब्ध हैं जो सिर्फ इंजन खराब होने के कारण खराब पड़ी हैं, जितने पैसे में हम एक नई बस खरीदेंगे उतने पैसे में इन गाड़ियों में नया इंजन डलवाकर दो या तीन गाड़ियाँ तैयार कर लेंगे। ऐसा करके व्यर्थ व्यय से बचा जा सकता है। पुनः मंत्री महोदय ने कहा तो क्यों नहीं किसी बड़े फर्म से एक भारी संख्या में बस ही ले ली जाये, जो रोड़वेज के नियंत्रण में चलायी जाये? मंत्री जी के इस सुझाव

पर प्रबन्धक महोदय ने यह विचार व्यक्त किया कि हम ऐसा करके परिवहन निगम जैसी महत्वपूर्ण संस्था को किसी एक व्यवसायी के हाथ में नहीं देना चाहेंगे। यहां भी मंत्री जी को एक साथ ही बड़ा लाभ मिलने की आशा बन रही थी। इस विचार मित्रता का परिणाम यह हुआ कि मंत्री महोदय ने स्वयं लाभ की आशा में उस योग्य और अनुभवी महाप्रबन्धक का स्थानान्तरण अविलम्ब करा दिये। इस प्रकार के आपसी मन-मुटाव सम्बन्धों के दौरान कभी-कभी सार्वजनिक धन का दुरूपयोग भी हो जाता है जो जनहित के विपरीत हो जाता है।

7. श्री जयवीर सिंह तथा श्रीमती नीता चौधरी विवाद- श्री जयवीर सिंह राज्य चिकित्सा एवं स्वास्थ्य मंत्री हैं तथा श्रीमती नीता चौधरी प्रमुख सचिव हैं। 13 फरवरी 2006, को चिकित्सा एवं स्वास्थ्य मंत्री घंटों अपने दफ्तर में इंतजार करते रहे, लेकिन वहां आयोजित दो बैठकों में न तो प्रमुख सचिव नीता चौधरी पहुंची, न कोई सचिव या विशेष सचिव। प्रमुख सचिव के व्यवहार से पहले से ही त्रास्त चल रहे राज्य मंत्री ने इसे अवमानना मानते हुए इसकी शिकायत प्रमुख सचिव से की और अफसरों के खिलाफ अनुशासनात्मक कार्यवाही करने का आग्रह किया। राज्य मंत्री व प्रमुख सचिव के बीच यह 'टकराव' की यह पहली घटना नहीं है। श्री सिंह इससे पहले भी मुख्यमंत्री और मुख्य सचिव से शिकायत कर चुके हैं कि प्रमुख सचिव न सिर्फ उनके निर्देशों की अवहेलना करती हैं बल्कि सत्तारूढ़ दल के वरिष्ठ नेताओं का नाम लेकर अनुचित व्यवहार भी करती हैं। अब तो स्थिति यह है कि राज्य मंत्री के मांगने पर शासन की पत्रवलियाँ भी नहीं भेजती। विधानसभा और विधान परिषद के सवालों की ब्रीफिंग बैठकों में भी शासन के अधिकारी नहीं पहुंचते। सोमवार को मुख्य सचिव को प्रेषित पत्र में श्री सिंह ने कहा कि यह प्रवृत्ति न सिर्फ विभाग के महत्वपूर्ण कार्यों के प्रति अफसरों के उदासीन रवैये की परिचायक हैं बल्कि संविधान के प्रावधानों की

अवमानना भी है। सूत्रों के मुताबिक राज्य मंत्री श्री सिंह ने सोमवार को अपने कार्यालय में ''एड्स नियंत्रण तथा यू.पी. हेल्थ सिस्टम डेवलपमेन्ट प्रोजेक्ट'' के बारे में बारह बजे और तीन बजे दो बैठकें आयोजित की थी। इनमें प्रमुख सचिव, सचिव और विशेष सचिवों से शामिल होने की अपेक्षा की गयी थी। लेकिन कोई अधिकारी बैठकों में नहीं पहुंचा। इस वजह से बैठकों में कोई निर्णय नहीं लिया जा सका। प्रमुख सचिव नीता चौधरी की तैनाती के बाद चिकित्सा एवं स्वास्थ्य विभाग में ऐसे विवादों की बाढ़ आ गयी है। उन पर कई अधिकारियों के साथ अनुचित बर्ताव का आरोप लग चुका है। राज्य मंत्री ने पिछले दिनों इस बारे में मुख्यमंत्री से लिखित शिकायत भी की थी।

8. श्री आजम खाँ तथा श्री वी.पी. सिंह विवाद-श्री आजम खाँ नगर विकास मंत्री हैं तथा श्री वी.पी. सिंह नगर आयुक्त। मंत्री से नाराजगी के चलते श्री सिंह को शुक्रवार 16 जून, 2006 की शाम स्थानांतरित कर दिया गया। उन्हें विज्ञान एवं प्रौद्योगिकी विभाग में संयुक्त सचिव बनाया गया है। इससे पहले दिसम्बर में आई.ए.एस. अधिकारी आलोक कुमार भी उनकी नाराजगी का शिकार हुए थे। उन्हें भाजपा व लालजी टंडन का एजेन्ट करार दिया गया था। इसके बाद उन्हें सिद्धार्थनगर का जिलाधिकारी बना दिया गया था। आलोक कुमार के जाने के बाद लगभग साढ़े तीन महीने तक नगर आयुक्त की कुर्सी खाली रही। कारण आजम खाँ को कोई भरोसेमंद अफसर नहीं मिल रहा था। पूर्व नगर आयुक्त एस.पी. सिंह आजम खाँ के सबसे भरोसेमंद आदमी माने जाते थे। वह सार्वजनिक मंच से भी उनकी सराहना कर चुके हैं। लेकिन उनके नगर आयुक्त रहने के दौरान पटरी-दुकानदार नेता व सपा कार्यकर्ता रफीक खान ने आत्महत्या कर ली थी जिसके बाद मुख्यमंत्री एस.पी. सिंह से खासे नाराज हो गये थे। इसी कारण श्री सिंह को निलम्बित कर दिया गया था। नगर विकास मंत्री के प्रयास से एस.पी. सिंह बहाल हो गये थे तथा उनकी तैनाती भी

बतौर विशेष सचिव नगर विकास विभाग में हो गयी। हालाँकि बीच-बीच में उनके नगर आयुक्त बनने की चर्चाएँ होती रहीं। जब भी ऐसी चर्चा होती पटरी दुकानदार आन्दोलन पर उतारू हो जाते। इसी कारण साढ़े तीन महीने तक नगर आयुक्त की कुर्सी खाली रही। इससे नगर निगम की गाड़ी पटरी से उतर गई। इस दौरान निगम में कई बड़े-बड़े घोटाले हुए। दर्जनों विवादित मामले लेन-देन के बाद निपटा दिये गये। करोड़ों रूपयों का फर्जी भुगतान हुआ। इसके बाद 10 अप्रैल को पी.सी.एस. अफसर वी.पी. सिंह नये नगर आयुक्त बनाये गये। लेकिन नगर विकास मंत्री उनकी तैनाती से खुश नहीं हुए। औपचारिक मुलाकात करने पहुंचे वी.पी. सिंह से आजम खाँ ने तबादला कराने की सलाह दे दी। इस पर श्री सिंह ने उनसे ही स्थानांतरण करने को कह दिया। इसको लेकर नगर विकास मंत्री व नगर आयुक्त में गर्मा-गर्मी हो गयी। इसके बाद दोनों की बात-चीत भी बन्द हो गयी थी।

9. मंत्री राजाराम पाण्डे बनाम देवीशंकर शर्मा-श्री राजाराम पाण्डे खादी मंत्री और देवीशंकर शर्मा उत्तर प्रदेश खादी एवं ग्रामोद्योग बोर्ड के मुख्य कार्यपालक। उत्तर प्रदेश खादी एवं ग्रामोद्योग बोर्ड की ऐतिहासिक इमारत ढ़हाने के लिए उन्होंने बोर्ड के मुख्य कार्यपालक अधिकारी देवी शंकर शर्मा पर दबाव डाला। श्री शर्मा ने अपनी रपट में कहा कि पुराना भवन गिराकर नया भवन बनाना बोर्ड के हित में नहीं है। बोर्ड के पास निर्माण के लिए पैसा नहीं हैं और न ही प्रस्तावित भवन का नक्शा पास है। जबकि मंत्री हर हाल में पुराना भवन गिराकर 'खादी माल' बनवाना चाहते थे क्योंकि इसमें मंत्री जी का व्यक्तिगत लाभ ज्यादा था। इस रिपोर्ट से नाराज मंत्री ने श्री शर्मा को अपने पद से हटवा दिया। अब नये मुख्य कार्यपालक अधिकारी के लिए यह रिपोर्ट गले की हड्डी बन गई। श्री शर्मा ने शासन को भेजी अपनी रिपोर्ट में कहा है कि बोर्ड के पुराने भवन को गिराकर नया भवन बनाया जाना उपयुक्त नहीं है। इसके लिए शासन

न तो बोर्ड को कोई अनुदान दे रहा है और न किसी प्रकार की कोई शासकीय गारण्टी। उन्होंने कहा कि बोर्ड के पास इतना धन नहीं है कि नई इमारत बना सके। बोर्ड के पस अर्जित ब्याज की धनराशि 4.77 करोड़ रूपया 31 मई सन् 2006 तक आरक्षित है, इसके अलावा बोर्ड के पास कोई पैसा नहीं है, और न अपना कोई आय का स्रोत है। उन्होंने पत्र में लिखा-''ब्याज मद में आरक्षित 4.77 करोड़ की धनराशि को कार्यदायी संस्था को अवमुक्त करने हेतु मा. मंत्री जी के स्तर पर मौखिक दबाव डाला गया।'' इस धनराषि से भी केवल प्रथम फेज का निर्माण हो सकता। इसमें केवल बेसमेन्ट और ग्राउण्ड फ्लोर ही बन सकता है। ग्राउण्ड फ्लोर पर प्रदर्शनी ओर दुकानों का निर्माण प्रस्तावित है। जिसमें अधिकारियों व कर्मचारियों के बैठने का इन्तजाम नहीं हो सकता। उपलब्ध धनराषि से केवल अधूरा भवन बनेगा। जो भविष्य में जाँच का विषय बनेगा। श्री शर्मा ने लिखा कि बोर्ड इसी मद से प्रति माह 2.28 लाख रूपये का भुगतान संविदा पर कार्यरत कर्मियों को कर रहा है। स्पष्ट है कि भवन का निर्माण इस धनराशि से नहीं हो सकता है। रिपोर्ट में श्री शर्मा ने लिखा कि-''प्रस्तावित भवन का नक्शा विकास प्राधिकरण के पत्र संख्या-26774/97-273 दिनांक 10.03.2006 द्वारा आपत्तियों सहित वापस किया गया। बिना नक्शा स्वीकृत हुए भवन निर्माण नियमानुसार नहीं होगा। साथ ही बोर्ड प्रांगण की 5600 वर्गफीट जमीन अधिग्रहण का प्रकरण शासन में लम्बित है जिस पर कुल 48.89 लाख रूपये का व्यय प्रस्तावित है। जिसके बढ़ने की सम्भावना रहेगी। ऐसे में भूमि अधिग्रहण और बोर्ड के पक्ष में भूमि स्थानांतरित होने से पहले निर्माण कार्य कराया जाना विधिक नहीं होगा। श्री शर्मा ने यह रिपोर्ट 12 जुलाई सन् 2006 को सचिव खादी एवं ग्रामोद्योग विभाग में भेजी और इसी शाम श्री शर्मा को बोर्ड के मुख्य कार्यपालक अधिकारी पद से हटाये जाने का आदेश जारी कर दिया गया। आनन-फानन में अब ब्रह्मानन्द को खादी बोर्ड का मुख्य कार्यपालक

अधिकारी बनाया गया। श्री शर्मा की यह रपट मंत्री जी के लिए मुसीबत बन गई।

10. खाद्य मंत्री एवं प्रमुख सचिव श्री राम विवाद-श्री सुरेन्द्र विक्रम सिंह, वर्तमान मुलायम सिंह यादव सरकार में खाद्य मंत्री थे, तथा श्रीरामप्रमुख सचिव खाद्य विभाग। लेवी चावल की खरीद को लेकर खाद्य मंत्री वहां के तत्कालीन आर.एफ.सी. श्रीराम से काफी नाराज थे क्योंकि श्रीराम मंत्री की हर बात को मानने के लिए तैयार नहीं थे। इसलिए खाद्य मंत्री ने श्रीराम को वहां से तबादला दूसरे जगह करवा दिया। श्रीराम के हटने के बाद पता चला कि जिन मुद्दों में 'शिथिलता' बरतने के चलते खाद्य मंत्री श्रीराम से नाराज थे उसके असली कारण आर.एम.ओ., एस.एन. राय हैं। कुछ समय बाद आर.एम.ओ., एस.एन. राय का भी तबादला करवा दिया गया, लेकिन श्री एन.एन. राय को उसी वर्ष दिसम्बर सन् 2006 में रिटायर होना था। इसलिए इसी आधार पर वह अपने तबादला आदेश के खिलाफ उच्च न्यायालय चले गये और वहाँ से उन्हें राहत भी मिल गयी। लेकिन इसी बीच खाद्य विभाग वहां एक-दूसरे आर.एम.ओर., सुधाकर मिश्र की तैनाती कर चुका था लिहाजा विभाग ने विधिक राय ली। जिसमें एन.एन. राय को वहाँ से हटाने पर अवमानना का मामला बनने की बात सामने आयी। इसको देखते हुये एन.एन. राय को डिस्टर्ब करने की जगह वहाँ दो आर.एम.ओ. की तैनाती करने का फैसला कर दिया गया। फैसले को अमलीजामा पहनाने में दिक्कत यह आ रही थी कि हर मण्डल में आर.एम.ओ. को एक पद होता है। इसलिए दसरे आर.एम.ओ. की तनख्वाह कैसे निकलेगी। रास्ता भी ढूंढ लिया गया। सहारनपुर मण्डल के आर.एम.ओ.के पद को बरेली मण्डल शिफ्ट कर दिया गया। इसके बाद दोनों आर.एम.ओ. के बीच कार्यों का बटँवारा भी कर दिया गया। दिलचस्प बात यह है कि एस.एन. राय को दूसरे कामों के साथ गेंहूँ खरीद की जिम्मेदारी दी गयी है।

11. खाद्य तंत्री एवं श्री ए.के. चतुर्वेदी विवाद-श्रीमती ओमवती बसपा सरकार में खादी ग्रामोद्योग विभाग की राज्यमंत्री (स्वतंत प्रभार) हैं, तथा श्री ए.के. चतुर्वेदी मुख्य कार्यपालक अधिकारी (सी.ई.ओ.) खादी एवं ग्रामोद्योग विभाग। मंत्री महोदया का कहना है कि मैं अपने विभागीय अधिकारियों से परेशान व लाचार हूँ। किसी भी प्रकरण की फाइल मांगने पर अधिकारी मुझ तक पहुंचाते ही नहीं है। राज्य मंत्री, रविवार 16 दिसम्बर, 2007 को खादी ग्रामोद्योग बोर्ड कर्मचारी यूनियन के महाधिवेशन में कर्मचारियों को सम्बोधित कर रही थी। अपने सम्बोधन के दौरान उन्होंने कहा कि मुख्य कार्यपालक अधिकारी (सी.ई.ओ.) से भवन बनाने के लिए फाइल मांगी तो नहीं मिली। आपके पदोन्नति, स्थायीकरण समेत अन्य मसलों की फाइल तलब की मगर अधिकारियों के कान तक जूँ नहीं रेंगी। आप बताओ ऐसे मैं आपकी कैसे मदद करूँ। श्रीमती ओमवती ने यह विचार जाहिर किये तो सभी चकित रहे गये। उन्होंने मायूसी से कहा कि खादी ग्रामोद्योग बोर्ड का पुराना भवन टूट गया है एक भवन में कर्मचारियों को बैठने में असुविधा होती है। केन्द्रीय मंत्री श्री महावीर प्रसाद नये भवन के लिए पैसा देने के लिए तैयार है पर सी.ई.ओ.ए.के. चतुर्वेदी ने आज तक अनुमानित खर्च की फाइल ही नहीं भेजी। कर्मचारियों की 16 सूत्रीय माँगों को व पूरा करने को तैयार हैं पर जब तक बोर्ड प्रशासन का सहयोग नहीं मिलेगा वह कुछ नहीं कर पायेंगे।

12. रघुराज प्रताप सिंह (राजा भैया) एवं श्री अनिल कुमार (प्रमुख सचिव) विवाद-स्टाम्प एवं निबंधन मंत्री रघुराज प्रताप सिंह राजा भैया फिर चर्चा में हैं। इस बार वह अपने ही विभाग के प्रमुख सचिव अनिल कुमार के फैसलों से खफा हैं। हाल ही में विभाग के 33 लिपिकों को प्रभारी सब रजिस्ट्रार के पद पर तैनात करने के प्रमुख सचिव के फैसले को राजा भईया ने अवैध करार दे दिया है। इसके अलावा अपर महानिरीक्षक निबंधन (एडीशनल आईजी) के दो पदों पर प्रमुख सचिव ने कार्मिक विभाग से डीपीसी करवाकर पाँच नाम तय करवाने का जो

फैसला लिया, वह भी विभागीय मंत्री को रास नहीं आया। जबकि फरवरी माह में इस फाइल पर सीएम से अनुमोदन लिया जा चुका है। हालांकि प्रमुख सचिव अनिल कुमार ने सीएम के अनुमोदन के बाद अपने विभागीय मंत्री से अनुमोदन लेने के लिए उनके पास भी फाइल भेजी मगर मंत्री ने फाइल पर यह लिख दिया कि सीएम से अनुमोदन वाला अंश फाइल में नहीं है, इसलिए वह अंश फाइल में नहीं है, इसलिए वह अंश भी भेजा जाए। इन दोनों ही मामलों पर विभाग के अन्य अफसर अब प्रमुख सचिव अनिल कुमार के साथ लामबंद हैं। नाम न छापने की शर्त पर अफसरों ने बताया कि प्रमुख सचिव के दोनों ही फैसले नियमों के मुताबिक हैं। चूंकि लोक सेवा आयोग में सब रजिस्ट्रार की नई भर्तियों पर रोक लगी हुई है और 25 प्रतिशत बाबुओं को कोटे से सब रजिस्ट्रार बनाने का प्रावधान है, इसलिए रोक की वजह से इन बाबुओं को प्रभारी रजिस्ट्रार बनाया गया है। जहाँ तक अपर महानिरीक्षक निबंधन के दो पदों पर भर्ती का सवाल है तो जब मुख्यमंत्री का अनुमोदन मिल चुका तो फिर विभागीय मंत्री के स्तर पर इस मामले में क्यों अडंगा लगाया जा रहा है।

निष्कर्ष एवं सुझाव

निष्कर्ष रूप में हम कह सकते हैं कि दोनों के क्रमशः राजनीतिक एवं प्रशासनिक दायित्व एक–दूसरे के पूरक हैं। अपने कार्यो के लिए दोनों एक–दूसरे पर निर्भर हैं, और इस प्रकार दोनों का सामूहिक लक्ष्य संवैधानिक दायित्वों को पूरा करना हैं। इसमें राजनीतिक तटस्थता, प्रत्यायोजित विधान, सत्तारूढ़ राजनैतिक दल की विचारधारा, मंत्री की मंत्रिपरिषद् में स्थिति, सामाजिक एवं राजनीतिक संस्कृति या परिवेश, दोनों का एक–दूसरे के प्रति विश्वास एवं दृष्टिकोण, वैयक्तिक रूचि, लोक सेवकों का स्थानांतरण, पदस्थापन, पदोन्नति, निलम्बन, वार्षिक गोपनीय प्रतिवेदन के रूप में उनके कार्य व्यवहार पर टिप्पणी, नीतियों एवं संवैधानिक आदर्शों के प्रति प्रतिबद्धता तथा राजनैतिक दल या असंतुलन पैदा करते हैं। इसमें

कुछ विषय ऐसे है। जिस पर ज्यादातर सत्तारूढ़ दल लोकसेवकों की निष्ठा को परखने की कोशिशि करते हैं, जैसे-प्रत्येक सत्तारूढ़ दल की उपर्युक्त इच्छाओं को पूर्ण करने में कोई लोकसेवक किल रहता है तो उसे स्थानांतरण, निलम्बन एवं चरित्र पंजिका में प्रतिकूल प्रविष्टि के लिए तैयार रहना चाहिए, भले ही उसने अपने दायित्वों के निर्वहन में कितनी ही ईमानदारी क्यों न दिखाई हो, यह कोई मायने नहीं रखता है। कुछ मामलों में मंत्री तो कुछ मामलों में सचिव प्रतिष्ठा का प्रश्न बना लेते हैं जो कि दोनों के सौहार्दपूर्ण सम्बन्धों के लिए उचित नहीं है। अत: मंत्री एवं सचिव के बीच सम्बन्धों की प्रकृति सहजीवी है। मंत्री के कई प्रकार के विधायिकी कार्य सौंपे गये हैं, जैसे-संसद में पूछे गये प्रश्नों का उत्तर तैयार करना, विधेयक के प्रतिरूप को तैयार करना, इत्यादि, परन्तु इन प्रत्येक कार्यों में सम्बन्ध में सचिव का योगदान एवं महत्व को देखा जा सकता है। मंत्री एवं सचिव के बीच का संचार महत्वपूर्ण विषय पर लिखित होना चाहिए, ताकि उत्तरदायित्व का निर्धारण किया जा सके। मंत्री एवं सचिव के बीच ऐसी भावना को विकसित किया जाना चाहिए, जहां सचिव सम्बन्धित मंत्री को अपना उच्चाधिकारी माने, परन्तु मंत्री अपने सचिव को अधीनस्थ न माने। प्रत्येक सचिव से यह अपेक्षा की जाती है कि, 'व्यापक दृष्टिकोण के आधार को मानते हुए वह भारत सरकार के सचिव के रूप में कार्य करे, परन्तु सबसे बुरी स्थिति तब होती है, जब कोई सचिव मंत्री के व्यक्तिगत सचिव के रूप में कार्य करता है। प्रशासनिक सुधार आयोग के अनुसार, जिन राजनीतिज्ञों को राजनीतिक कार्यपालिका का पद सौंपा जाये, उसे प्रशासनिक प्रशिक्षण दिया जाना चाहिए ताकि दोनों के मध्य दृष्टिकोण में एकरूपता बनायी जा सके। राजनीतिज्ञों और सिविल सेवकों के सम्बन्धों को बेहतर बनाने हेतु यह आवश्यक है कि सिविल सेवकों की नियुक्तियों और स्थानान्तरण सम्बन्धी शक्तियों के दुरप्रयोग पर अंकुश लगाया जाय। सिविल सेवाओं में सम्बन्धित आचार संहिताओं में इस तरह के परिवर्तन लाये जाने की

आवश्यकता है, ताकि राजनीतिक तटस्थता जैसे सिद्धांतों को आधुनिक आवश्यकता के अनुरूप उपयोगी बनाया जा सके। अपराध प्रक्रिया की धारा 197 में इस तरह के परिवर्तन लाये जाने की आवश्यकता है ताकि सत्ताधारी राजनीति, भ्रष्ट लोकसेवकों को संरक्षण न प्रदान कर पायें। भ्रष्टाचार के विरोध के सम्बन्ध में प्रभावी कदम उठाये जाने की आवश्यकता है, जैसे कि राज्यों में लोक आयुक्त संस्था को प्रभावी बनाया जाना, संघ में लोकपाल व्यवस्था, नियमों और विनियमों का सरल एवं स्पष्ट रूप दिया जाना, भ्रष्ट लोकसेवकों का सम्पत्ति अधिग्रहण अधिनियम, शासनिक और प्रशासनिक तंत्र में पारदर्शिता इत्यादि। मंत्रालय और विभिन्न तरह के स्वायत्त पूर्ण संगठनों को बेहतर और स्पष्ट बनाये जाने की आवश्यकता है। मंत्री और सिविल सेवाओं के सम्बन्धों को आधुनिक परिस्थितियों के अनुसार प्रभावी करने की आवश्यकता है। मंत्रियों को भी लोक नीति प्रक्रिया में पूर्ण जानकारी दिये जाने की आवश्यकता है। पदोन्नति व्यवस्था में वरिष्ठता के साथ-साथ योग्यता को उपर्युक्त रूप से ध्यान में रखे जाने की आवश्यकता है। योग्यता मूल्यांकन के सम्बन्ध में कार्य निष्पाद एवं मूल्यांकन को बेहतर एवं वैज्ञानिक बनाये जाने की अति आवश्यकता है।

सन्दर्भ

1. भाम्भरी, चन्द्र प्रकाश, लोक प्रशासनः सिद्धांत एवं व्यवहार, जय प्रकाश नाथ एण्ड कम्पनी, मेरठ, 2003।
2. जैन, आर.बी., भारतीय समाज अधिकारी तंत्र और सुशासन, हिन्दी माध्यम कार्यान्वयन निदेशालय, दिल्ली विश्वविद्यालय, दिल्ली, 2007।
3. माहेश्वरी, श्रीराम, भारतीय प्रशासन, ओरिएण्ट लॉग्मैन, नई दिल्ली, 2002।
4. माहेश्वरी, एस.आर., पब्लिक एडमिनिस्ट्रेशन इन इण्डिया, मैकमिलन इंडिया लिमिटेड, नई दिल्ली, 2007।

5. भट्टाचार्य, मोहित, इंडियन एडमिनिस्ट्रेज़न, दि वर्ल्ड प्रेस, कलकत्ता, 2000।
6. बसु, रूमकी, लोक प्रशासनः संकल्पनाएं एवं सिद्धांत, जवाहर पब्लिशर्स एण्ड डिस्ट्रीब्यूटर्स, नई दिल्ली, 2008।
7. दुबे, अशोक कुमार, प्रशासनिक विचारधाराएं, टाटा मैग्राहिल, नई दिल्ली, 2008।
8. शर्मा, पी.डी.एण्ड शर्मा बी.एम., इण्डियन एडमिनिस्ट्रेशन, रावत पब्लिकेशन्स, जयपुर, 2009।
9. बसु, रूमकी, पब्लिक एडमिनिस्ट्रेशन इन इण्डिया, स्टर्लिंग पब्लिशर्स, नई दिल्ली, 2015।
10. भट्टाचार्य, मोहित, न्यू होराइजन ऑफ पब्लिक एडमिनिस्ट्रेशन, जवाहर पब्लिशर्स एण्ड डिस्ट्रीब्यूटर्स, नई दिल्ली, 2013।
11. रामचन्द्रन, पद्म, पब्लिक एडमिनिस्ट्रेशन इन इण्डिया, नेशनल बुक ट्रस्ट, इंडिया, नई दिल्ली, 2011।
12. फाड़िया, बी.एल., भारत में लोक प्रशासन, साहित्य भवन प्रकाशन, आगरा, 2003।
13. सिंह, राम रणविजय प्रसाद, एवं लोक प्रशासनः विकास सिंह रामरणवीर, पब्लिशिंग हाउस, दिल्ली, 1987।
14. शर्मा, प्रभुदत्त एवं शर्मा, हरिशचन्द्र, लोक प्रशासनः सिद्धांत एवं व्यवहार, जयपुर कालेज बुक डिपार्ट, त्रिपोलिया बाजार, 2002।
15. राठौर, ए.एस., लोक सेविवर्गीय प्रशासनः रिसर्च पब्लिकेशन, जयपुर, 2004-05।
16. भाम्भरी, चन्द्र प्रकाश, ब्यूरोक्रेसी एण्ड पॉलिटिक्स इन इंडिया दिल्ली, विकास पब्लिकेशन्स, 1971।

17. खान, मुहम्मद अकबर अली, कौशिक, एस.एल., साहनी, प्रदीप, पालिटिक्स एण्ड एडमिनिस्ट्रेशन्स इन ए वेलफेयर स्टेट इन इंडिया, किताब महल, इलाहाबाद, 1983।

18. शर्मा, एम.पी., सड़ाना, बी.एल., लोक प्रशासनः सिद्धांत एवं व्यवहार, किताब महल, इलाहाबाद, 1966।

19. गोयल, एस.एल., पर्सनल एडमिनिस्ट्रेशन्स एण्ड मैनेजमेण्ट, स्टरलिंग पब्लिशर्स, नई दिल्ली 1993।

20. माया पत्रिका, 25 फरवरी–10 मार्च, 2000।

21. शर्मा, घनश्याम, उ.प्र. सिविल सेवा का संगठन एवं कार्य प्रणाली, बी.के. तनेजा क्लासिकल पब्लिशिंग कम्पनी, नई दिल्ली, 1992।

22. दैनिक जागरण, समाचार पत्र, लखनऊ, 14 फरवरी, 2006।

23. हिन्दुस्तान, समाचार पत्र, लखनऊ, 17 जून, 2006।

24. हिन्दुस्तान, समाचार पत्र, लखनऊ, 18 जुलाई, 2006।

25. हिन्दुस्तान, समाचार पत्र, लखनऊ, 20 अगस्त, 2006।

26. सिविल सर्विसेज क्रॉनिकल, नई दिल्ली, मार्च, 2003।

27. हिन्दुस्तान, समाचार पत्र, लखनऊ, 25 अप्रैल, 2016।

16

संसदीय प्रजातन्त्र एवं लोक सेवाएँ चुनौतियाँ व सम्भावनाएँ

– कमलेश गुप्ता, मंजरी दमेले

1990 के दशक के बाद वैश्विक स्तर पर राजनीतिक गतिविधि, सामाजिक, अन्तर्राष्ट्रीय घटनाक्रम व प्रौद्योगिकीय क्षेत्रों में जो व्यापक परिवर्तन हुए है, उनके कारण विकासशील देशों के प्रजातंत्रीकरण का मार्ग अत्यधिक सबल हुआ है। कल्याणकारी राज्य की अवधारणा के साथ प्रभावी नियामकीय राज्य की अवधाराणा को भी मान्यता मिली है, ऐसे में समसामयिक समस्याओं के चलते प्रजातांत्रिक व्यवस्थाओं में कुछ नई अभिवृत्तियाँ विकसित हुई हैं, जिसके कारण प्रजातंत्र के महत्व में अत्यधिक वृद्धि हुई है, जिसके फलस्वरूप लोक सेवा सशक्त रूप से उभरकर सामने आयी है। निसंदेह लोकतंत्र दुनिया की बेहतरीन शासन व्यवस्था है, लेकिन यह हर देश में समान सुचारु तरीके से चल रही हो, ऐसा नहीं है। इस व्यवस्था में भी निरंतर सुधार व परिशोधन की आवश्यकता है। नई दिल्ली में 6 जनवरी, 2010 को आयोजित संगोष्ठी में पूर्व प्रधानमंत्री डॉ. मनमोहन सिंह ने कहा कि ''लोकतंत्र हमेशा बेहतरीन तरीके से ही नहीं चलता, वह धीरे-धीरे रफ्तार पकड़ता है

क्योंकि आम राय बनानी आसान नहीं होती। लेकिन भारत में बहुदलीय शासन प्रणाली चल निकली है और उसने समाज के अनेक दबे-कुचले आबादी समूहों को आवाज दी है। देखना यह चाहिए कि समाज के लोकतंत्रीकरण की प्रक्रिया किस रफ्तार से चल रही है। यदि हम अपने देश के संदर्भ में देखें, तो निःसंदेह लोकतंत्र अपनी जड़ें जमा रहा है, लेकिन उसमें कमियां भी हैं। अमेरिका जैसे देश में भी, जहां लोकतंत्र की जड़ें अपेक्षाकृत कम गहरी हैं, सबको साथ लेकर चलने की यह प्रक्रिया लगभग ठीक-ठाक चल रही है, जबकि भारत में आम राय बनाने में सत्ताधारियों को नाकों चने चबाने पड़ जाते हैं।'' लोकतंत्र में निर्वाचन प्रक्रिया इतनी महंगी हो गई है कि योग्य और ईमानदार लोगों का चुनकर आना समसामयिक परिस्थतियों में असंभव है। जनता का, जनता के लिए और जनता के द्वारा वाला लिंकन का फार्मूला वर्तमान परिस्थितियों में कल्पना बन गया है। लोकपाल, न्यायिक सक्रियता, तो सूचना का अधिकार जैसे देकर जनता की एक मृग-मरीचिका सी दिखाई जाती है, लेकिन जल्दी ही उन कानून के तोड़-खोज लिए जाते हैं। ऐसे में लोक सेवा का शसक्त रुप से उभरना संसदीय प्रजातन्त्र में मजबूती का द्योतक हैं । सूचना प्रौद्योगिकी के क्षेत्र में आयी क्रांति में लोक सेवा को नई दिशा दी है जिससे समसामयिक परिप्रेक्ष्य में लोक सेवा के प्रति आमजन के रूझान में सकारात्मक परिवर्तन आया है। ऐसे में लोकतंत्र को कैसे जनोन्मुखी बनाया जाए, यह एक गंभीर प्रश्न बन गया है। प्रस्तुत शोध पत्र में संसदीय प्रजातंत्र एवं लोक सेवा के समीक्षात्मक विश्लेषण के साथ समसामयिक चुनौतियाँ व सम्भावनाओं पर भी प्रकाश डाला गया है।

प्रजातन्त्र एवं लोक सेवा का सैद्धान्तिक परिप्रेक्ष्य

प्रजातन्त्र वर्तमान में एक लोकप्रिय अवधारणा ही नहीं अपितु शासन संचालन की सर्वोत्तम पद्धति है। वर्तमान शासन व्यवस्था में शासन के सर्वोत्तम संचालन हेतु विभिन्न देशों द्वारा उपयुक्त पद्धति को अपनाया है।

इस पद्धति ने विभिन्न साम्राज्यों व तानाशाही व्यवस्था को ध्वस्त किया है, इसलिए प्रजातन्त्र के विभिन्न विचारक स्वीकार करते हैं कि मानव शक्ति को उन्मुक्त करने के लिए कोई भी व्यवस्था प्रजातन्त्र के समान कारगर नहीं है। वर्तमान में विभिन्न देशों में कल्याणकारी राज्य के उदय के फलस्वरूप प्रजातन्त्र की अवधारणा अत्यधिक शक्तिशाली हुई है इसी सन्दर्भ में विद्वान रावर्ट दहल ने आधुनिक प्रजातन्त्र को लोकतन्त्रीय शासन या बहुलतन्त्र कहा है।

ब्राइस के अनुसार, ''प्रजातन्त्र, शासन का एक प्रकार है, जिसमें राज्य के शासन की शक्ति किसी विशेष वर्ग या वर्गों के हाथों मे निहित न होकर, सम्पूर्ण जन समुदाय मे निहित होती है।''[1] विभिन्न विचारकों के प्रजातन्त्र से सम्बन्धित विचार यह दर्शाते हैं कि प्रजातन्त्र किस प्रकार कार्य करता है। गिडिग्स के अनुसार ''प्रजातन्त्र केवल सरकार का ही रूप नहीं, अपितु राज्य, समाज का रूप अथवा इन तीनों का मिश्रण है।'' ''साधारणतः यदि प्रजातन्त्र को परिभाषित किया जाये तो प्रजातन्त्र के तीन आयाम है। पहली सरकार जनता की है, दूसरा सरकार जनता द्वारा चुनी गयी है, तीसरा जनता के लिए है। अर्थात् लोकतन्त्र शासन की वह व्यवस्था है जो जनता के हित के लिए कार्य करती है।''[2] बेजमीन बारबार ने लाकतंत्र कों आधुनिक परिपेक्ष्य में परिभाषित किया, उनके अनुसार ''लोकतंत्र किसी बहुमत सरकार या प्रतिनिधि सरकार का नाम नहीं अपितु यह नागरिकों की स्वस्थ सरकार होती है, और इस तरह की सरकार की स्थापना लोक समाज के सहयोग से संम्भव है।''[3] उपयुक्त विश्लेषणात्मक व्याख्या से स्पष्ट है कि प्रजातन्त्र मे सम्भवतया तीन मूलभूत विशेषताएं पायी जाती है–

- जनता का प्रतिनिधित्त्व
- जनता के हितों का रक्षण
- जनता के प्रति उत्तरादायित्त्व

प्रजातन्त्र के विकास की एक लम्बी परम्परा रही है, जिसमें प्लेटो, अरस्तू, सिसरो से लेकर मध्यकाल के प्रमुख राजनीतिशास्त्र के विद्वानों ने भी योगदान दिया, किन्तु इसकी प्रमाणिक व औपचारिक अभिव्यक्ति लॉक व रूसो द्वारा की गयी, विभिन्न प्रजातन्त्र समर्थक अवधारणाओं का प्रतिपादन कर प्रजातन्त्र की नींव मजबूत की। ''इन विचारकों ने प्रत्येक व्यक्ति के प्राकृतिक अधिकार, प्रजा द्वारा परिवर्तन की न्यायोचित सम्भावना, सरकार द्वारा सहमति के आधार पर शासन, नागरिकों द्वारा शासन मे सहभागिता, सामान्य इच्छा में राज्य की इच्छा का स्रोत तथा उसकी सर्वोच्चता आदि धारणाओं को प्रतिपादित कर प्रजातन्त्र को मजबूत किया। इसी दिशा में जॉन स्टूअर्ट मिल सहित, अन्य उपयोगितावादी विद्वानों के योगदान के परिणामस्वरूप पश्चिम में प्रजातन्त्र एक सर्वमान्य शासन व्यवस्था के रूप में स्वीकार एवं आत्मसात कर लिया गया।''[4] औद्योगिक क्रान्ति ने प्रजातन्त्र के सिद्धान्त को आर्थिक क्षेत्र में प्रयुक्त किया। इस तरह लोकतन्त्र का विकास भी एक प्रक्रिया के रूप में धीरे-धीरे हुआ, बढ़ती जनजागरूकता ने इस व्यवस्था को बल प्रदान किया।

प्रजातन्त्र की अवधारणा की वास्तविकता यह है कि 2500 वर्ष पूर्व विकसित किया गया प्रजातन्त्र संम्भवतः पश्चिम की देन है, लेकिन प्राचीन भारतीय वैदिक समाज में भी इस तरह की व्यवस्था समकक्ष स्वरूप में विद्यमान थी। उपर्युक्त प्रजातन्त्र की अवधारणाओं को यदि वर्तमान परिप्रेक्ष्य में वर्गीकृत किया जाय तो सामान्यतः व्यावहारिक रूप में प्रजातन्त्र के तीन स्वरूप सामने आते है-

प्रजातन्त्र
- पश्चिमी प्रजातन्त्र
- साम्यवादी प्रजातन्त्र
- गाँधीवादी प्रजातन्त्र

वर्तमान प्रजातान्त्रिक व्यवस्था पर टिप्पणी करते हुए क्लाइल नामक विद्वान ने कहा था कि प्रजातन्त्र असम्भव है, इसी प्रकार समस्त जनता

द्वारा शासन भी असम्भव है, अतः हमें केवल न्यून शासन की बात करनी चाहिए, जो कि निर्वाचन एवं प्रतिनिधि प्रणाली के माध्यम से सम्भव है, किन्तु अधिकांश जन समूहों की उदासीनता के कारण अधिकांश राज्य व्यवस्थाओं में वास्तविक शक्ति सक्रिय जनों के हाथों मे आ गयी है। ये अल्प संख्यक समूह का प्रतिनिधित्व करते हैं, लेकिन मेरे विचार से उपयुक्त परिभाषा अब इस रूप में परिवर्तित हो गयी है कि सम्पूर्ण प्रजातंत्रीयकरण असम्भव है अब सिर्फ प्रजातन्त्र के कुछ मूलभूत सिद्धान्तों को ही स्वीकार किया जा सकता है। क्योंकि इसमें निर्वाचन से समस्त नागरिकों को शासन में सहभाग करने का अवसर मिलता है, लेकिन वर्तमान परिवेश में कल्याणकारी राज्य के उद्देश्यों को पूरा सक्षम बनाए जाने की आवश्यकता है। इस सन्दर्भ में सरटोरी ने ठीक ही कहा है प्रजातन्त्र के शास्त्रीय सिद्धान्त की अपर्याप्ताओं एवं अपूर्णताओं को दूर किया जाना चाहिए।

लोक सेवा की अवधारणा पश्चिमी यूरोप के प्रशा में 18वीं सदी में अस्तित्व में आयी। जबकि प्राचीन काल में लोक सेवाओं का जन्म छटवी शताब्दी में चीन में हुआ। लोक सेवा शब्द का पहली बार प्रयोग सर रावर्ट बलपोल ने 1841-1842 में किया। लोक सेवा सबद का सुरूवाती प्रयोग ईस्ट इंडिया कपनी के व्यापारिक व प्रशासनिक कार्य करने बाले कार्मिको के लिए किया गया 1954 मैं नार्थकोर्ट त्रावेलियन रिपोर्ट मैं इस शब्द का प्रयोग किया। विभिन्न आयोगों ने लोक सेवा के सुधार हेतु सुझाव दिये जिसके फलसवरूप लोक सेवा का वर्तमान स्वरूप अस्तित्व में आ सका। ग्लैन स्टाल का यह मत लोक सेवा के संबंध मे सर्वाधिक उपर्युक्त प्रतीत होता है कि किसी भी देश की सरकार उससे अच्छी नहीं हो सकती जितना लोक सेवा उसे इजाजत देती है यह वक्तव्य समसामयिक राज्य में लोक सेवा की अवधारणा को स्थापित करता है। लोक सेवा संसदीय प्रजातन्त्र व प्रशासनिक व्यवस्था का अपरिहार्य अंग है। लोक सेवा के संदर्भ में व्यापक सुधार हेतु प्रयास 1967 में प्रथम प्रशासनिक सुधार

आयोग के साथ शुरु हुआ जोकि वर्तमान आधुनिक राज्य तक जारी है'' उदारीकरण निजीकरण व वैश्वीकरण के वातावरण ने लोक सेवा के समक्ष न्यूनतम लागत के साथ प्रर्दशन के उत्तमता को संभव बनाने की चुनौती उत्पन्न की है।[5] वैश्वीकरण के कारण राज्य व लोक सेवा की प्रकृति में बदलाव देखने को मिल रहे है, इन बदलावों के मुख्य रूप से तीन कारक है।

- सूचना एवं प्रौद्योगिकी का विकास
- वैश्विक संस्थाओं की सक्रियता
- कार्य कुशलता व उत्पादकता पर अधिक बल

सूचना प्रौद्योगिकी का निश्चित रूप से लोक सेवा पर प्रभाव पड़ा है, सूचना प्रौद्योगिकी सामान्यत: सेवा की कार्य कुशलता व दक्षता को बढ़ाती है जिससे प्रशासन नागरिकों को बेहतर सुविधाए मुहैया कराने की ओर अग्रसर होता है वर्तमान में इस संदर्भ में ई–प्रशासन को भी महत्व दिया जाने लगा है जो प्रशासन को मितव्ययी बनाता है, अत्याधुनिक तकनीकी की शुरुआत, सूचना सेवाओं की संयुक्तिकरण व वितरण, लचीली पर्यवेक्षण प्रणाली व नियंत्रण प्रणाली आदि ऐसी प्रविधियाँ है जिनके माध्यम से लोक क्षेत्र को कार्यकुशल व जबावदेह बनाया जा सकता है। वर्तमान में लोक सेवा के समक्ष मुख्य चुनौती स्वयं को परिवर्तित व जन आँकांक्षाओं के अनुरुप परिवर्तित करने की है तथा समसामायिक परिप्रेक्ष्य में प्रशासनिक सुधारों की महती आवश्यकता है। ई–गर्वनेन्स व सूचना का अधिकार वास्तव में वैश्वीकरण के बाद ही अस्तित्व में आये है। जिनसे समसामायिक प्रशासनिक सुधारो को करने की पहल की ओर सरकारों का रुझान बढ़ा है।

प्रजातन्त्र एवं लोक सेवा: समसामायिक परिप्रेक्ष्य

जे.एल.मिल, मैक्स वेवर, वेरिग्हन मूर और ऐलेक्स डी ताक्विले जैसे विद्वानों व अतुल कोहली जैसे शिक्षकों ने अपने विचारों के माध्यम से यह

स्थापित करने का प्रयास किया कि प्रजातन्त्र की स्थापना औद्योगिक रूप से विकसित, एक समान रूप वाले समान और पूंजीवादी व्यवस्थाओं में ही हो सकती है, वे भारत को प्रजातन्त्र की स्थापना के लिए उपयुक्त नहीं मानते, क्योंकि भारतीय समाज, कृषि आधारित, रूढ़िवादी और विभिन्नताओं से भरा समाज है, इसलिए उनका पक्ष है कि प्रजातन्त्र भारतीय समाज में नहीं पनप सकता, परन्तु इन विविधताओं के बावजूद भारत में विशेष प्रकार की प्रजातन्त्र स्थापित हुआ हैं, और भारतीय प्रजातन्त्र विश्व की वृहद लोकतान्त्रिक व्यवस्थाओं में से एक हैं। भारतीय प्रजातन्त्र पर विचार करने से पहले यह समझना आवश्यक होगा कि भारतीय प्रजातन्त्र किन आधारभूत तत्वों को लेकर चलता है। जिसके कारण विभिन्न देशों ने भारतीय लोकतान्त्रिक प्रणाली का समर्थन किया है। स्वतन्त्रता, समानता, सम्प्रभुता एवं बन्धुत्व भारतीय प्रजातन्त्र के आधारभूत तत्व हैं। लोकतन्त्र के द्वारा व्यक्ति व समाज के बीच प्रभावशाली सम्बन्ध सूत्र स्थापित होता है। प्रजातन्त्र में जनता के पास सत्ता की चाबी होती है।

भारत में प्रजातन्त्र की अवधारणा को संसदीय प्रजातन्त्र के रूप में व्यवहारिक मान्यता दी गयी हैं। संसदीय लोकतन्त्र से आशय सरकार की उस प्रणाली से है जिसमें जनता अपने प्रतिनिधियों के माध्यम से शासन करती है। ये प्रतिनिधि वयस्क मतदाताओं द्वारा स्वच्छ एवं निष्पक्षतापूर्वक चुने जाते हैं, अर्थात् आमजन को प्रतिनिधि चुनने का अधिकार दिया गया है, भारतीय संसदीय लोकतन्त्र की मुख्य विशेषता दोहरी कार्यपालिका का उपस्थित होना है। भारतीय राष्ट्रपति औपचारिक प्रधान होते हुए नाममात्र की कार्यपालिका की तरह कार्य करता है, जबकि प्रधानमन्त्री व उसका मन्त्री परिषद् वास्तविक कार्यपालिका की भूमिका मे रखते हैं। भारत में केवल संसदीय प्रजातन्त्र ही प्रजातान्त्रिक व्यवस्था अपनाने का साक्ष्य नहीं है अपितु विभिन्न राज्यों मे अन्य नगर निकायों व ग्राम स्तर तक में भी प्रजातान्त्रिक प्रक्रिया को अपनाया गया है तथा प्रतिनिधि चुनने का

अधिकार जनता को प्रदान किया गया है। इस सन्दर्भ में डॉ. सुभाष कश्यप ने सही लिखा है कि "भारतीय मतदान किसी भी दल को सत्ता से वंचित कर सकता है और अपने देश की राजनीतिक संरचना एवं इतिहास के प्रवाह को बदल सकता है, यही तथ्य प्रजातन्त्र का सार एवं आधार है।"[6]

भारतीय प्रजातन्त्र के मूल आधार

- भारतीय संसद वास्तव में भारतीय प्रजातन्त्र का आधार स्तम्भ है, कार्यपालिका की राजनीतिक शक्ति का स्रोत संसद है।
- भारतीय प्रजातन्त्र के बुनियादी सिद्धान्त धर्मनिरपेक्ष व समानता की अवधारणा है, इन दोनों के आधार पर ही बिना भेदभाव किए आम जन को लोकतान्त्रिक पद्धति में भाग लेने का अवसर प्रदान किया गया है।
- भारतीय प्रजातन्त्र में आर्थिक नियोजन की विकेन्द्रीकरण प्रणाली को अपनाया गया है, जिससे आर्थिक विषमताओं को काफी हद तक कम करने का प्रयास किया गया है।
- भारत में सिर्फ केन्द्रीय स्तर पर ही प्रजातान्त्रिक प्रणालियों को नहीं अपनाया गया है, अपितु राज्य जिला एवं ग्राम स्तर पर भी प्रजातान्त्रिक प्रणाली को अपनाया गया। जिससे ग्रामीण परिवेश का आम व्यक्ति भी इस व्यवस्था को समझे व अपना योगदान दें।

भारतीय प्रजातन्त्र के अब तक के व्यवहारिक पक्ष का विश्लेषण इस बात की ओर ध्यान इंगित कराता है कि संसदीय प्रणाली मे जब एक दल बहुमत में आता है, तो उस दल की व्यवस्थापिका तथा कार्यपालिका मे निरंकुशता व्याप्त रहती है। दूसरी ओर यदि लोकसभा में किसी भी दल को बहुमत नहीं मिलता तो अस्थायित्व की स्थिति बन जाती है। "चुनाव कराने का हमारा रिकॉर्ड हमें लोकतांत्रित देशों की श्रेणी हमें तो खड़ा करता है, पर सही कहें, तो हमारा लोकतंत्र आपाधापी का लोंकतंत्र हैं।

देश में करीब 70 करोड़ वोटर हैं, और सिर्फ 4,617 उम्मीदवार! इतने कम लोग इतनी बड़ी आबदी को उंगलियों पर नचाकर अपना उल्लू सीधा कर रहे है।''[7] द इकोनोमिस्ट ने दुनिया भर में प्रजातन्त्र की सेहत पर एक सर्वे किया हैं। उसके अनुसार, करीब आधी दुनिया किसी न किसी प्रकार के प्रजातन्त्र में रहती है। पत्रिका ने दुनिया में लागू शासन प्रणालियों को पांच श्रेणियों में बांटा। उसके मुताबिक, प्रथम दस प्रजातांत्रिक देशों में स्वीडन, नाँर्वे, आइसलेंड, नीदरलैंड, डेनमार्क, फिनलैंड, न्यूजीलैंड, स्विटजरलैण्ड, जर्मनी, आँट्रिया और स्पेन है। अमेरिका और इंग्लैंड को पूर्ण प्रजातांत्रिक देशों की दूसरी सूची में स्थान मिला है। भारत अधूरें या अपूर्ण प्रजातंत्रों की सूची में 35 वें स्थान पर हैं। एक अन्य सूची ऐसे देशों की है, जहां थोड़ा लोकतंत्र और थोड़ा कोई और शासनतंत्र हैं, इसमें पाकिस्तान जैसे देश आते है। अंतिम सूची ऐसे देशों की है, जहां पूरी तरह तानाशाही है। ''सैद्धान्तिक दृष्टि से देखें, तो लोकतंत्र एक बेहद आकर्षक प्रस्ताव का नाम है। पर व्यवहार में यह हमेशा से अभिजनों का तंत्र रहा है। हजारों साल पहले एथेंस का प्रत्यक्ष लोकतंत्र भी ऐसा ही था, और आज यूरोप के लोकतंत्रों से लेकर भारत के लोकतंत्र तक ऐसा ही है। इसीलिए लोकतंत्र के कई आलोचक कहते है कि इस व्यवस्था में हमेशा अभिजनों का एक सेट दूसरे की जगह लेकर परिवर्तन का भ्रम पैदा करता है। मनु शर्मा का प्रकरण बताता है कि भारत में यह परिवर्तन किस प्रकार घटित हुआ है।''[8]

''ऐसा प्रतीत हो रहा है कि हमारा संसदीय प्रजातन्त्र पहले के मुकाबले अधिक राजनीतिक स्थिरता के दौर में प्रवेश कर चुका है। अब सरकार बदलने के लिए वोटरों को पटाना आसान नहीं रह गया है, या तो सरकार खुद अपने ही पैरों पर कुल्हाड़ी मार ले, या फिर विपक्ष के पास वास्तव में कोई ढंग का विकल्प मौजूद हो, केवल गद्दी पर बैठने वाले नेताओं में परिवर्तन की खातिर होने वाला बदलाव अब लोगों को बेतुका लगने लगा है, चूंकि किसी विपक्षी राजनीतिक पार्टी के पास कोई नया

एजेंडा होता ही नहीं और वे केवल सरकार के खिलाफ पांच साल में जमा हुई नाराजगी के दम पर जीतना चाहते हैं, इसलिए भी वोटर सत्तारूढ़ पार्टी की तरफ ही झुकना मुनासिब समझता है।''[9]

वर्तमान में संसद के महत्व कमी आ गई है, विधि निर्माण के क्षेत्र में संसद का महत्व कम हो गया है और सरकार की निर्णय प्रक्रिया पर उसका उतना अधिक प्रभाव नही रह गया है, वर्तमान में संसद केवल सीमित सतर्कता का साधन बन कर रह गयी है। प्रमुख नीति निर्माण अधिकरण होने के बाद भी संसद सरकार की नीतियों पर महत्वपूर्ण प्रभाव नही छोड़ पा रही, जो कि संसदीय प्रजातांत्रिक व्यवस्था के लिये शुभ संकेत नही है? इसमें सुधार आपेक्षित हो जिसके लिय मजबूत व सक्रिय विपक्ष के साथ नागरिक समाज संगठनों की आवश्यकता है, जो सरकार के समक्ष जनांकाक्षी मुद्दों को उठायें व उन पर प्रभावी निर्णय लेने के लिए बाध्य करें।

समसामयिक परिप्रेक्ष्य में लोक सेवा, प्रजातन्त्र व समाज के विकास के लिये व्यक्तियों को संगठित करके प्रशासनिक गतिविधियों के प्रति संवेदनशीलता विकसित करता है। नागरिक समाज के विकास से संबंधित अंतरराष्ट्रीय प्रयत्नों ने अभिशासन व लोकतंत्र को स्थापित करने तथा मानव अधिकार के संरक्षण में महत्वपूर्ण भूमिका निभाई है सामाजिक पूंजी का विकास कर नागरिक समाज ने अभिशासन को स्थापित करने की दिशा सकारात्मक माहौल विकसित किया है। नागरिक समाज के माध्यम से जहां एक तरफ व्यवसायिक व यांत्रिक संगठनों का मानवीय तत्वों के साथ जोड़ने का प्रयास किया जा रहा है वही दूसरी तरफ जन चेतना का विकास कर विश्व में भ्रष्टाचार पर अंकुश लगाकर पारदर्शिता को बढ़ावा देने का प्रयास किया है।

लोक सेवा लोक उत्तरदायित्व की अवधारणा को विकसित कर शासन व प्रशासन ने आम जन की भागीदारी सुनिश्चित करता है तथा आन्तरिक

गुणवत्ता को बढ़ाता है। शासन व प्रशासन में पारदर्शिता संवेदनशीलता, प्रभावशीलता, सहभागिता तथा विकास के तत्व को विकसित करने तथा सरकार व समाज के मध्य संबंध स्थापित करने का प्रयत्न किया जाता है। वास्तव में लोक सेवा की राजनीतिक सदस्यता सरकारों के प्रति समय के सापेक्ष मे विधि समिति तार्किक व्यवहार को सुनिश्चित करती है लेकिन स्वतंत्रता के 57 वर्षो बाद संसदीय लोक तंत्र की प्रकृति में बदलाव आया है जिससे लोक सेवा की प्रकृति में भी बदलाव देखने को मिल रहा है। संसद के प्रति सामूहिक उत्तरदायित्व का सिद्धांत आज भी अस्तित्व मे है किन्तु लोक जवाबदेयता के संन्दर्भ में लोक सेवा का राजनीतिकरण हुआ है समाजिक न्याय की स्थिति व व्यवहार मे भी बदलाव आया है जिससे लोक सेवा का व्यवहार बदला है और उसे नया रुप देने की कोशिश की जा रही है। जिसके लिये कुछ हद तक राजनीतिक सक्रियता भी जिम्मेदार है। राजनीति प्रशासन विभाजन संबंधी गुडनाऊ का चितन समसामयिक परिपेक्ष्य में प्रसांगिकता खो चुका है।

संसदीय प्रजातन्त्र एवं लोक सेवा की चुनौतियाँ

किसी राष्ट्र की प्रजातान्त्रिक व्यवस्था आदर्श प्रजातान्त्रिक व्यवस्था नहीं हो सकती, क्योंकि उसे उत्कृष्ट स्तर पर पहुचनें हेतु निरन्तर, सतत् सुधार की आवश्यकता होती है। उस प्रजातान्त्रिक व्यवस्था में विभिन्न परिस्थितियों के अन्तर्गत चरणबद्ध तरीके से सुधार होते रहने चाहिए। प्रजातन्त्र पर विचार करते समय जरूरत इस बात की है, कि प्रजातन्त्र एवं नागरिक समाज के समक्ष जो चुनौतियाँ हैं उन पर विचार किया जाए तथा उन चुनौतियों के समाधान के मुख्य विकल्प क्या हो सकते हैं इस बात पर चर्चा की जाए।

जागरूक जनमत

भारतीय प्रजातन्त्र के सफल क्रियान्वयन एवं नागरिक समाज के विकास में एक प्रमुख चुनौती जागरूकता है। जागरूकता की कमी शिक्षा

से जुड़ी हुई है। विश्व के सबसे बड़े प्रजातन्त्र की एक विड़म्बना है कि अशिक्षित व्यक्ति भी मन्त्री व मुख्यमन्त्री बन जाता है व बड़े राजनीतिक पदों पर पहुंच जाता है, फिर वह शासन व प्रशासन का संचालन किस प्रकार कर पाएगा। ऐसी स्थिति में शासन का संचालन नौकरशाही के हाथों में आ जाता है। भारतीय प्रजातन्त्र के सम्बन्ध में स्पष्ट है कि इस स्थिति में सत्ता का संचालन किसी और के द्वारा किया जाता है। देश की सत्ता संचालन करने वाले के लिए कोई योग्यता नहीं है, और न ही जनता के प्रति कार्य के लिए कोई जवाबदेही। अत: भारतीय लोकतन्त्र की सफलता हेतु आवश्यकता इस बात की है, कि जनप्रतिनिधियों की योग्यता के निर्धारण के साथ-साथ उम्र को भी निर्धारित किया जाना चाहिए तथा उनकी जवाबदेही सुनिश्चित की जानी चाहिये। प्रजातन्त्र को सशक्त व प्रभावी बनाने के लिए वर्तमान परिस्थितियों मे आम नागरिक की प्रजातान्त्रिक व्यवस्था में नागरिक समाज के माध्यम से भागीदारी सुनिश्चित करने की आवश्यकता है। यह भागीदारी तभी सुनिश्चित की जा सकती है जब आम जन जागरूक हो क्योंकि जागरूक जनमत ही वह प्रभावशाली अस्त्र है जो कि न केवल प्रजातान्त्रिक व्यवस्था की रक्षा करेगा वरन् उसे सुदृढ़ व उत्कृष्ट स्तर पर ले जाएगा।

सहभागी प्रजातन्त्र

भारतीय संसदीय प्रजातन्त्र को मजबूत करने के लिए इसे सहभागिता आधारित प्रजातन्त्र में बदलना होगा जिसके अन्तर्गत शासन की भूमिका को परिवर्तित करना होगा, जिसमें नागरिक समाज को भी प्रयत्न करने होंगे। उसमें विकेन्द्रीकरण नामक तत्व की अधिकता लानी होगी, क्योकि सत्ता जितनी केन्द्रीकृत होगी उसमें निरंकुशता की सम्भावना उतनी ही बढ़ेगी। शासन तन्त्र को अपनी भूमिका में परिवर्तन करते हुए व्यवस्थापिका की भूमिका में आना होगा। जब तक नागरिक समाज के माध्यम से नागरिकों की सहभागिता प्रशासन में नहीं होगी तब तक समस्याएं कम

नहीं होंगी। अत: सहभागिता आधारित प्रजातन्त्र वर्तमान भारतीय प्रजातान्त्रिक व्यवस्था को सुदृढ़ स्तर पर ले जाने हेतु आधार तत्व है।

बहुदलीय व्यवस्था

"भारतीय संसदीय व्यवस्था के समक्ष बहुदलीय व्यवस्था भी मुख्य चुनौती बन गई है। दलों की बढ़ती संख्या न केवल प्रजातन्त्र के लिए हानिकारक है बल्कि भारतीय लोकतंत्र के अस्तित्व के लिए भी खतरनाक है।"[10] भारतीय राजनीति में छोटें राजनीतिक दल अधिक लाभ की स्थिति में होते है, इसलिये इनकी संख्या बढ़ती जा रही है। ये दल गठबंधन सरकार में महत्वपूर्ण भूमिका निभाते हैं। भारतीय प्रजातन्त्र की प्रमुख चुनौती खण्डित जनादेश है, लेकिन यह संसदीय शासन प्रणाली का दोष नहीं, अपितु जातिवादी राजनीति के कारण है। जातिवादी राजनीति के कारण जातियां ध्रुवों में बट गयी हैं। सामाजिक विरोधाभाषी प्रजातन्त्र, देश की अखण्डता व एकता के लिए सबसे बड़ा खतरा है। इसकी शुरुआत वी.पी. सिंह के समय से हुई, जिन्होंने मण्डल कमीशन के माध्यम से जातिवादी राजनीति को सुदृढ़ आधार प्रदान किया।

राजनीतिक अपराधीकरण

राजनीतिक अपराधीकरण भी संसदीय व्यवस्था के समक्ष मुख्य चुनौती है। वर्तमान में राजनीतिक दलों ने अपने सिद्धांतों से समझौता कर लिया है व व्यक्तिवादी विचारधारा के आधार पर अपराधिक छवि व अन्य निम्न प्रवृत्ति के व्यक्तियों का चयन राजनीतिक दल कर लेते है, जिसके फलस्वरूप भ्रष्टाचार व अपराधीकरण जैसी प्रवृत्तियों को बढ़ावा मिला है। वर्तमान में भारतीय संसदीय शासन व्यवस्था के समक्ष राजनीतिक सौदेबाजी भी मुख्य चुनौती है, जिसमें मुख्य पार्टियों की महत्वपूर्ण भूमिका है, दलों द्वारा बहुमत जुटाने के लिए भी जोड़ तोड़ की प्रक्रिया को अपनाया जा रहा है। राजनीतिज्ञ भी मंत्री पद पाने के लिए अपने सिद्धान्तों से समझौता कर लेते है, जिसके फलस्वरूप राजनीति में मधु कोड़ा की तरह के भ्रष्टाचार

के प्रकरण हमारे सामने आते हैं। इसके लिये आवश्यक है राजनीतिक दल राष्ट्रवादी विचारधारा का अनुशरण करें व सिद्धातों से समझौता न करें।

वापस बुलाने का अधिकार

17 जून 2008 के दिन भारतीय लोकतंत्र में एक महत्त्वपूर्ण घटना हुई, जिससे हमारे राजनेताओं को सबक लेने की जरूरत है। इस दिन छत्तीसगढ़ राज्य के तीन स्थानीय निकाय प्रमुखों को उनके पद सें वापस बुला लिया गया। यह वास्तव में सच्चें लोकतंत्र की ताकत का आमजन में एहसास था। ये स्थानीय निकाय के प्रमुख वहां की जनता की अपेक्षाओं पर खरे नही उतर रहे थे। वे चुनाव से पहले किए गये वायदे भूल गये थे, इन लोगों को शायद यह गलतफहमी हो गई थी, कि अब तो अपना कार्यकाल पूरा करके ही वापस आयेगें। भारतीय प्रजातंत्र में इस प्रक्रिया को सांसदों और विधायकों पर भी लागू करने की बात काफी समय से की जा रही है, लेकिन अभी तक संभव नहीं हुआ है। कई विकसित देशों और विकासशील देशों में चुने गए प्रतिनिधियों को वापस बुलाने का अधिकार हैं। *व्लादीमीर लेनिन* के अनुसार "कोई भी चुनी गई संस्था या प्रतिनिधि सभा तब तक सही मायने में लोकतांत्रिक और लोगों का प्रतिनिधि करने वाली नहीं मानी जा सकती है जब तक कि मतदाता के पास चुनकर भेजने वालों को वापस बुलाने का अधिकार न हो।"

देश में वापस बुलाने मध्य प्रदेश में पंचायत स्तर पर, छत्तीसगढ़ में नगर निकाय स्तर पर लागू है, जबकि महाराष्ट्र में कानून बना पर लागू नहीं हो सका है। छत्तीसगढ़ नगर पालिका एक्ट 1961 के सेक्शन 47 में स्थानीय निकाय के सदस्यों को घटिया प्रदर्शन करने का वापस बुलाने का प्रावधान है। अमेरिका में 18 राज्यों में जनप्रतिनिधियों को वापस बुलाये जाने के लिए चुनाव कराने का प्रावधान हैं, 1921 में उत्तरी डाकोटा के गवर्नर लिन फ्रेजियर को पद से वापस बुलाया गया जबकि 2003 में कैलीफोर्निया के गवर्नर ग्रे डेविस को राज्य के बजट की अव्यवस्था के

चलते इसी प्रक्रिया द्वारा हटाया गया। कनाडा में जनप्रतिनिधियों को अनुशासन में रहने के लिए वापस बुलाने के अधिकार का प्रभावकारी प्रयोग किया जाता है। 1995 में ब्रिटिश कोलंबिया में इस कानून को अमल में लाया गया। इस क्षेत्र में मतदाता याचिका द्वारा वर्तमान जनप्रतिनिधि को हटाने की मांग कर सकते है। वेनेजुएला के 1999 के संविधान में राष्ट्रपति सहित किसी भी चुने गये जनप्रतिनिधि को वापस बुलाने का प्रावधान है। यहाँ के संविधान की धारा 72 के अनुसार पॉपुलर मतों द्वारा प्राप्त किए गए किसी भी पद को निरस्त किया जा सकता है। किसी भी जनप्रतिनिधि का आधा कार्यकाल बीत जाने के बाद उस चुनाव क्षेत्र के 20 फीसदी पंजीकृत मतदाता याचिका द्वारा फिर से चुनाव करा सकते हैं। स्विटजरलैंड में आधुनिक प्रत्यक्ष लोकतंत्र का सबसे सशक्त उदाहरण हैं, यहां पर स्थानीय और केंद्र दोनों स्तरों पर फिर से चुनाव कराने की व्यवस्था है। यहां के नागरिकों या नागरिकों कें समूहों द्वारा हस्ताक्षरित याचिका मतदाताओं के सामने स्वीकार या अस्वीकार करने के लिए रखी जाती है, हालांकि इस प्रक्रिया का ज्यादा प्रयोग यहाँ नही किया जाता है।

चुनाव प्रक्रिया में पारदर्शिता

प्रजातन्त्र में सुधार करने के लिए चुनाव प्रक्रिया को और अधिक पारदर्शी बनाना होगा, इसी दिशा में चुनाव आयोग ने कुछ राज्यों में फोटों मतदान लिस्ट जारी कर एवं ई. वी. एम. सम्बन्धी शिकायतों के निवारण हेतु पर्ची प्रणाली को अपनाकर पहल की है, जो पर्याप्त नहीं है, अभी और अधिक सुधार की जरूरत है। जिससे मतदान प्रक्रिया को पारदर्शी बनाया जा सके, सूचना के अधिकार जैसे नियमों को अधिक कारगार बनाने की जरूरत है जिससे लालफीताशाही व भ्रष्टाचार जैसी समसामायिक समस्याओं पर अंकुश लगाया जा सके। इस व्यवस्था में सुधार हेतु नागरिक समाज का सहयोग आपेक्षित हैं।

दलीय व्यवस्था

भारत में लोगों को अपनी सरकार पर अत्यधिक भरोसा है। भारत मे गरीब व आमजन भी मतदान के लिए समर्पित है, परन्तु जागरूकता के अभाव में वे उनके सही हितैशियों का चयन नही कर पा रहे हैं। चुनावों मे लगभग 63 प्रतिशत वोटिंग होती है, जो कि अमेरिका की तुलना में अधिक है। लेकिन आमजन जातीय समीकरण व अन्य मुद्दों में बन्द चुका है। साथ ही बहुदलीय शासन व्यवस्था के कारण भारतीय संसदीय प्रजातन्त्र में 20 से 22 प्रतिशत मत प्राप्त करने वाला दल सत्ता पर काबिज हो जाता है, इसमें सुधार के लिए भारतीय संसदीय प्रजातन्त्र को द्विदलीय प्रजातान्त्रिक व्यवस्था को अपनाना चाहिए। वर्तमान निर्वाचन व्यवस्था का अर्थ है कि जिस भी उम्मीदवार को सबसे अधिक मत मिले उसे चुना हुआ माना जाता है, लेकिन यह जरूरी नही कि उसे बहुमत का समर्थन मिला ही हो। वर्तमान में इतने पंजीकृत दल है, इतने प्रत्याशी हैं, वहां कोई प्रत्याशी 15 से 20 प्रतिशत मत पाकर भी विजयी हो जाता है। संविधान आयोग में ने 2002 में एक अध्ययन किया, जिसमें लोकसभा के तीन और विधानसभा के तीन चुनावों के अध्ययन किए गए थे। तब नतीजा यह निकला कि जो लोग जीतकर आते है उनमें से 70 प्रतिशत लोग ऐसे हैं, जिनके विरोध में मत अधिक है, पक्ष में कम। ऐसे लोग भी जनता के प्रतिनिधि बनकर सामने आ रहे हैं, तो अब जब 70 प्रतिशत लोग जिसके खिलाफ हैं वह भी जीत रहे हैं, ऐसे कैसे इस प्रक्रिया को प्रजातांत्रिक प्रक्रिया कह सकते हैं, प्रत्याशी वोट बैंक बनाते हैं। आंकड़े बताते है कि जिस निर्वाचन में 15 प्रतिशत लोग एक ही जाति-बिरादरी के हो वहां कोई भी उम्मीदवार वह इसी बात पर केंद्रित होकर चुनाव लड़ता है, उसे किसी और मुद्दे की जरूरत ही नहीं होती है।

राजनीतिक गठबंधन

वर्तमान में एक अन्य चुनौती यह है कि अगर विभिन्न राजनीतिक

दलों के बीच कोई राजनीतिक गठबंधन बने तो वह चुनाव के पहले बने या चुनाव के बाद। अगर चुनाव के पूर्व कुछ दलों के बीच चुनावी गठबंधन बनता है तो सामाजिक और राजनीतिक, दोनों ही स्तरों पर इसका औचित्य नजर आता हैं। ऐसे हालात में सामान्यतः यह संदेश जाता है कि विभिन्न दल एकसमान कार्यक्रम और समझ के साथ जनता के सामने जा रहे हैं तब वह इसी आधार पर अलग-अलग रहते है, चुनाव प्रचार के दौरान एक-दूसरें से भिड़ते है, आरोप-प्रत्यारोप की राजनीति करते है, चुनाव के बाद एक-दूसरें के साथ आते हैं तो दल जनता के साथ धोखाधड़ी करते है। छोटे दल चुनाव के बाद फिर उसी दल से समझौता कर लेते है जिसकी कल तक आलोचना कर रहे थे तो इसका सीधा-अर्थ है कि उस दल ने जनता को गुमराह किया है। चुनाव के बाद जो भी गठबंधन बनते है, उनके पीछे उनका उद्देश्य जन सेवा नहीं, बल्कि सत्ता के प्रति आकर्षण होता है जिसके तहत दल अपने सिद्धांतों से समझौता कर लेता है । "ऐसे में चुनाव के बाद गठबंधन बनाना सिर्फ सत्तालोलुपता की निशानी है और यह जनता के साथ छलावा है। हमारी व्यवस्था में एक बहुत ही दुर्भाग्यपूर्ण बात यह है कि जिन्हें निर्वाचक कहा जाता है, उनकी उम्मीदवार के चयन में कोई भूमिका ही नहीं होती। यदि इस दिशा में प्रावधान किए जाएं तो निगेटिव वोटिंग और इस तरह के दूसरे चुनाव सुधार के कार्यक्रमों की जरूरत ही नहीं पड़ेगी।"[11] इसके लिए ऐसा प्रावधान हो कि पार्टी अपना उम्मीदवार चुनने से पहले संबंधित उम्मीदवार के निर्वाचन क्षेत्र में पब्लिक मीटिंग कर प्रत्याशी अपनी बात रखें। लेकिन वर्तमान में वास्तकिता यह है कि पार्टी को ही पता नहीं होता कि उसका प्रत्याशी कैसा है, फिर जनता को कैसे मालूम होगा। "संविधान आयोग ने इस बाहर में कुछ सुझाव दिए है। पहला तो यह है कि किसी भी प्रत्याशी के चुनाव जीतने के लिए यह सुनिश्चित किया जाए कि उसे कुल मतों के 50 प्रतिशत से अधिक मत मिले हों। अगर किसी को 51 प्रतिशत मत न मिले हों तो जो पहले दो उम्मीदवार हों उनकें बीच चुनाव कराया जाए।

शुरूआत में तो इसमें दिक्कतें आएंगी, लेकिन जब एक बाहर ऐसी व्यवस्था लागू हो जाएगी तो यह लोगों के हित में ही होगा।''[12]

आदर्श आचार संहिता

चुनाव सुधारों को लागू करने के साथ-साथ हमें आदर्श आचार संहिता को कानूनी रूप देना होगा। चुनाव का जो खर्च हो, वह सभी राज्यों की सरकारें वहन करें एवं मतदान को मौलिक कर्तव्य बनाने के साथ-साथ अनिवार्य भी बनाया जाए, वर्तमान व्यवस्था में मतदान के अधिकार के साथ-साथ मतदान न करने का अधिकार भी शामिल है। यह व्यवस्था खत्म की जानी चाहिए। मतदान के बाद एक कार्ड दिया जाए और उसकी उपयोगिता सुनिश्चित की जाये, ड्राइविंग लाइसेंस, राशन कार्ड, पासपोर्ट आदि बनवाते समय यह कार्ड दिखाना अनिवार्य किया जाए। इस कार्ड के माध्यम से आयकर में कुछ छूट भी दी जा सकती है।

संसदीय व्यवस्था में मंत्री लोक सेवक संबध

ऐतिहासिक रुप से राजनीतिक मंत्री अपने वर्तमान स्वरुप मे 1921 मे प्रकट हुआ जब मॉटेस्क्यू चेन्सफोर्ड ने दोहरे की व्यवस्था कायम की उस समय सामान्यता स्थाई प्रशासक (सचिव) व राजनीतिक स्वामियों की सेवा करने की अपनी भूमिका के साथ समायोजित की कोशिश की। 1935 मे भारत शासन अधिनियम से प्रांतीय स्वायत्ता स्थापित की जिसके तहत प्रांतो में पूर्ण उत्तरदायी शासन प्रदान किया गया। इसके साथ ही सचिव व मंत्री के बीच संबंधों को प्रश्न भी महत्वपूर्ण होता चला गया। इसी क्रम मे समय-समय पर संबंधों मे सुधार हेतु प्रयत्न किये जाते रहे लेकिन स्वतंत्रता के 69 वर्ष पश्चात भी मंत्री व लोक सेवको के बीच स्वस्थ संबंधों का विकास नही हो पाया है भारत मे अनेक राजनीतिज्ञों ने मंत्री पद धारण करते हुये लोक सेवा की कार्यप्रणाली पर टिप्पणियां की है।

भारतीय संसदीय प्रणाली मे सरकार मे कार्यपालिका के दोनों स्वरुप राजनीतिक कार्यकारी व स्थाई कार्यकारी स्वरूपों को स्वीकार किया गया है राजनीतिक कार्यकारी की शैली में मंत्री तथा दूसरी स्थाई कार्यकारी मे लोक सेवक आते है। भारतीय संसदीय प्रणाली जनता की प्रभुसत्ता सिद्धान्त पर आधारित है इसलिये राजनीतिक कार्यपालिका के अधीन स्थाई कार्यपालिका को रखा गया है। इस संदर्भ मे मोहित भट्टाचार्य ने ठीक कहा है कि ''संसदीय प्रणाली में मंत्री की सर्वोच्यता एवं सचिव की अधीनस्था स्वतः सिद्ध है।'' संसदीय में सुचारु ओर कार्य कुशल निष्पादन के लिये मंत्री एवं लोक सेवक के मध्य प्रभावी संबंध होना आवश्यक व सरकार के स्वरुप कार्य संचालन मे दोनों एक दूसरे के पूरक हो। सामान्यतः अच्छे संबंधों के तीन महत्वपूर्ण बिन्दू है।

- मंत्री एवं लोक सेवकों को अपने कर्तव्यो को निभाते समय संवैधानिक प्रवधानों और संसदीय कानूनों का अनुपालन करना चाहिए।
- लोक संदशों को मंत्रियों (सरकार) की नीतियों ओर निर्णयों को पूर्ण निष्ठा से कार्यान्वित करना चाहिये इन्हे यह नही सोचना चाहिए कि नीतियाँ उनके परामर्श से अलग है।
- लोक सेवकों को तटस्थता, अनामिकिता व निष्पक्षता के सिद्धांतो का पालन करना चाहिए गैर राजनीतिक होना चाहिये तथा बिना भेद भाव के कार्य करना चाहिए।

मत भेद के सामान्य कारण

व्यवहार मे ऐसे कई प्रकरण है यह दर्शाते है कि मंत्री लोक सेवक संबंध अच्छे नही रहे है।[13]

- सामन्यता मंत्री लोक सेवको स्पष्ट व निष्पक्ष सलाह को प्रोत्साहित नही करते। जिससे दोनों में मध्य पर स्थिर समझ ओर सहयोग की भावना विकसित नहीं हो पाती।

- मंत्रियों एव लोक सेवकों में दलीय प्रतिवद्धिता, जातीवाद व गुटवाजी की स्थिति भी संबंधों को सही स्वरुप में विकसित नही होने देती।
- मंत्रियों द्वारा प्रशासक के दैनिक कार्यों में हस्तक्षेप करना व लोक सेवकों द्वारा महत्वपूर्ण मामलो को मंत्रियों की जानकारी में न लाना भी सबंधों में मतभेद का कारण है।

भारतीय लोकसेवा राजनीतिक दबाव से ऊपर नही उठ पा रही है। इस वजह से इसका तस्टस्थ स्वरूप नहीं रह गया है। जो इससे आपेक्षित था राजनीतिक लोक सेवकों सत्ता का प्रभाव दिखाकर उन्हे अपनी मर्जी से चलाना चाहते है तो लोक सेवक ऐसा नही करते है उन पर प्रत्यक्ष या परोस रुप से दबाव बनाया जाता है जिससे लोक सेवकों की प्रशासनिक क्षमता में ह्यास होता है कार्यशैली मे निष्पक्षता और पारदर्शिता नही रह जाती राजनेताओं की अवेलहना करने वाले अधिकारियों महत्वहीन पदों पर स्थानातरित कर दिया जाता है। जिसके भय से अनेक पदलोलुप स्वार्थ अधिकारियों की प्रतिबद्धता राष्ट्र के प्रति न रहकर राजनीतिज्ञों के प्रति हो जाती है। शासन में ऐसी व्यवस्था अस्तित्व में आने पर आलोचना अधिक होती है लेकिन राजनीतिक संरक्षण के चलते लोकसेवक राजनीतिक गठजोड़ बना रहता है जिससें शासन मे विक्रतियां बढ़ती जाती है। इस सन्दर्भ में वोरा समिति का कथन उल्लेखनीय है ''जहां माफियां तत्व एवं नक्सली संगठन समानांतर सरकार चलाते है उसमे कुछ नौकरशाहों/राजनीतिज्ञों की मिली भगत होती है। इसलिए अपराधी तत्त्वों व नक्सलियो की हिम्मत बढ़ती जा रही है। समसामयिक परिपेक्ष्य में मथुरा (उ.प्र.) की घटना इससे प्रेरित प्रतीत होती है।

प्रशासनिक सुधार आयोग के सुझाव[14]

प्रशासनिक सुधार आयोग द्वारा बेहद महत्वपूर्ण सुझाव दिये गये।

- जिसमें कुछ ऐसे मामलों मे जहां सरकार की नीति मे स्पष्ट न

हो किसी विषय पर मंत्री व सचिव में मतभेद हो वहा निर्णय का संक्षेप रूप मे लिखित उल्लेख होना चाहिए।

- लोक सेवकों द्वारा गंभीर चूक व कुशासन के मामलों को छोड़कर मंत्रियों को रोजमर्रा के कार्यों में हस्तक्षेप नही मंत्रियों नही करना चाहिए।
- सचिवों व लोक सेवकों को भी मंत्रियों की कठिनाईयों के प्रति अधिक संवेदनशील रहकर समझना चाहिए तथा उनके प्रति जागरुकता दिखनी चाहिए।
- मंत्रियों को वरिष्ठ अधिकारियों के मध्य निड़रता तथा न्याय का वातावरण विकसित करना चाहिए तथा उन्हे निष्पक्ष परामर्श देने के लिए प्रोत्साहित करना चाहिए सचिव का मंत्री के प्रति सरकारी सम्बन्ध निष्ठा तथा मंत्री सचिव का विश्वास होना चाहिए।

चुनौतियाँ व सम्भावनाएँ

वर्तमान में राज्य व्यवस्थाओं में प्रजातन्त्र का मुख्य लक्ष्य सुरक्षा, न्याय, समानता, स्वतन्त्रता व लोक कल्याण जैसे आदर्श मूल्यों की स्थापना करना है। 21वीं शताब्दी में प्रजातन्त्र का मुख्य लक्ष्य लोककल्याण बन गया है, क्योंकि इसी में अन्य सभी आदर्श मूल्य भी समाहित हैं। विभिन्न विद्वानों द्वारा प्रजातन्त्र को मूलतः एक भावनात्मक एवं मूल्यात्मक अवधारणा के रूप में परिभाषित किया जाता रहा है, लेकिन प्रजातन्त्र एक ऐसी संवेदनशील प्रशासनिक पद्धति, यंत्रा या निष्पादक अंग है जो प्रशासन में जनता की भागीदारी की प्रकृति के आधार पर निर्धारित होता है। ''प्रजातन्त्र का यह दर्शन न केवल बहुमत के शासन को स्वीकारता है, बल्कि उस प्रकार की केन्द्रीय व्यवस्था को नहीं अपनाता, जिससे सत्ता शक्ति लोगों द्वारा प्राप्त न हो, अतः वास्तव में लोकतान्त्रिक प्रक्रिया निचले स्तर से

शुरू होनी चाहिए।''[15] वर्तमान में विचारात्मक विभिन्नताओं की आंधी में विकासशील नवोदित देशों के लिए प्रजातन्त्र को परिशुद्ध एवं सूक्ष्म रूप को समझने की आवश्यकता है। ''सरटोरी नामक विद्वान ने इस अवस्था के कारण वर्तमान अवस्था को प्रजातान्त्रिक भ्रान्ति का युग कहा तथा बताया कि उससे उन्मुक्त होने की आवश्यकता है''[16] अर्थात् सरटोरी का कहना है कि वर्तमान में सभी देशों में प्रजातन्त्र के मूलभूत सिद्धान्तों को लागू किया जाना चाहिए तथा जो विचारधारा जिस देश की परिस्थतियों के अनुसार उपयुक्त हो उसे अपनाना चाहिए।

भारतीय संसदीय प्रजातन्त्र में दो संयुक्त गठबन्धनों का अस्तित्व है, जिनमें कोई भी बहुमत के आधार पर क्षेत्रीय दलों के साथ मिलकर शासन चला सकता है। यह स्थिति वास्तव में जातिवादी राजनीति के अस्तित्व मे आने से एवं क्षेत्रीय पार्टियों के उभरते सशक्त स्वरूप के कारण बनी है। पन्द्रहवीं लोकसभा में भी यही स्थिति बनी है। भारतीय संसदीय लोकतन्त्र को सशक्त स्वरूप प्रदान करने के लिए राजनीतिक दलों निजी हितों से ऊपर उठकर राष्ट्र विकास एवं राष्ट्रीय हितों के बारे में सोचना चाहिए और शासन के संचालन में सहभागिता प्रणाली को अपनाना चाहिए। ''भारतीय प्रजातन्त्र को सुदृढ़ आधार प्रदान करने हेतु वर्तमान परिप्रेक्ष्य में जरूरत इस बात की है कि लोकतान्त्रिक विकेन्द्रीकरण के सन्दर्भ मे जो संस्थाएँ स्थापित की गयी है, उन्हें शक्तिशाली बनाया जाए। इससे भारतीय लोकतन्त्र की जड़ें सुदृढ़ हो सकती हैं।''[17] उपयुक्त सुधारों के साथ-साथ वर्तमान भारतीय परिवेश में लोकतंत्र को सुदृढ़ आधार प्रदान करने हेतु संरचनात्मक, प्रक्रियात्मक, व्यवहारात्मक सुधारों की आवश्यकता है, जिसमें नागरिक समाज को महत्वपूर्ण भूमिका का निर्वहन करना होगा, जिसके माध्यम से भारत में गुणात्मक प्रजातन्त्र की स्थापना की जा सके।

समसामयिक परिप्रेक्ष्य में लोक सेवा का स्वरूप जनहित के मुद्दों के प्रति संरक्षणात्मक प्रकृति अपनाने के कारण चर्चा में आया है। जिससे जन

समस्याओं के निपटारे एवं जनहित के मुद्दों के प्रति सरकारों का रूझान बढ़ा है। समसामयिक परिप्रेक्ष्य में प्रशासनिक पारदर्शिता (ई. प्रौद्योगिकी का उपयोग) नागरिक सक्रियता तथा लोकतंत्रीकरण वंचित वर्ग का कल्याण आदि मुख्य मुद्दों चर्चा में है वैश्वीकरण के कारण राज्य की प्रकृति में बदलाव के साथ-साथ लोक सेवा की प्रकृति में भी बदलाव अया है। अतः समसामयिक परिप्रेक्ष्य में यह कहा जा सकता है कि लोक सेवा प्रजातांत्रिक व्यवस्था को सुदृण करने हेतु आवश्यक है क्योंकि वैश्वीकरण के दौर में पूंजीवाद स्वस्थ प्रतियोगिता अपनाकर उदारवादी सोच के साथ सभी राष्ट्रो का विकास का मार्ग प्रशस्त कर रहा है तब लोक सेवा का दायित्व इस बात को लेकर अधिक बढ़ जाता है इसके साथ ही समसामयिक परिप्रेक्ष्य में UNDP, UNFEM, UNV आदि संस्थाओं ने वैश्विक अभिशासन तेज को सह संबंधित करने का प्रयास किया है।[18] वर्तमान में विकासशील देशों में ऐसा वातावरण बनाने की आवश्यकता है जिससे निजी क्षेत्र भी सामाजिक उत्तरदायित्व के साथ कार्य करें।

सामान्यतः विभिन्न लोक प्रशासन के विद्वान यह मानते है कि 1988 के द्वितीय मिन्नोवुक सम्मेलन के बाद लोक सेवा के महत्व में बढ़ोत्तरी हुई है तथा लोक सेवा लोकतांत्रिक संरचना को सशक्त करने के सन्दर्भ में महत्वपूर्ण रूप से सामने आया है जिसे समसामयिक परिप्रेक्ष्य की घटनाओं से समझा जा सकता है। समसामायिक परिपेक्ष्य मे स्वच्छ व सुद्रण प्रशासन हेतु सुधार व परिवर्तन की प्रक्रिया राजनीति व प्रशासन दोनों स्तर पर की जानी चाहिए। भारतीय लोकसेवा उचित लक्ष्य एवं जन अपेक्षाओं के साथ लोगों के प्रति सेवा प्रतिवद्धता सुनिश्चित कर जवाबदेय व पारदर्शी प्रशासन संभव बनाती है तो भारत में आर्थिक व अच्छे अभिशासन की अवधारणा को व्यवाहरिता प्रदान करना संभव हो सकेगा।[19]

लोक सेवकों को व्यवसायिक आचरण के मानदंडों का अनुपालन करना चाहिए। ऐसा करने से न केवल बेहतर शासन की कार्यसूची को

प्रमुख्यता मिलती है बल्कि देश की वृद्धि व समृधि के लिए एक फ्रेम के रूप में सम्मानित अखिल भारतीय सेवा की प्रतिष्ठा बढ़ाने में मदद मिलती है।[20] प्रशासनिक पादरर्शिता व जवाबदेहता के संन्दर्भ मे बदल रहे चिन्तन ने लोक सेवा मे नागरिक विश्वास को बनाये रखने के लिए नये सिरे से संरचना को संगठित करने का मार्ग प्रशस्त किया।''[21] लोक सेवा का प्रभावी होना भी हमारी संसदीय व्यवस्था की विशेषता है, जिसका मुख्य कारण मंत्रियों का अपने राजनीतिक कार्यक्रमों में व्यस्त्ता है, जिससे उन्हें अपने विभाग के प्रशासनिक कार्यकलापों की गहन जानकारी नहीं होती। गठबंधन सरकारों में मंत्रीगण अपने स्थिति सुदृढ़ करने हेतु प्रयास करते रहते हैं, विभागीय कार्य अधिकारियों द्वारा अपने तरीके से सम्पादित किये जाते है और इस व्यवस्था में लोक सेवक उत्तरदायित्व से बच जाते हैं। इस व्यवस्था में सुंधार हेतु प्रयत्न करने होंगे।

भारत मे कॉरपोरेट अभिशासन के तत्वों को लोक सेवा से संबंध किया जाये भारतीय लोक सेवा में असीमित क्षमता है अतः यादि लोक सेवा को उचित ढंग से अभिप्रेरित किया जाये तो देश को दक्ष, कुशल व पारदर्शी प्रशासन मिलेगा। साथ ही भारत को आर्थिक महाशक्ति बनाया जा सकेगा जिसके लिये प्रशिक्षण व्यवस्था में भी वैज्ञानिकता व नवीनता लाने की आवश्यकता है साथ ही होता समिति[22] की 64 संसतुतियो पर विचार करने की आवश्यकता है। लोक सेवा में बहस उस चुनौती के संदर्भ में है जिसका संबंध तटस्तता के साथ प्रतिवद्धता के मुद्दे से है सकीर्ण मूल्यात्मक राजनीति में तटस्थ रहते हुये लोक सेवा को संविधान के प्रति प्रतिबंद्ध कर जनकल्याण के प्रति सकारात्मक सोच विकसित करने की चुनौती है।

भारतीय लोक सेवा के यदि सकारात्मक पक्षों पर पर विचार किया जाये तो यह स्पष्ट है लोक सेवा का सामाजिक न्याय व आर्थिक विकास में महत्वपूर्ण योगदान है। इस संदर्भ में द्वितीय प्रशासनिक सुधार आयोग ने

प्रशासन मे नैतिकता को बनाये रखे हुए देश में सामाजिक आर्थिक विकास को तीव्रता प्रदान करने का आवाहन किया। लोक सेवा की प्रसांगिकता को बनाये रखने के लिये उचित वातावरण मे प्रशिक्षण के कार्यक्रम राष्ट्रीय, राज्यकीय व स्थानीय स्तर पर बनाये जाने व प्रशिक्षण के तौर तरीको में सुधार हो।[23] 21 वीं सदी के वर्तमान दशक में प्रजातन्त्र को मानव विकास के लक्ष्य की प्राप्ति तथा चुनौतियों से निपटने हेतु विकास के नये आयामों जिनमें सतत् विकास, जनभागीदारी, एवं सशक्तिकरण आदि के साथ जोड़ने का प्रयास किया जा रहा है। संसदीय प्रजातन्त्र नई सदी की आवश्यताओं के सन्दर्भ में अपनी प्रासंगिकता को बनाये रखने हेतु अपनी प्रकृति में सकारात्मक बदलाव लाने का प्रयत्न कर रहा है। जिससे वास्तव में भारत में गुणात्मक लोकतंत्र की स्थापना की जा सके।

फूटनोट

1. एस.एल. वर्मा, उच्चतर आधुनिक राजनीतिक सिद्धान्त, नेशनल पब्लिशिंग हाउस, जयपुर, 2006, पृ. 218-19।
2. ए.पी.एस. चौहान एवं कमलेश गुप्ता, विकेन्द्रीकरण के उभरते प्रतिमान, एसोसिएटेड पब्लिशिंग हाउस, आगरा, 2009, पृ. 33।
3. वेजमीन बारबार "स्ट्राग्गं डेमोक्रेसी, पर्टिसिपेटरी पॉलिटिक्स फॉर ए न्यू ऐज," कैलीफोर्नियाँ यूनिवर्सिटी प्रेस, वर्कले, 1984, पृ. 11।
4. एस.एल. वर्मा एवं मधु मिश्रा, महात्मा गाँधी एवं धर्मनिरपेक्षता, राजस्थान हिन्दी ग्रन्थ अकादमी जयपुर, 1999, पृ. 36।
5. अशोक दुबे, 21वीं सदी लोक प्रशासन, टाटा मेक्ग्राहिल, नई दिल्ली, पृ. 282-310।
6. सुभाष कश्यप, दिनमान, दिसम्बर 6, 1970, पृ. 6-7।
7. सुनील शाह, क्या हम वाकई मजबूत लोकतंत्र है? अमर उजाला (इलाहाबाद), मई, 1, 2008।
8. अभय कुमार दुबे, तक्षकों के हाथ में हमारा लोकतंत्र, अमर उजाला, नवम्बर 13, 2009।
9. अभय कुमार दुबे, भाजपा ही नहीं, बदहाल है पूरा विपक्ष, अमर उजाला, अक्टूबर 28, 2009।

10. रजनी कोठारी, भारत में राजनीति, टिलकी हिन्दी ग्रंथ अकादमी प्रकाशन पृ. 174।
11. सुभाष कश्यप, दोषपूर्ण चुनावी प्रक्रिया, जागरण (इलाहाबाद) अप्रैल 9, 2009।
12. सुभाष कश्यप, दोषपूर्ण चुनावी प्रक्रिया, जागरण (इलाहाबाद) अप्रैल 9, 2009।
13. मोहित भट्टाचार्य, रिकन्सट्रक्सन ऑफ पब्लिक एडमिनिस्ट्रेसन, जवाहर पब्लिकेशन हाऊस, नई दिल्ली, 2008 प्र.।
14. प्रथम प्रशानिक सुधार आयोग की सिफारिसे, भारत सरकार।
15. राजकुमारी सुरणा, भारत मे लोकतन्त्रिक विकेन्द्रीकरण व नवपंचायती राज, राज पब्लिशिंग हाउस, जयपुर, 2000 पृ. 41।
16. एस.एल. वर्मा, उच्चतर आधुनिक राजनीतिक सिद्धान्त, नेशनल पब्लिशिंग हाउस, जयपुर, 2006, पृ. 720-21।
17. रमेश दुबे, हरीशचन्द्र शर्मा, भारत में लोक प्रशासन, कॉलेज बुक डिपों जयपुर, 1996 पृ. 485-86।
18. नीरा चंदोक, स्टेट एण्ड सिविल सोसाइटी 'एक्सप्लोरेशन इन पॉलिटिकल थ्योरी, सेज पब्लिकेशन, नई दिल्ली, 1995, पृ. 107-112।
19. सोफी अली, रिविल्डिंग सिविल सर्विस कैसफोर ह्यूमन डवलपमेन्ट सर्विस ए कोन्सेप्चयुल फ्रेमवर्क, आई.जे.पी.ऐ., बॉ. 50, अप्रैल-जून 2004, पृ. 449-63।
20. बी.के. चर्तुवेदी, शासन में नौकरशाही व राजनीतिज्ञों के संबंध, योजना, मार्च 2014, पृ. 6-9।
21. एस.के. दास, सिविल सर्विस रिफोर्म एण्ड स्टक्चरल एडजस्ट मेंट, ऑक्सपोर्ट यूनिवर्सिटी प्रेस, नई दिल्ली, 1998।
22. पीसी. होता, एक्सीलेन्स इन पब्लिक सर्विस, आई.जे.पी.ऐ., बॉ. 52, नं. 3, जुलाई-सितम्बर 2006, पृ. 399-342।
23. द्वितीय प्रशासनिक सुधार आयोग का प्रतिवेदन, भाग-2, भारत सरकार, नई दिल्ली।

17

प्रशासन में मन्त्री सचिव सम्बन्धः भारत में एक अध्ययन

– *रीना सिंह*

सारांश

लोक प्रशासन जनता की सेवा करने वाला प्रशासन है। लोक प्रशासन राज्य का एक यन्त्र है, जो विद्यायिका और कार्यपालिका की नीतियों और निर्णयों को लागू करने का काम करता है। इस लेख में मन्त्री और सचिव के कार्यात्मक सम्बन्धों पर ध्यान केन्द्रित किया गया है। एक मन्त्री की सफलता उसके सचिव पर निर्भर करती है। क्योंकि सचिव व्यक्तिगत और व्यावसायिक तौर पर योग्य व्यक्ति होता है। उसे प्रशासन सम्बन्धी प्रशिक्षण प्राप्त होता है। इसके विपरीत मन्त्रीगण प्रशासनिक मामलों के विशेषज्ञ नही होते और उन्हें प्रशासन सम्बन्धी बारिकीयों का ज्ञान नही होता है। सिडनी लौ ने कहा है। *''वित्त मंत्रालय में द्वितीय श्रेणी के लिपिक का पद प्राप्त करने के लिए एक नवयुवक को अंकगणित की परीक्षा में अवश्य उत्तीर्ण होना पड़ेगा, पर वित्त मन्त्री अधेड़ उम्र का एक ऐसा सांसारिक व्यक्ति भी हो सकता है, जो अंक के विषय में अपनी उस थोड़ी बहुत जानकारी को भी भूल चुका हो जो उसने ईरान अथवा ऑक्सफोर्ड में प्राप्त*

की हो और दशमलव में लगाए गए खजाने के हिसाब को उसके सामने रखे जानें पर अंजान की तरह उन अंकों का मतलब जानने के लिए उत्सुक हों'' यदि कोई मन्त्री अपनी सचिव की सलाह नही मानता तो यह उसकी सबसे बड़ी गलती होती है। लोकतन्त्र में राजनीतिक (मन्त्री) और सचिव दोनो एक दूसरे से एक कड़ी की भांति बंधे हैं इस लेख में मन्त्री और सचिव के राजनीति, आर्थिक और सामाजिक सम्बंधों का अवलोकन किया गया है। और उनके सम्बन्ध प्रशासन में किस प्रकार के होते हैं, यह प्रदर्शित करने का प्रयास किया गया है।

क्योंकि लोकतन्त्र में मंत्री एवं सचिव दोनों से एक टीम वर्क की अपेक्षा की जाती है। एक तरफ जहाँ मन्त्री से अपने स्वार्थ हित से कार्य करने की अपेक्षा की जाती है, वहीं प्रशासनिक अधिकारियों से यह आशा की जाती है, कि वह अपना कार्य भय एवं पक्षपातरहित होकर करेंगें। प्रशासन का पहला सिद्धान्त यही हैं कि सचिव अपने पद पर सकारात्मक निर्णयों को लेने एवं लोक हित में परियोजनाओं को कार्यान्वित करने हेतु बिना किसी राजनीतिक दबाव के स्वतन्त्र हैं। वह अपने पद पर सुरक्षित हैं ''किसी की इच्छा पर उन्हें सेवाओं से पृथक नही किया जा सकता''।

परिचयः-हमारी संसदीय शासन-प्रणाली एवं प्रशासनिक व्यवस्था दोनो ही ब्रिटिश शासन की देन हैं, इस व्यवस्था में शक्तियां मुख्य रूप से मन्त्री में निहित होती हैं। मन्त्री पर संसद का नियन्त्रण रहता है। मन्त्री अपने प्रशासनिक कार्यो के लिए प्रत्यक्ष रूप से संसद के प्रति उत्तरदायी रहते है। मन्त्री द्वारा अपने दल के उद्देश्यों तथा व्यापक सामाजिक परिपेक्ष्य में नीति का निर्माण संसद की स्वीकृति से किया जाता है। तथा उसका क्रियान्वयन लोक सेवकों को सौंप दिया जाता है। सरकार के कार्य संचालन में मन्त्री और सचिव महत्वपूर्ण भूमिका निभाते हैं।

प्रेस्थस के अनुसार, *''लोकतन्त्र में नौकरशाही निर्वाचित व्यवस्थापकों के बृहत निर्देशन में कार्य करती है, जिसके लिए कि मुख्य कार्यकारी*

प्रमुख रूप से विद्यायिका के प्रति उत्तरदायी होता है। परन्तु नीति निर्माण के विशिष्ट कार्य में लोक सेवक महत्वपूर्ण भूमिका निभाते है।''

मन्त्रीमण्डल राजनीतिक कार्यपालिका है। और मन्त्री लोग विभिन्न विभागों के प्रशासनिक प्रधान है। तथ्य यह है। कि *''मन्त्री लोग अपने अपने विभागों की साधारण नीति निर्धारित करते है। और विभाग के वास्तविक प्रशासक उच्च प्रबन्धक होते है।''* विभिन्न विभागों का काम चलाने के लिए अध्यक्ष मन्त्री लोग होते है। मन्त्रियों की सहायता के लिए अनेक स्थायी पदाधिकारी होते है।

मन्त्री सचिव के बीच सम्बन्ध

सचिव एक प्रशासनिक प्रमुख-प्रमुख होता है। उसका पद स्थायी और कार्यकाल निश्चित होता है। चाहे सरकार किसी भी राजनीतिक दल की हो। यह व्यवस्था सरकार को सन्तुलित बनाये रखने के लिए की गई है। लोकतन्त्र मे मन्त्री और सचिव दोनों ही महत्वपूर्ण है। मन्त्री का पद अस्थायी होता है। क्योंकि वो एक राजनीतिक व्यक्ति होता है। अपने मंत्रालय का राजनीतिक प्रमुख होता है। मन्त्री पर संसद का नियन्त्रण रहता है। मन्त्री अपने कार्यों के लिए प्रत्यक्ष रूप से संसद के प्रति उत्तरदायी होता है। और उसके इस कार्य में सचिव सहायता करता है।

इस प्रकार सचिव प्रशासन में निम्न प्रकार से भूमिका निभाते है।

नीति सलाहकार के रूप में: सचिव प्रशासनिक नितियों से सम्बन्धित मुद्दों पर मन्त्रियों को सलाह देता है। और उनके क्रियान्वयन के लिए विकल्प उपलब्ध कराता है। सचिव नीति से सम्बन्धित सभी तकनीकी, प्रबन्धकीय विधिक और वित्तीय पहलुओं पर मन्त्रियों को सलाह देता है। नीति निर्माण में यह महत्वपूर्ण है कि मन्त्रीगण इन मुद्दों पर दी गई सलाह को समझने का प्रयास करें। मन्त्री नीति निमार्ण के उद्देश्य को निश्चित करता है। और सचिव इन्हे प्राप्त करने के लिए एक यन्त्र का काम करता है।

विभाग के प्रमुख के रूप मे: सचिव अपने विभाग का प्रशासनिक प्रमुख होता है। उस विभाग की प्रशासनिक जिम्मेदारी उसी की होती है। मन्त्री विभाग का राजनीतिक प्रमुख होता है। जिसके कारण सचिव यह देखता है। कि विभाग राजनीतिक प्राथमिकताओं को निश्चित करें क्योकि राजनीतिक प्रमुख प्रशासन के कार्यो को प्रभावित करते है। एक ईमानदार लोकसेवक, एक सचिव अपने दायित्वों का सम्मान करता है। और राजनीतिक स्तर पर बैठे लोकतन्त्रात्मक सत्ता की नीतियों को पूरा करने का प्रयास करता है।

लोक सेवक के रूप में: सचिव लोक सेवक के रूप में भी अपनी भूमिका का निर्वाह करता है। लोक सेवक के रूप में वह निरन्तर सरकार के कुशलतापूर्वक संचालन में सहयोग करता है।

मन्त्रीगण की भूमिका: राजनीतिक एक, *"गैर-तर्कसगत साँचा"* है यह एक बदलाव और अनिश्चिकता का क्षेत्र है। प्रशासन में मंत्रियों की भूमिका इस प्रकार है-

नीतियों और व्यवस्था को विनिर्देष्ट करना: मन्त्री अपने विभाग की प्रशासनिक नीति बनाता है, प्रशासनिक ढाँचे का निर्धारण करता है। अपने विभाग के अधिकारी व कर्मचारियों की नियुक्ति, सेवास्थिति तथा अनुशासन की समस्याएं सुलझाता है। दैनिक प्रशासन पर परिवेक्षण करता है। समन्वय उसका विशेषाधिकार है। और संसदीय नियन्त्रण भी उसी माध्यम से संचालित होता है।

नौकरशाही पर प्रभाव बनाना: मन्त्री अपने राजनीतिक दल का एक प्रभावशाली नेता होता है। उसका नौकरशाह पर बहुत प्रभाव इस बात पर निर्भर होता है। कि वह कहां तक सुगठित है। उसकी विचार धारा विभिन्न विषयों पर कहा तक सुस्पष्ट है। तथा जनता के मध्य कितनी मान्यता है। यदि मन्त्रीमण्डल में सम्बद्ध मन्त्री की स्थिति प्रभावपूर्ण है। तथा उसके

पीछे राजनीतिक समर्थन विद्यमान है। तो वह अपने सचिव व अन्य विभागीय अधिकारीयों के समक्ष प्रभावशाली सिद्ध होगा।

उपरोक्त विवरण से स्पष्ट है कि मन्त्रियों को लोक सेवा के विशेषज्ञों से अनेक मामलों में परामर्श लेने पड़ता है। प्रशासन का तकनीकी पक्ष मन्त्रियों के समक्ष लोक सेवा के लोग ही प्रस्तुत करते है। मन्त्रीगण प्रत्येक कार्य को लोक सेवा के विशेषज्ञों से परामर्श लेकर करना ही अधिक अच्छा समझते है। समस्त आंकड़ों और सूचनाएं मन्त्रियों को लोक सेवक से ही मिलते है। अपनी आगामी योजनाओं को भूत से सम्बद्ध करने के लिए और उन्हे असफलता से बचाने के लिए मन्त्रियों को लोक सेवा के लोगो के परामर्श पर निर्भर रहना पड़ता है। मन्त्री नए होते है। और लोक सेवक अनुभव के कारण पुराने फलस्वरूप अनेक मन्त्रियों को लोक सेवको के प्रभाव में ही कार्यो करना पड़ता है।

डॉ. सी.पी. भाम्भरी ने अपने ग्रन्थ 'Bureaucracy and politics in India' मे लिखा है, 'political weak faction ridden cabinet proves a blessing for the I.C.S to thrive".

मन्त्री लोक सेवकों के सम्बन्ध को निर्धारित करने वाले तत्वः- मन्त्री और लोक सेवकों के सम्बन्धों पर अब तक हुए अध्ययनों के आधार पर जो तत्व उभरकर सामने आए है। वे ये दर्शाते है कि मन्त्री और लोक सेवक किन परिस्थितियों में शक्तिशाली है किन परिस्थितियों में शक्तिहीन है। तथा किन परिस्थितियों में एक दूसरे पर निर्भर करते है।

मन्त्री और लोक सेवक (सचिव) सम्बन्ध निम्न परिस्थितियों एवं कारकों पर निर्भर करते है।

राजनीतिक दल की प्रकृतिः राजनीतिक दल जैसे होगा नेता की स्थिति भी वैसी ही होगी। जनता मे उस दल की मान्यता कैसी है या विभिन्न दलो के सहयोग से सत्तारूढ़ है। या विधानमण्डल में स्पष्ट बहुमत है।

मन्त्रीमण्डल में स्थितिः यदि मन्त्रीमण्डल में सम्बद्ध मन्त्री की स्थिति प्रभावपूर्ण है तथा उसके पीछे राजनीतिक समर्थन विद्यमान है तो वह अपने सचिव के समक्ष प्रभावशाली सिद्ध होगा।

सामाजिक एवं आर्थिक कारकः- प्रायः मन्त्री तथा लोक सेवकों के मध्य मतभेद उनकी विभिन्न सामाजिक संस्कृतियों के कारण होते है।

लक्ष्य सम्बन्धी समरूपता का न होनाः मन्त्रियों तथा सचिवों के मध्य न तो लक्ष्यों की समरूपता होती है न ही वे एक दूसरे के प्रति सद्भाव रखते है, क्योकि प्रशासक समझते है। कि वे एक उच्च शिक्षा प्राप्त वर्ग के प्रतिनिधि है तथा वे ही समग्र राष्ट्रीय दृष्टिकोण तथा जनहित को समझते है। उनका सामाजिक, आर्थिक, सास्कृतिक एवं राजनीतिक स्तर उसके मन्त्री के साथ सम्बन्धों को निर्धारित करता है।

जातिवाद की भावनाः-जाति, धर्म, भाषा, विचार व पृष्ठभूमि सम्बन्धी एकता मन्त्री एवं प्रशासक के पारस्परिक सम्बन्धों को बड़ा प्रभावित करती है। भारतीय मन्त्री यह प्रयास करते है। कि किसी तरह वह अपने जानकार सचिव को अपने साथ लाए ताकि उन पर भरोसा किया जा सके। स्वयं सचिव के अपने उद्देश्य उसको प्रेरित करते है। और वह शीध्र पदोन्नतियां, सेवानिवृति के पश्चात् नियुक्तियों, आर्थिक लाभ, स्वजनों की नियुक्तियों आदि की दृष्टि से मन्त्री का अनुगामी बन जाए।

नीति-निमार्ण का स्तर तथा अभिकरणों का प्रकार 'राजनीतिज्ञ एवं लोक सेवकों के सम्बन्ध विभागीय, नीति या निर्णय निर्माण के स्तरों पर निर्भर करते है। उच्च स्तर पर उनके सम्बन्ध बराबरी और सहयोग मध्य स्तर पर आदेश अनुपालक तथा निम्न स्तर पर स्वामी सेवक जैसे होते है।

भारत में मन्त्री-सचिव सम्बन्धः कतिपय उल्लेखनीय मामलेः भारत में मन्त्री सचिव सम्बन्धों की शुरूआत सर्वप्रथम सन् 1921 से होती है जबकि 1919 के मॉण्टेग्यू चेम्सफोर्ड सुधार एक्ट के अन्तर्गत पहली

बार प्रान्तीय शासन में निर्वाचित मन्त्रियों का प्रावधान किया गया पहली बार भारत के प्रशासनिक इतिहास में "सचिव" को अपने अनिपुण मन्त्री के मातहत होकर कार्य करने की आदत डालनी पड़ी। यह एक नवीन प्रयोग था जिसमें मन्त्री–सचिव सम्बन्धों मे तनाव पैदा होना स्वभाविक था। सुधार जाँच समिति (1924) के समक्ष अनेक मन्त्रियों ने शिकायत की उन्हें अपने सचिव से पूर्ण सहयोग नही मिला।

सी. वाई, चिन्तामणि जो कि संयुक्त प्रान्त में शिक्षा मन्त्री थे इसलिए त्याग पत्र दे दिया कि उनके सचिव ने उपेक्षा करते हुए गवर्नर से सीधे सम्पर्क स्थापित कर लिया।

1935 के भारत शासन अधिनियम पारित होन के बाद प्रान्तों में उत्तरदायी शासन की स्थापना की ओर अन्मुख होने से मन्त्री सचिव सम्बन्ध और अधिक विवाद का विषय बन गया। मन्त्री विद्यानसभा के प्रति उत्तरदायी बनाए गए अतः सचिव से उनके नियन्त्रण में रहने की अपेक्षा करने लगे। मैक्सवेल समिति 1937 की धारणा थी कि विभाग का सचिव प्रशासनिक मुखिया है। जो कि मन्त्री के अधीन रहकर मन्त्री को परामर्श देगा। स्वाधीनता प्राप्ति के बाद भी मन्त्री सचिव सम्बन्धों को लेकर मामले प्रकाश में आते रहे है। पाकिस्तान में तत्कालिक भारतीय हाई कमिश्नर श्री प्रकाश ने अपने संस्मरणों मे लिखा है। कि उनके द्वारा लिए गए निर्णयों के क्रियान्वयन में उनका 'डिप्टी' जो कि आई.पी.एस. का सदस्य था, रोड़े अटकाता रहता था। जवाहर लाल नेहरू जैसे व्यक्ति ने भी अपने प्रारम्भिक दिनों में महसूस किया था कि सिविल सेवा के अधिकारी अपनी मर्जी से शासन चलाने की मंशा रखते थे न कि मन्त्रियों की मंशा से।

स्वतन्त्र भारत में मन्त्री सचिव सम्बन्धों की दृष्टि से निम्नलिखित मामले अत्यन्त रोचक एवं उल्लेखनीय है–

टी.टी. कृष्णामचारी बनाम एच.एम. पटेल विवाद– सन् 1957 में पहली बार मन्त्री सचिव विवाद साफ झलकने लगा।

टी.टी. कृष्णामचारी वित्तमन्त्री थे और एच.एच. पटेल वित्त सचिव दोनों में मतभेद का मुद्दा था राष्ट्रीयकृत जीवन बीमा निगम द्वारा निजी कम्पनियों के शेयर खरीदने से सम्बन्धित घटना थी कृष्णामचारी का कहना था कि वित्त सचिव पटेल ने केवल सरसरी तौर पर उन शेयर की खरीदारी की उनसे मौखिक चर्चा की थी। जबकि वित्त सचिव पटेल का कहना था कि उन्होने हमेशा मन्त्री स्वीकृति से और उनकी जानकारी से काम किया था। इस मामले में अलसी सवाल संवैधानिक उत्तर-दायित्व का हैं संसदीय दबाव के कारण उत्तरदायित्व के सिद्धान्त की पालना मे टी.टी. कृष्णामाचारी ने त्याग पत्र दे दिया और एच.एम. पटेल ने भी स्वेच्छा से अवकाश ग्रहण कर लिया, जबकि अन्त में उन्हे भी दोषमुक्त पाया गया था।

गुलजारी लाल नन्दा बनाम एल.पी. सिंह विवाद सन् 1966 में सामने आया। इसमे गृह मन्त्री तथा और सचिव उलझे हुए थे। और यह विवाद भारत मन्त्री सचिव सम्बन्धों के साथ-साथ उत्तरदायित्व लोक सेवक की सीमाओं आदि तथ्यों पर प्रकाश डालता है। गृह मन्त्री नन्दा ने प्रधान मन्त्री से शिकायत की कि गृह सचिव एल.पी. सिंह उन्हें आवश्यक सहयोग प्रदान नही कर रहे है अतः उन्हें हटा दिया जाए। नन्दा ने अपने पत्र में प्रधानमन्त्री को लिखा कि लोक सेवक से जैसी आशा की जाती है वैसा सहयोग व सहायता गृह सचिव से नही मिल रही है। नीति निर्धारण के स्तर पर निर्णय लेने में मेरी बात नही मानी जाती। क्या आपने (प्रधानमन्त्री) कभी सोचा कि आपके द्वारा दिए गए उपकरणों (सचिव) से में कैसे काम कर सकूंगा?

इस प्रकार की अनेक घटनाएं जैसे के हनुमन्तैया बनाम बी.सी. गागुली विवाद (1971) प्रधानमन्त्री राजीव गांधी और सी. श्रीनिवासी शास्त्री डॉ. बोद्यपाध्याप तथा ए.पी. वेंकटेश्वरन का मामला तथा राम जैठमलानी किरन अग्रवाल मतभेंद 1988 में तात्कालिक रोजगार एवं शहरी विकास

मन्त्री राम जेठमलानी ने अपने विभाग की सचिव किरन अग्रवाल से सभी दायित्व छीन कर विशेष सचिव एस.एस. चट्टोपाध्याय को सौप दिए।

उपरोक्त घटनाओं के अतिरिक्त आज भी वर्तमान भारत में हमें मन्त्री सचिव विवाद निरन्तर देखने को मिलते है। जो इस प्रकार है:-

मन्त्री ए. राजा बनाम डी.एस. माथुर विवाद: टेलीकॉम मंत्रालय के पूर्व सचिव डी.एस. माथुर के मुताबित मंत्री ए. राजा ने उन्हे मोबाइल कम्पनी को सस्ते में मोबाइल नेटवर्क बांटने के लिए लाइसेंस के लिए एप्लीकेशन देने का कट ऑफ डेट कुछ दिन पहले करने को कहा जिसके लिए उन्होंने मना कर दिया था। सचिव डी.एस. माथुर ने मन्त्री ए. राजा से कहा कि किसी पारदर्शी नीति के बगैर पहले आओ पहले पाओ नीति को लागू नही करना चाहिए और पूछा कि इस सिद्धान्त का अर्थ क्या है, लेकिन ए. राजा ने उनकी बात नही मानी। और दोनों में विवाद बढ़ा तथा एक दूसरे पर आरोप व प्रत्यारोप करने लगें।

मन्त्री गिरीश बापट सचिव दीपक कपूर विवाद: अन्न व नागरिक आपूर्ति मन्त्री गिरीश बापट और विभाग के सचिव दीपक कपूर के बीच टकराव ने प्रदेश में दाल का संकट बढ़ा दिया । इस मुद्दे पर बापट ने कपूर को पत्र लिखकर मौजूदा संकट के लिए जिम्मेदारी ठहराया ।

मन्त्री सचिव सम्बन्धी के इन मामलों से स्पष्ट होता है कि कि कुछ मामलो में सचिवों ने अपनी भूमिका सही ढ़ग से नही निभायी तथा कुछ मामलों मे मन्त्री विशेष ने अनावश्यक हस्तक्षेप किया।

निष्कर्ष

प्रशासन में मन्त्री सचिव सम्बन्धों तथा उनके विवादों का अवकोलन करने स्पष्ट होता है। कि मन्त्री और सचिव दोनों एक साथ एक टीम के रूप में काम नही कर पाते है क्योकि मन्त्री एक राजनीतिक व्यक्ति होता है और उसे जनता द्वारा चुना जाता है। और हमारे संविधान में मन्त्रियों की

योग्यता का भी निर्धारण नहीं किया है जिस वजह से अशिक्षित व्यक्ति भी मन्त्री बन जाते है। इसके विपरित एक सचिव या लोक सेवक प्रशासनिक प्रशिक्षण प्राप्त योग्य व्यक्ति होता है। जिस प्रशासन का पूरा ज्ञान होता है। जिस कारण मन्त्री और सचिव में सहयोगात्मक भावना बहुत कम देखने को मिलता है और विवाद अधिक। उदाहरण के तौर पर हम हाल ही हुए आई.पी.एस. अमिताभ ठाकुर और मुलायम सिंह का विवाद को देखा जा सकता है। जिसमे मुलायम सिंह यादव पर अमिताभ ठाकुर को फोन पर धमकाने का आरोप लगा उसके बाद प्रदेश सरकार ने उन्हे निलंबित कर दिया और उन पर मुकदमे दर्ज करायें।

इस प्रकार के राजनैतिक फैसलों के कारण ही सचिव मन्त्री के फैसले के विपरीत जाने की कोशिश नही करना चाहते वह गलत हो या सही। यदि कभी किसी सचिव ने कोशिश की भी है तो उसके परिणाम हमारे सामने हैं लेकिन सबसे बड़ा सवाल आज भी ये है कि प्रशासन में होने वाली अनियमता, अव्यवस्था, घोटालों और विवादों का उत्तरदायित्व किस पर है? उत्तर है: मन्त्री और सचिव दोनो पर अत: दोनों को ही अपने उत्तरदायित्व का निर्वाह ईमानदारी से करना चाहिए।

मोरिस जोन्स के अनुसार "मन्त्रियों और प्रशासको के सम्बन्ध में विकार पैदा हो सकता है यदि प्रशासक मन्त्री की जी-हुजूरी करता है। प्रत्येक कार्य मन्त्री को खुश रखने के लिए करता है। उचित कार्य भी मन्त्री की नाराजगी का डर नही करता और इस प्रकार प्रशासन के मानदण्डों को गिरा देता है। भारत मे ऐसे अफसरों की कमी नहीं जो अपने दृष्टिकोण के कारण मन्त्री के पैर छूते है और उनके गलत कार्यों की आलोचना करके उनका बेड़ा भी गर्क कर देते है।"

संक्षेप में यह कहा जा सकता है कि सचिव व मन्त्री का सम्बन्ध अत्यन्त घनिष्ठ व महत्वपूर्ण होता है। यह पति-पत्नि के सम्बन्ध से भी अधिक गोपनीय व पवित्र रहना चाहिए। जहां तक दोनों को केवल

लोकहित के लिए काम करना है इनमे कटुता आने का कोई कारण नही है। पर जहां एक को दूसरे के कन्धे पर रखकर अपना निशाना साधने का स्वार्थ पैदा हो जाता है वही पर परस्पर सन्देह व चालबाजी का माहौल पैदा हो जाता है जो सरकारी कार्यों की प्रगति के लिए सबसे बड़ा रोड़ा बन सकता है सामाजिक व व्यक्तिगत पृष्ठभूमि समानान्तर ने होते हुए भी मामूली शिष्टता के सहारे दोनों एक दूसरे के पूरक और सहायक बन सकते है। इनके कार्यकलापों को सम्पूर्णतः नियमों द्वारा नही बांधा जा सकता, बहुत कुछ अनौपचारिकता अवश्यम्भावी है।

सुझावः-आधुनिक लोकतन्त्रों मे व्यावहरिक दृष्टि से कोई भी समस्या इतनी जटिल एवं विचारणीय नही है। जितनी की मन्त्री अर्थात् राजनीतिज्ञ एवं सचिव अर्थात् लोक सेवकों के मध्य सम्बन्धों की समस्या है। संसदीय लोकतन्त्र में यह समस्या और भी अधिक गम्भीर हो जाती है। क्योकि उसमें शासन को लोक सेवा (सचिव) के माध्यम से ही संचालित करना पड़ता है। राजनीतिज्ञ मन्त्री आते-जाते रहते है, किन्तु लोक सेवा निरन्तर बनी रहती है। वस्तुतः संसदीय शासन प्रणाली की सफलता तथा लोक प्रशासन का कुशलतापूर्वक संचालन मन्त्री सचिव सम्बन्धों के सन्तुलित स्वरूप पर ही निर्भर है। और इस सन्तुलन को बनाने कि लिए मन्त्री और सचिव दोनों को अपने कर्त्तव्यों की अनिवार्यता का पालन करना चाहिए।

इन कर्तव्यों को पूरा करने के लिए निम्न सुझाव इस प्रकार है-

1. **लोक सेवकों के लिए कानून सम्बन्धी अनिवार्यताः** प्रत्येक प्रशासनिक अधिकारी को कानून के अनुसार कार्य करना पड़ता है और यह सतर्कता रखनी पडती है। कि कानून के अन्तर्गत कर्तव्य निर्वाह करने मे राजनीतिक या वैयक्तिक हस्ताक्षेप न हो पाए।

2. **नीतियों का क्रियान्वयन पक्षपात रहितः** लोक सेवको को नीतियों का क्रियान्वयन भय व पक्षपात रहित होकर करना चाहिए क्योंकि नीतियां वैधानिक रूप से स्वीकृत होती है।
3. **आदेश का लिपिबद्ध होनाः** प्रशासनिक अधिकारियों को अपने मन्त्रियों से जो आदेश मिलते है उन्हे लिपिवृद्ध कर लेना चाहिए। क्योकि ऐसे भी मामले सामने आए है कि मन्त्रियों के मौखिक आदेशों का अधिकारियों ने पालन किया और बाद में जब दोनों मे मतभेद उत्पन्न हो गया तो उसका परिणाम उन अधिकारियों को भुगतान पड़ा।
4. **नीति निर्माण मे सहायताः** लोक सेवकों अथवा सचिव को नीति निर्माण में मन्त्री की सहायता करनी चाहिए क्योंकि मन्त्री राजनीतिक व्यक्ति होता है। प्रशासनिक नही जैसे की एस. एस. खेडा ने उच्च प्रशासनिक अधिकारी के रूप मे प्राप्त अपने विस्तृत अनुभव के आधार पर कहा है– एक प्रशासनिक अधिकारी तथा राजनीतिज्ञ के सम्बन्ध का स्वरूप अद्वितीय होता है। यह पारस्परिक विश्वास सहानुभूति तथा भरोसा किए जाने जैसे असाधारण गुणों की अपेक्षा करता है। मन्त्री अपने सचिव का स्वामी है लेकिन उसका सचिव न केवल उसका विभागीय सहायक होता है बल्कि यह सरकार का सचिव भी होता है।

मन्त्रियों के लिए सुझाव

1. मन्त्रियों को नीतियों कार्यक्रमों को समझने के लिए सचिव से सहायता लेनी चाहिए क्योंकि सचिव को इनके विषय में ज्यादा जानकारी रहती है।
2. मन्त्रियों को अपने सचिव से सद्व्यवहार करना चाहिए और उसमें किसी भी तरह का भय उत्पन्न नही करना चाहिए।

3. मन्त्रियों को किसी भी प्रशासनिक या सचिव के अनुचित कार्यो का नैतिक उत्तरदायित्व लेते हुए आगे से ऐसा न करने की सलाह देनी चाहिए।
4. मन्त्री द्वारा सचिव को अपने हाथों की कठपुतली नही समझना चाहिए।
5. राजनीतिज्ञ तथा प्रशासनिक कर्मचारियों के बीच विश्वास तथा सद्भावना होनी चाहिए।

सन्दर्भ सूची

1. भारतीय प्रशासन (डॉ. वी.एल.फडिया)।
2. 2जी स्पेक्ट्रम घोटाला 2010 Newspaper अमर उजाला।
3. मन्त्री सचिव विवाद R.K. राघवन (Dec. 9, 2011)।
4. वेबसाइट-मन्त्री सचिव विवाद M dailyhant.in news India
5. साभार Janokti.com बुधवार 2 फरवरी 2011।
6. Newspaper and NDTV इण्डिया: मन्त्री व प्रशासनिक अधिकारी विवाद।
7. March 2011 newsofmanasa monthly archives

18

देश के विकास के लिए राजनेताओं व नौकरशाहों में समन्वय आवश्यक

– दीप्ती श्रीवास्तव

भारत में प्रचलित संसदी प्रणाली की सरकार में कार्यपालिका के दोनों रूपों को स्वीकार किया गया है, अर्थात राजनीति कार्यकारी और स्थायी कार्यकारी। राजकीय कार्यकारिणी की श्रेणी में प्रधानमंत्री, कैबिनेट मंत्री राज्यमंत्री और उपमंत्री आते है। दूसरी ओर स्थायी कार्यकारियों की श्रेणियों में लोक सेवक (अर्थात सचिव, अपर सचिव, संयुक्त सचिव, उप सचिव और अन्य व्यावसायिक प्रशासक आते है। किसी मंत्रालय/विभाग में कार्यरत लोक सेवाओं का राजनीतिक प्रमुख मंत्री होता है और प्रशासनिक मुख्य सचिव राजनीतिक कार्यपालक को सत्ता आवधिक चुनावों के माध्यम से जनता से प्राप्त होती है और वह उस सत्ता का प्रयोग अपनी संवैधानिक स्थित के अनुसार करता है। स्थायी कार्यकारी का चयन उसकी योग्यता और प्रवीणता के आधार पर होता है वह शक्ति अपनी प्रशासनिक पदस्थिति और तकनीकी कुशलता से प्राप्त करता है। सरकार की प्रणाली जनता की प्रभुसत्ता के सिद्धान्त पर आधारित है इसलिए स्थायी कार्यपालिका–राजनीतिक कार्यपालिका के नीचे है क्यों कि वह जनता का प्रनिधित्व

करता है। मोहित भट्टाचार्य ने इस संबंध में ठीक ही कहा है कि संसदीय प्रणाली की सरकार में मंत्री की सर्वोच्चता और सचिव की अधीनस्थता स्वतः सिद्ध है।

सरकारी तंत्र को सुचारू रूप से कुशलता के साथ चलाने के लिए राजनीतिक कार्यपालिका और लोक सेवक के बीच यथोचित और सद्भावपूर्ण संबंधों का भारी महत्व है। राजनीतिक कार्यपालिका अपनी शक्ति समय-समय पर होने वाले चुनावों की प्रक्रिया के द्वारा जनता से प्राप्त करती है और संवैधानिक स्थिति के कारण उसका प्रयोग करती है। दूसरी ओर, लोकसेवकों का चयन उनकी योग्यता के आधार पर होता है और उसको अपनी शक्ति प्रशासनिक पदों एवं तकनीकी विशेषज्ञता दोनों से प्राप्त होती है। जनता की प्रभुसत्ता के सिद्धान्त पर आधारित जनतांत्रिक सरकार में लोकसेवक जनता का प्रतिनिधित्व करने वाली राजनीतिक कार्यपालिका के अधीन होते हैं। जैसा कि पीटर सेल्फ का मत है, ''राजनीतिक कार्यकारियों और लोकसेवकों के बीच परस्पर क्रिया कुछ विशेष रूपों में होती है। ये रूप भागीदारों के दो समूहों की विशिष्ट शैलियों तथा हितों का परिणाम होते हैं। उन्होंने दोनों के बीच परस्पर क्रिया के चार क्षेत्र बताए हैं-

1. नीति निर्माण
2. हितों की मध्यस्थता
3. व्यक्तिगत और स्थानीय दावों का उपचार
4. राजनीतिक दायित्व तथा प्रशासनिक विवेक के बीच संतुलन

उनके बीच की परस्पर क्रिया का आगे विश्लेषण करते हुए उन्होंने कहा, ''पहले दोनों मामलों में राजनीतिज्ञों का औपचारिक उत्तरदायित्व होता है। परन्तु राजनीतिक निर्णयों के अनुपस्थित तत्वों की आपूर्ति प्रशासक करते हैं। तीसरे मामले में, विशेष निर्णयों को प्रभावित करने में राजनीतिज्ञों के अक्सर पैदा होने वाले हितों के विपरीत प्रशासक अपनी विशिष्ट पद्धतियों की एकरूपता बनाए रखते हैं। चौथा मामला दोनों समूहों

They would do the politicians' biddings rather than adhere to rules. Lest the situation becomes more vicious, it is necessary that a better arrangement be conceived under the Constitution. The question of appointments, transfers and placements is not to be left to the discretion of the politicians or administrative bosses but be entrusted to independent and autonomous boards. The Commission, therefore, recommends that the questions of personnel policy including placements, promotions, transfers and fast-track advancements on the basis of forward-looking career management policies and techniques should be managed by autonomous Personnel Boards for assisting the high level political authorities in making key decisions. Such civil service boards should be constituted under statutory provisions. They should be expected to function like the UPSC. Reputed management experts from institutes of management, well known for their excellence, should be inducted into these boards to provide a broad based pool of expertise. The principle is not to take politics out of personnel policy but to make knowledge and information institutionally available to the political decision-makers on the basis of appropriate parliamentary legislation under Article 309. The sanctity of parliamentary legislation under Article 309 is needed to counteract the publicly known trends of the play of unhealthy and destabilising influences in the management of public services in general and higher civil services in particular."

Arbitrary and motivated transfers of government servants which are not in public interest and good governance have become a matter of great concern particularly in some States although the position is somewhat better at the Union Government level.

The Union Government has initiated several measures in order to ensure security of tenure to civil servants. The Rules governing the All India Services have been amended and provision made for fixation of tenures of posts encadred with the AIS. For example, the Indian Administrative Service (Cadre) Rules, 1955, have been amended and a new clause inserted: *"7(c)"*

(i) The Central Government, in consultation with the State Government or State Governments concerned, may determine the tenure of all or any of the cadre posts specified for the

State concerned in item 1 of the Schedule to the Indian Administrative Service (Fixation of Cadre Strength) Regulation, 1955.

(ii) A cadre officer, appointed to any post for which the tenure has been so determined, shall hold the minimum tenure as prescribed except in the event of promotion, retirement, deputation outside the State or training exceeding two months.

(iii) An officer may be transferred before the minimum prescribed tenure only on the recommendation of a Committee on Minimum Tenure as specified in the Schedule annexed to these rules."

The tenure of several posts has been notified accordingly for many States. The Commission has tried to address this issue in the Chapters 8 and 9 by suggesting a mechanism for posting of officers and for fixation of tenures. The Commission would like to reiterate that the tenure of all posts above a certain level should be fixed in Government of India by making a provision in the new civil services law. State Governments should also take similar steps.

Recommendations

(a) There is a need to safeguard the political neutrality and impartiality of the civil services. The onus for this lies equally on the political executive and the civil services. This aspect should be included in the Code of Ethics for Ministers as well as the Code of Conduct for Public Servants.

(b) The Commission would like to reiterate its recommendation made in its Report on "Ethics in Governance" while examining the definition of corruption under the Prevention of Corruption Act, 1988, wherein it has been recommended that "abuse of authority unduly favouring or harming someone" and "obstruction of justice" should be classified as an offence under the Act.

(c) It is essential to lay down certain norms for recruitment in government to avoid complaints of favouritism, nepotism, corruption and abuse of power. These norms are:

  (i) Well-defined procedure for recruitment to all government jobs.

(ii) Wide publicity and open competition for recruitment to all posts.

(iii) Minimisation, if not elimination, of discretion in the recruitment process.

(iv) Selection primarily on the basis of written examination or on the basis of performance in existing public/board/ university examination with minimum weight to interview.

These principles could be included in the 'Civil Services Bill' as recommended by the Commission.

Index

R

S

की आवश्यकताओं और हितों के बीच संघर्ष के अपरिहार्य बिंदु का प्रतिनिधित्व करता हैं। भारत जैसे विकासशील समाजों में लोक सेवा अत्यंत महत्वपूर्ण भूमिका अदा करती है। इसके निम्नलिखित कार्यकलाप हैं-

1. **नीति कार्यान्वयन**-राजनीतिक कार्यपालिका द्वारा तय की हुई नीतियों का कार्यान्वयन लोकसेवा का सबसे महत्वपूर्ण और बुनियादी कार्य है। कल्याणकारी राज्य के लक्ष्यों अर्थात सामाजिक समानता, आर्थिक विकास इत्यादि को प्राप्त करने के लिए लोक सेवक कानूनों और नीतियों को लागू करते हैं।

2. **नीति निरूपण**-राजनीतिक कार्यपालिका का कार्य है नीति निरूपण और नीति निर्धारण। लेकिन इसमें लोकसेवकों की भूमिका सक्रिय होने लगी है। नीति निर्माण में सूचना उपलब्ध कराकर वे मंत्रियों की सहायता करते हैं तथा उनको सलाह देते हैं। राजनीतिक कार्यपालक गैर पेशेवर होते हैं, अतः वे नीतियों की जटिलताओं को समझ नहीं सकते हैं और इसलिए उनको पेशेवर लोकसेवकों की विशेषज्ञ सलाह पर निर्भर होना पड़ता है।

3. **प्रदत्त विधि निर्माण**-इस अर्द्ध-विधायी कार्य को लोकसेवकों द्वारा किया जाता है। समय की कमी, काम के दबाव और विधि-निर्माण की बढ़ती हुई जटिलताओं के कारण विधायिका कानूनों की रूपरेखा तैयार करती है और इसके विवरण तैयार करने का अधिकार कार्यपालिका को सौंप देती है। इस प्रकार विद्यायिका द्वारा अनियमित मूल कानमन की सीमा में उप-कनूनों, नियमों एवं विनियमों के निर्माण का कार्य लोकसेवक करते हैं।

4. **प्रशासनिक अधिनिर्णय**-इस अर्द्ध-न्यायिक कार्य को लोकसेवकों द्वारा किया जाता है। राज्य और नागरिकों के बीच विवादों का निपटारा लोकसेवक करते हैं। इस कार्य के लिए न्यायधीश लोकसेवकों के साथ

प्रशासनिक अधिकरण स्थापित करते हैं। भारत में आयकर अपील अधिकरण, औद्योगिक अधिकरण, किराया अधिकरण और रेलवे दर अधिकरण इत्यादि ऐसे अधिकरणों के कुछ उदाहरण हैं। ये अधिकरण सामान्य न्यायालय प्रणाली से बाहर काम करते हैं।

उपरोक्त के साथ-साथ लोकसेवक निम्न कार्य भी करते हैं-

1. प्रशासनिक नियोजन।
2. सार्वजनिक उपक्रमों का प्रशासन। संसद तथा इसकी समितियों के प्रति मंत्रियों के प्रति मंत्रियों के उत्तरदायित्वों को पूरा करने में उनकी सहायता करना।
3. राज्य के वित्तीय कार्यों का संचालन करना।
4. संगठन और उपायों द्वारा प्रशासन में सुधार लाना।
5. जनसंपर्क।

व्यवहार में सम्बन्ध

व्यवहार में मंत्री और लोक सेवक के बीच सम्बन्ध परस्पर मतभेदों, विवादो, बेचैनी और शंकाओं से घिरा रहता है। इस कुछ महत्वपूर्ण उदाहरण यह है-

मंत्री और लोक सेवक के बीच परस्पर मतभेद की घटना स्वतंत्रता के बाद पहली बार वर्ष 1957 में मूंधड़ा सौदा के मामले मे हुई। इसमें राष्ट्रीयकृत जीवन बीमा निगम की 1.25 करोड़ रूपये की राशि निजी क्षेत्र के शेयरों की खरीद के लिए व्यय की गयी। जब इस मामले ने जोर पकड़ा तो तत्कालीन वित्ती मंत्री (टी.टी. कृष्णभाचारी) और प्रधान वित्त सचिव (एच.एम. पटेल) ने दोष एक दूसरे पर मढ़ा। फलस्वरूप भारत सरकार ने तथ्यों और मूंधड़ा सौदे के औचित्य की जांच के लिए वर्ष 1958 में एम.सी. छांगला की अगुवाई में एक सदस्यीय आयोग की नियुक्ति की। छागला आयोग ने अपने रिपोर्ट में उल्लेख किया कि "सवैधानिक तौर पर

मंत्री उस कार्य लिए जिम्मेदार है जिसे उसके सचिव ने किया। मंत्री महोदय न तो सचिव के कुकृत्व का आश्रय ले सकते है और न ही अपने कार्य को नकार सकते है।

पुनः वर्ष 1966 में तत्कालीन गृहमंत्री (गुलजारी लाल नन्दा) ने अपने गृह सचिव (एल.पी. सिंह) के असहयोगपूर्ण रवैये की शिकायत प्रधानमंत्री से करते हुए यह अनुरोध किया कि एल.पी. सिंह की जगह कोई नया सचिव नियुक्त किया जाये। प्रधानमंत्री ने नन्दा के अनुरोध को स्वीकार नहीं किया। फलस्वरूप गुलजारी लाल नन्दा ने त्याग पत्र दे दिया।

वर्ष 1987 में भारत के पूर्व प्रधानमंत्री राजीव गांधी ने कृषि सचिव (सी.एस. शास्त्री) ग्रामीण विकास सचिव (डी. बांधोपाध्याय) और विदेश सचिव (ए.पी. वेंकटेशन) के साथ दुर्व्यवहार किया था।

वर्ष 1993 में गृह सचिव ने गृहमंत्री की कार्यशैली के कारण मतभेद होने पर अपने पद से त्याग पत्र दे दिया था।

परस्पर मतभेद के कारण

1. मंत्री आमतौर पर लोक सेवकों की स्वतंत्र, स्पष्ट और निष्पक्ष सलाह को प्रोत्साहित नहीं करते। इससे परस्पर समझ और सहयोग की भावना को ठेस लगती है।
2. मंत्री और लोक सेवक के बीच राजनीतिक सम्बन्ध बनने के कारण लोक सेवा का राजनीतिकरण।
3. मंत्री द्वारा अपनी अनुशासनात्मक शक्तियों का प्रयोग कर लोक सेवकों को स्थानान्तरित और निलम्बित किये जाने के कारण लोक सेवकों द्वारा ठीक कार्य न किया जाना।
4. मंत्रियों और लोक सेवकों में गुटबाजी, दलीय प्रतिद्वंदिता और जातिवाद की भावना का व्याप्त होना।
5. एक प्रबल दलीय प्रणाली (अर्थात कांग्रेस) का अंत और फलस्वरूप राजनीतिक अस्थिरता का माहौल।

6. मंत्रियों और लोक सेवकों को अपनी-अपनी भूमिका के बारे में उचित समझबूझ का अभाव। मंत्रियों द्वारा प्रशासक के दिन प्रतिदिन के कार्य में आमतौर दखल देना और लोक सेवकों द्वारा महत्वपूर्ण मामलों को मंत्रियों की जानकारी में न लाया जाना।
7. मंत्रियों की असफलता का आरोप लोक सेवकों के मत्थे मढ़ा जाना। छंगला आयोग ने इस संदर्भ में कहा है कि ''मंत्री की जिम्मेदारी के सिद्धान्त के दो आयाम है। अपने प्राधिकार के क्षेत्र में मंत्री को पूर्ण स्वायत्ता प्राप्त है। सिद्धान्ततः मंत्री को अपने सेवकों द्वारा किये गये कार्यों की पूरी जिम्मेदारी लेनी चाहिए।''
8. लोक सेवकों द्वारा अपनी सामाजिक और निजी मंडली में मंत्रियों की आलोचना किये जाने के कारण मंत्रीगण की भी वैसी ही प्रतिक्रिया होनी।
9. लोक सेवकों का मंत्री की कठिनाईयों और समस्याओं के प्रति संवेदनशील न होना। लोक सेवक उन मंत्रियों की राजनीतिक भूमिका को नजर अंदाज करते है। जो व्यक्तियों और समूहों दोनों के हितो का ध्यान रखने की कोशिश करते है।
10. मंत्री और लोक सेवक, ऐतिहासिक भूमिका, सामाजिक पृष्ठ भूमि, व्यवसायिक प्रतिबद्धता, मानसिक योग्यता और दृष्टिकोण आदि की दृष्टि से एक दूसरे से भिन्न हैं।

प्रशासनिक सुधार आयोग की सिफारिशे-प्रशासनिक सुधार आयोग ने राजनेताओं तथा लोक सेवकों में समन्वय स्थापित करने हेतु निम्नलिखित सिफारिशें प्रस्तुत की-

1. ''ऐसे मामलों में जहां सरकार की नीति स्पष्ट नहीं हो या नीति में कुछ विचलन अथवा किसी महत्वपूर्ण विषय पर मंत्रियों और सचिव में मतभेद हो, वहां सभी प्रमुख निर्णयों को कारण बताते हुए संक्षेप में लिखित में ला देना चाहिए।

2. मंत्रियों को निर्भीकता का वातावरण तैयार करना चाहिए। उन्हें अपनी नीतियों और आदेशों कार्यान्वित करने में सचिवों का आवश्यक मार्गदर्शन करना चाहिए।
3. प्रधानमंत्री को मंत्रिमंडल और केन्द्रीय कार्मिक एजेंसी के माध्यम से लोक सेवकों में किसी मंत्री विशेष से व्यक्तिगत और अहितकर सम्बन्ध को रोकने की ओर विशेष ध्यान देना चाहिए।
4. लोक सेवकों द्वारा किये गये घोर अन्याय, उसकी गम्भीर चूक अथवा कुप्रशासन के मामलों में सिवाय मंत्रियों को रोजमर्रा के प्रशासन में हस्तक्षेप नहीं करना चाहिए। अगर किसी नागरिक का अनुरोध या उसकी शिकायत किसी नियम, कार्यविधि अथवा नीति में संशोधन में मांग करती है, तो समस्या का समाधान करने के लिए सिर्फ संशोधन करना चाहिए। किसी व्यक्तिगत मामलों में उपकार करने के लिए नियमों में ढील नहीं देनी चाहिए।
5. सचिवों तथा अन्य लोक सेवकों को मंत्रियों की कठिनाइयों के प्रति अधिक संवेदनशीलता प्रदर्शित करनी चाहिए और उनको बेहतर ढंग से समझानी चाहिए। उनको छोटे मोटे समायोजनों तथा मूल सिद्धान्तों से समझौता करने वाले अथवा ऐसे कार्यों के बीच अन्तर करना चाहिए जो सेवाओं की कार्यकुशलता और उनके मनोबल पर भारी या स्थायी प्रभाव डाल सकते हो।
6. मंत्री के प्रति सचिव का आधिकारिक सम्बन्ध निष्ठा का तथा सचिव के प्रति मंत्री का रिश्ता विश्वास का होना चाहिए।

वस्तुतः संसदीय शासन प्रणाली की सफलता तथा लोक प्रशासन का कुशलतापूर्वक संचालन मंत्री–सचिव संबंधों के संतुलित स्वरूप पर ही निर्भर है। **लॉस्की** के अनुसार, ''दोनों का सम्बन्ध वस्तुतः उनके व्यक्तित्व

पर आधारित है। यदि मंत्री का व्यक्तित्व शक्तिशाली है तो वह लोक सेवा के सदस्यों पर हावी रहेगा, पर यदि मंत्री ढीला-ढाला व्यक्ति है तो उसे लोक सेवा के इशारों पर चलना पड़ेगा। "**प्रोफेसर आर्डवे टीड** के अनुसार, "लोकतंत्र में प्रशासन एक नैतिक कार्य है और प्रशासक एक नैतिक अभिकर्ता।" अर्थात् सार्वजनिक पदों पर बैठे लोगों से नैतिक कार्यों की उम्मीद की जाती है जो भारत की सामाजिक परम्पराओं एवं संवैधानिक मूल्यों के अनुरूप आचरण एवं व्यवहार करने से पूर्ण होती है। किन्तु वर्तमान परिवेश में नौकरशाह राजनेताओं की राजनीति का शिकार हो रहें हैं। जिस प्रकार लूट की प्रणाली बढ़ती जा रही है उससे नौकरशाहों की कार्यकुशलता पर प्रतिकूल प्रभाव पड़ रहा है। राजनेताओं द्वारा अपने भरोसेमंद तथा लाभकारी नौकरशाहों को विशिष्ट पदों पर नियुक्त करने तथा राजनीतिक लाभ के लिए अनियंत्रित रूप से स्थानान्तरण करने की प्रवृत्ति के कारण नौकरशाहों की कार्यकुशलता और दक्षता में कमी आ रही है। जिसके कारण वे न तो स्वतंत्रतापूर्वक कार्य कर पा रहें है, और योजनाओं का कुशलतापूर्वक संचालन कर पा रहें हैं। नौकरशाहों के कार्य राजनीतिक प्रभुत्व से प्रभावित रहते हैं, तथा वे अपने स्थानान्तरण के प्रति आशंकित रहते है। इसके कारण नौकरशाह स्वविवेक से निर्णय न लेकर राजनीतिक हित में कार्य करने को विवश हो जाते हैं। अतः कुशल नेतृत्व तथा प्रशासनिक दक्षता के लिए आवश्यक है कि राजनेता और नौकरशाह परस्पर हितों का त्याग कर जन कल्याणोन्मुख होकर निष्पक्ष रूप से कार्य करें। लोक प्रशासन लोक भावनाओं के प्रति तभी संवेदनशील रह सकता है जब यह ठोस राजनीतिक अधीनता, नियन्त्रण तथा निदेशन में निरन्तर कार्य करें। इसके लिए दोनों के बीच सुव्यवस्थित तालमेल होना अत्यन्त आवश्यक है।

सन्दर्भ सूची

1. इन्द्रजीत कौर, लोक प्रशासन, साहित्य भवन पब्लिकेशन, आगरा।

2. अशोक कुमार दुबे, इक्कीसवीं सदी में लोक प्रशासन, टाटा मैग्रा हिल्स संस्करण।
3. डॉ. सुरेन्द्र कटारिया, भारत में लोक प्रशासन, आर.बी.एस.ए. पब्लिशर्स, जयपुर।
4. एस.सी. मेहता, लोक प्रशासन सिद्धान्त एवं व्यवहार, राजस्थान हिन्दी ग्रंथ अकादमी, जयपुर।
5. सडाना शर्मा, लोक प्रशासन सिद्धान्त और व्यवहार, किताब महल, इलाहाबाद। अवस्थी एवं माहेश्वरी, लोक प्रशासन, आगरा।
6. एम. लक्ष्मीकांत, लोक प्रशासन, टाटा मैग्रा हिल्स संसकरण।
7. क्रानिकल, मासिक पत्रिका, राजनातिक प्रशासन, सितम्बर 2010।
8. योजना, मासिक पत्रिका, जुलाई 2013।
9. योजना, मासिक पत्रिका, सितम्बर 2014।

Annexure

Recommendation of Second ARC on Politician-Civil Servant Relationship

In a democracy, power vests with the people. This power is exercised through its elected representatives who have the mandate to govern them for a specific period. The civil services by virtue of its knowledge, experience and understanding of public affairs assist the elected representatives in formulating policy and are responsible for implementing these policies. Parliamentary democracies are usually characterised by a permanent civil service which assists the political executive. Under the Presidential form of government (like in the US), the higher echelons of the civil services are, in contrast, appointed by the government of the day (spoils system). India has adopted the British model.

Some advantages of having an independent, permanent and impartial civil service are as follows:

(i) The spoils system has the propensity to degenerate into a system of patronage, nepotism and corruption. Having a credible recruitment process through an impartial agency provides a defence against such abuse.

(ii) Public policy today has become a complex exercise requiring in-depth knowledge and expertise in public affairs. A permanent civil service provides continuity and develops expertise as well as institutional memory for effective policy making.

(iii) A permanent and impartial civil service is more likely to assess the long-term social payoffs of any policy whereas the political executive may have a tendency to look for short-term political gain.

(iv) A permanent civil service helps to ensure uniformity in public administration and also acts as a unifying force particularly in vast and culturally diverse nations.

(v) A permanent civil service like any other reputable profession is likely to evolve over time an ethical basis for its functioning.

A healthy working relationship between ministers and civil servants is critical for good governance. While the principles governing the roles and responsibilities of ministers and civil servants are well defined in political theory, in the actual working of this relationship this division of responsibility becomes blurred with both sides often encroaching upon the other's sphere of responsibility. In any democracy, ministers are responsible to the people through Parliament and therefore the civil servants have to be accountable to the minister. However, an impartial civil service is responsible not only to the government of the day but to the Constitution of the land to which they have taken an oath of loyalty. At the same time, implementing the policies of the duly elected government is a core function of civil servants. That is why the division of responsibility between the civil servants and ministers needs to be more clearly defined. A framework in which responsibility and accountability is well defined would be useful.

Constitutional Provisions in India

The Indian Constitution provides for separation of powers between the legislature, executive and judiciary with well-defined roles and responsibilities for each one of them. Since India is a parliamentary democracy, there is an interface between the legislature and the executive at the level of the Council of Ministers, which is collectively responsible to the legislature. In terms of Articles 53 and 154, the executive power of the Union and the States vests in the President or Governor directly or through officers subordinate to him. These officers constitute the permanent civil service and are governed by Part XIV of the Constitution.

The other part of the executive is the 'political'. The President or Governor is required to act according to the aid and advice of his/her Council of Ministers, appointed under Articles 73 and 163 of the Constitution. The President and Governor frame rules for the conduct of business in the government. Work is allocated among ministers as per the Government of India (Allocation of Business) Rules and the manner in which the officers are required to help the President or Governor to exercise his/her executive functions is governed by the Government of India (Transaction of Business) Rules. What this means is that though officers are subordinate to the President or Governor, they carry out the orders of the Council of Ministers in accordance with the rules framed in this behalf. The Rules of Business of Government do provide for the Secretary to the Government to advise his/her minister about the course of action proposed in a particular matter and to submit to him a note which tells him about the propriety or legality of his/her orders and suggest that either such orders not be given or that they be suitably modified. The relationship between the Secretary and the minister is organic. The Minister has the mandate of the people to govern, but the Secretary has an equivalent constitutional mandate to advise the minister. Once his/her advice has been suitably considered, unless the minister passes an illegal order, the Secretary is bound to implement it. The minister, on his/her part, is required to support the Secretary who is implementing his/her order. Once a law is framed or rules and regulations are approved, they apply to everyone, whether a member of the political executive or of the permanent civil service. A civil servant is required to implement the orders of government without bias, with honesty and without fear or favour. It is precisely in this area that a degree of difference of opinion often occurs between the political executive and the civil servants.

The Civil Services in Post Independence India

In the initial years after Independence, relations between ministers and civil servants were characterised by mutual respect and understanding of each other's respective roles, with neither encroaching upon the other's domain. However, in subsequent years, matters started changing for the worse. While some civil servants did not render objective and impartial advice to their ministers, often some ministers began to resent advice that did not fit in with short-term political interests. There was also a tendency for some ministers at the Union and the State levels to focus more on routine administrative matters such as transfers in preference to policy making. At the same time, some civil servants learnt the art of 'manoeuvering' for favours in return for pliability in their decision making. This trend was further accentuated by rising materialism and acquisitiveness in society as well as decline in values across the board. As a result, 'political neutrality' which was the hallmark of the civil service in the pre-Independence era as well as in the period right after Independence, was gradually eroded. These trends led to the phenomenon of 'politicisation of the civil service' in India.

Areas of Friction

The areas of potential conflict in the relationship between the political executive and the permanent civil service can be identified as follows:

(a) The concept of neutrality.

(b) Advisory role of civil servants in policy making.

(c) Statutory role of the civil servants.

(d) Discharge of delegated functions.

(e) Appointments/Recruitment to the civil services.

(f) Transfers and postings of civil servants.

The Concept of Neutrality

Sardar Patel had made the following observations in the Constituent Assembly to support the continuance of the pre-independence civil service structure:-

> "It needs hardly to be emphasised that an efficient, discipline and contended civil service assured of its prospects as a result of diligent and honest work, is a sine-qua non of sound administration under democratic regime even more than under an authoritarian rule. The service must be above party and we should ensure that political considerations, either in its recruitment or in its discipline and control, are reduced to the minimum if not eliminated altogether."

Unfortunately, this vision of civil service neutrality no longer holds good. Changes in governments particularly at the state level often lead to wholesale transfer of civil servants. Political neutrality is no longer the accepted norm with many civil servants getting identified, rightly or wrongly, with a particular political dispensation. There is a perception that officers have to cultivate and seek patronage from politicians for obtaining suitable positions even in the Union Government. As a result, the civil services in public perception are often seen as increasingly politicised.

The Commission is of the view that the political neutrality and impartiality of the civil services needs to be preserved. The onus for this lies equally on the political executive and civil servants. The Commission in its Report on "Ethics in Governance" while examining the ethical framework for ministers has recommended that a code of ethics for ministers should inter-alia include the following:

> "Ministers must uphold the political impartiality of the civil service and not ask the civil servants to act in any way which would conflict with the duties and responsibilities of the civil servants."

As observed by Paul Appleby civil servants should not confuse 'political neutrality' with 'programme neutrality'. At the stage of policy formulation, the role of civil servants is to render free and frank advice which should not be coloured by any political considerations. Once a policy or programme has been approved by the elected government, it is the duty of the civil servant to faithfully and enthusiastically see to its implementation. Not carrying out this task in the right spirit would amount to misconduct inviting appropriate sanctions.

Advisory Role of Civil Servants in Policy Making

Rendering policy advice to the political executive is the most important "staff function" of the civil servant. Policy-making is the ultimate responsibility of the minister. After a policy is approved by the elected government, it is duty of the civil servant to implement such policy in the right earnest whether he/she agrees with it or not. At the same time, it is the duty of the civil servant to provide the factual basis, thorough analysis of all possible implications of any measure under consideration and free and frank advice, without fear or favour, at the stage of policy formulation. It is unfortunate that at times senior civil servants get bogged down in routine administrative decision-making and are unable to contribute adequately to this crucial aspect of their functions. However, for civil servants to be able to provide appropriate policy inputs, they must acquire the necessary combination of a broad perspective of the sector as well as of the government as a whole, combined with conceptual clarity and requisite knowledge.

If a policy that is being formulated is perceived by the civil servant to be against public interest, his/her responsibility is to convince the political executive about the adverse implications of such a policy. However, if the political executive does not agree with such an advice, there is little that the civil servant can do other than putting his/her views clearly on record. It is for the other institutional mechanisms such as Parliament, the CAG, Judiciary and ultimately the electorate to hold the political executive to account for bad policy.

In order to ensure that senior civil servants have adequate time to focus their attention on their 'policy advice role', the Commission is making detailed recommendations on separation of staff and line functions, in a separate report. The issue of getting the most suitable civil servants to staff leadership positions has been examined in the Chapter 9.

Statutory Role of the Civil Servants

Civil servants are required to discharge statutory functions under various legislative enactments which may sometimes be quasi-judicial in nature. The role of the executive magistrate under the Cr. PC, the role of an Assessing Officer under the Income Tax Act and of the SHO under the Cr. PC and the respective Police Acts are some examples of such functions. It has been observed that there is an increasing trend on the part of the senior functionaries both in the civil services as well as elected representatives including ministers to interfere in such statutory functions. Acquiescence in the face of such interference is primarily the fault of the officer who has been entrusted with these statutory functions although those bringing such extraneous pressures should also be held to account.

The Commission in its Report on "Ethics in Governance" while examining the definition of corruption under the Prevention of Corruption Act, 1988 has recommended that "abuse of authority unduly favouring or harming someone" and "obstruction of justice" should be classified as an offence under the Act.

Discharge of Delegated Functions

In a democracy, the ultimate executive authority for all purposes lies with the political executive which is accountable to the people through Parliament. However, like in any large organisation, government also has to function through a hierarchy of functionaries to carry out defined tasks at different levels and in different locations. This necessitates on practical considerations the delegation of authority and responsibility to the civil servants at different levels in government. Such delegation is in line with the principles of subsidiarity which helps to take government closer to the people. The principles of sound management demand that authority and responsibility should go hand-in-hand.

It has been observed that there is an increasing tendency in government departments to centralise authority and also after having first delegated authority downwards, to interfere in decision-making of the subordinate functionaries. This is an unfortunate trend and it is for those holding leadership positions in government both in the political executive and in the civil services to correct it since such centralisation leads to inefficiencies and poor service delivery. It is also for the legislature to correct this trend by means of legislative enactments in certain critical areas as has been done for local bodies through Constitutional amendments (73rd and 74th) followed by State laws.

There is perhaps a perception that decentralisation and delegation of authority to field functionaries may lead to more corruption and abuse of power. The Chapter on Accountability and Disciplinary Procedures in this Report has provided for an elaborate mechanism for enforcing accountability among civil servants at all levels. Therefore, once these mechanisms are in place, there is no reason for decentralisation to be held back. In both decentralisation and delegation the underlying principle is that powers delegated should be exercised by the authority to whom the delegation has been done. Also, the exercise of such delegated authority should be allowed without any formal or informal interference.

Appointments/Recruitment to the Civil Services

The Constitution of India provides for an independent Union Public Service Commission (UPSC) and State Public Service Commissions

(PSCs). It lays down that it shall be the duty of the Union and the State Public Service Commissions to conduct examinations for appointments to the services of the Union and the services of the States respectively. However, while the UPSC enjoys an untarnished reputation for having developed a fair and transparent recruitment system, the same cannot be said for all the State PSCs. In addition, a large number of recruitments to various positions is done by departments of government and different organisations under their control both at the Union and the State government levels. Examples of such large scale recruitments which have often been the subject of complaints and controversies are recruitments to the posts of Police constables, teachers, bus-drivers and conductors etc. The Commission feels that it is essential to lay down certain principles/norms for such recruitments to avoid complaints of favouritism, nepotism, corruption and abuse of power that have often characterised these recruitment exercises. These principles are:

(i) Well-defined merit-based procedure for recruitment to all government jobs.

(ii) Wide publicity and open competition for recruitment to all posts.

(iii) Minimisation, if not elimination, of discretion in the recruitment process.

(iv) Selection primarily on the basis of written examination or on the basis of performance in existing public/board/university examination with minimum weightage to interview.

Postings and Transfers of Civil Servants

The National Commission to Review the Working of the Constitution made the following observations regarding transfers and postings of civil servants:

> "Arbitrary and questionable methods of appointments, promotions and transfers of officers by political superiors also led to corrosion of the moral basis of its independence.
>
> It has strengthened the temptation in services to collusive practices with politicians to avoid the inconvenience of transfers and to gain advantages by ingratiating themselves to political masters.